Developing Business Applications with OpenStep™

Springer
New York
Berlin
Heidelberg
Barcelona
Budapest
Hong Kong
London
Milan
Paris
Santa Clara
Singapore
Tokyo

Nik Gervae   Peter Clark

Developing Business Applications with OpenStep™

With 37 Illustrations

Springer

Nik Gervae
Pacific Data Images, Inc.
3101 Park Boulevard
Palo Alto, CA 94306, USA

Peter Clark
Integrity Solutions, Inc.
2900 Lone Oak Parkway
Eagan, MN 55121, USA

Library of Congress Cataloging-in-Publication Data
Gervae, Nik.
    Developing business applications with OpenStep / Nik Gervae, Peter
Clark.
      p.   cm.
    Includes bibliographical references and index.
    ISBN 0-387-94852-X (softcover)
      1. Application software—Development. 2. OpenStep 3. Business—
Data processing. I. Clark, Peter. II. Title.
QA76.76.A65G46 1996
005.2—dc20   96-32683

Printed on acid-free paper.

© 1997 Springer-Verlag New York, Inc.
All rights reserved. This work may not be translated or copied in whole or in part without the written permission of the publisher (Springer-Verlag New York, Inc., 175 Fifth Avenue, New York, NY 10010, USA), except for brief excerpts in connection with reviews or scholarly analysis. Use in connection with any form of information storage and retrieval, electronic adaptation, computer software, or by similar or dissimilar methodology now known or hereafter developed is forbidden.
The use of general descriptive names, trade names, trademarks, etc., in this publication, even if the former are not especially identified, is not to be taken as a sign that such names, as understood by the Trade Marks and Merchandise Marks Act, may accordingly be used freely by anyone.

Production managed by Frank Ganz; manufacturing supervised by Johanna Tschebull.
Photocomposed pages from the authors' FrameMaker files.
Printed and bound by R.R. Donnelley & Sons, Harrisonburg, VA.
Printed in the United States of America.

9 8 7 6 5 4 3 2 1

ISBN 0-387-94852-X Springer-Verlag New York Berlin Heidelberg SPIN 10524315

Contents

Foreword xi

Preface xiii

Acknowledgments and Disclaimers xvii

Part One: OpenStep

Chapter 1: What Is OpenStep? 3
The OpenStep Specification 4
    Components of the OpenStep Specification 6
User and Development Environments 12
    NeXT's OPENSTEP Release 4 for Windows NT 12
    SunSoft's OpenStep 1.0 for Solaris 13
    NeXT's OPENSTEP Release 4 for Mach 14

Chapter 2: The Object Model 15
Principles of Object-Oriented Programming 15
    Encapsulation 16
    Inheritance 17
    Polymorphism 18
    Dynamism 18
Basics of the Objective-C Language 20
    Objects and Messages 21
    Implementing Objects: Classes and Protocols 22
Run-Time Features 27
    Class Objects 27

      The Root Class 28
      Object Lifetime. 28
      Archiving. 30
Objective-C and C++. 31
      Mixing Objective-C and C++. 33

Chapter 3: The Foundation Framework. 35
The Classes. 37
      Core Run-Time Classes. 37
      Value and Collection Classes 44
      Classes for Distributed Objects and Concurrency 48
      Process Environment Classes 50

Chapter 4: The Application Kit 53
Preliminaries 54
Core Application Functionality. 55
      Graphical Structure. 56
      Driving the Application 60
      Standard User Interface Controls. 64
Other Functional Areas. 65
      Text and Fonts 65
      Drawing Aids. 67
      Printing. 68
      System Services 69

Chapter 5: NeXT's OPENSTEP for Windows NT 73
The User Interface 74
User System Programs 75
      Background Programs .75
      Demo Applications. 76
The Development Environment 76
      Project Builder 77
      Interface Builder 81
      Other Tools 82

Chapter 6: SunSoft's Solaris OpenStep 85
The User Interface 85
User System Programs 88

    Workspace Manager 88
    Mail 89
    Edit. 89
    Terminal 90
    Preview 91
    Preferences 91
The Development Environment 91
    Project Builder 92
    Interface Builder 96
    Header Viewer 96

Chapter 7: Building an Application 99
PayPerView: The Design 100
Creating the Project 101
Building the Interface. 103
    Laying Out the Window 104
    Creating the Controller Objects 107
    Connecting Interface Objects. 109
Fleshing Out the Classes 110
    The ProgramController Class. 111
    The Program Class 114
    The OrderController Class 115
Building and Debugging 118
    NeXT's Way 118
    SunSoft's Way 120

Part Two: Business Applications

Chapter 8: The Character of a Business Application 125
The Business Environment 125
    Data, Process, and Policy 126
The Elements of a Business Application 127
    Databases. 127
    Business Components 128
    Business Entities 128
    Presentation of Information 129
Elements as Objects 129

| Component Objects 129
| Business Objects 130
| Presentation Objects 130
| A Unified Approach to Business Applications 131

Chapter 9: Distributed Applications 133
What Distributed Objects Does 133
PayPerView with Distributed Objects 134
How It Works 137
    Advertising an Object. 137
    Contacting the Server. 139
    Remote Message Processing 142
    Transferring Data and Objects 146
    Handling Failures. 148
Other Distribution Models. 149
    Microsoft OLE Automation 149
    OMG's CORBA 152
Where Distributed Objects Falls Short 153
    Limitations in the Distribution Mechanism 154
    Absent and Incomplete Services 154
    Missing Tools. 155
Design with Distributed Objects 156
    Performance 157
    Reliability. 158
    Concurrency 159
    Interoperability. 160
Perspective 161

Chapter 10: Database Applications 163
What the Enterprise Objects Framework Does 164
    What's an Enterprise Object?. 165
    Model–View–Controller Revisited 166
    Specific Features 167
PayPerView with Enterprise Objects 168
    Defining the Relational-to-Object Mapping 169
    Revising the User Interface and Code. 174
    Changes to Existing Code 180
How It Works 181

    The Access Layer 182
    The Control Layer 188
    The Interface Layer. 194
Perspective 196

Chapter 11: World Wide Web Applications. 197
What WebObjects Does 199
    The Parts of a Page 199
    Reusable Components 200
    Session State Management 201
A Sample Page Definition 202
How It Works 204
    The Request–Response Loop 205
    Following Hello World. 206
Perspective 207

Part Three: Development Topics

Chapter 12: Development Topics 211

Chapter 13: Project Management
and the Development Life Cycle. 213
Building Business Models. 216
    Constructing the Model 216
    Verifying the Model 218
    Choosing a Methodology. 219
Rapid Prototyping 220
Iterative Development 222
Scheduling and Milestones 224
    Defining Milestones 225
    Revising the Schedule. 227
    The Benefits of Reuse. 228

Chapter 14: Portability 231
Guaranteed Portable 232
Guaranteed Nonportable 232
Gray Areas 233

System-Neutral Libraries and Tools 234
Additions to OpenStep 234
Noncode Resources 235

Chapter 15: Testing and Debugging 237
Debugging in OpenStep 238
Common Problem Areas 239
    Reference Counts 239
    Run-Loop Asynchrony 240
    Noncode Logic: Nib Files and Models 240
    Exceptions 241
    Weak Typing 242
    Distributed Objects 243

Chapter 16: Performance 245
Measuring Performance 245
Improving Performance 246
    Tuning Algorithms 247
    Reducing Memory and Disk Usage 247
    Managing Autoreleased Objects 248
    Loading Resources on Demand 248
    Using C++ and Standard C 249
    Using Threads and Distribution 249
    Overriding Reference-Count Methods 250
    Overriding Objective-C Dynamism 250

Appendices

Appendix A: PayPerView Source 255

Appendix B: PayPerView with Distributed Objects 265

Appendix C: PayPerView with Enterprise Objects 271

Suggested Reading 281

Index 283

Foreword

OpenStep™ is a landmark development. It brings together many of the features we have all been striving for in a software development environment: true object orientation, the drive for open systems, interoperability, robust class libraries, and the ability to separate the user interface from business logic in a way that allows applications to be deployed on the World Wide Web.

This book is also a landmark. It is one of the first books that give the rest of the world an unbiased perspective of what OpenStep really has to offer. It does this without the hype surrounding objects and from the perspective of mature and seasoned programmers who have already used these technologies in a business setting. Because the authors also have experience with mainstream languages such as C and C++, they give a fresh perspective of OpenStep that many of us will appreciate.

This book is honest to its readers. It explains the strengths of OpenStep but doesn't try to hide its few warts. Having a balanced view of any innovative technology helps us understand the business reasons for why we need to take a close look at the technology. We should never rush blindly into something because a consultant told us it was the "hottest new thing."

You will also find this book unique in its focus on the true business benefits of the object-oriented software development environment. There have been and will continue to be books written by academics that give fine introductions to other aspects of object-oriented systems like drawing, graphics, and mathematical visualization. But this book really focuses on the business reasons to invest in object-oriented technologies: They help you get your software developed faster, and the results are easily adapted to the changing business environments in which we work. The authors have an intimate knowledge of the differences between systems programming, where performance is the first priority, and applications programming, where time to market and adaptability are the benefits for which business managers strive.

This book is well-rounded. It looks at a bigger picture than just the technology—it also looks at the human side of managing object-oriented projects. This is critical since people who have been through the process of helping an organization transition from a traditional procedural programming culture to a truly object-oriented culture know that many times companies fail because they don't take into account the human side of the equation. The authors also know that understanding the process of object-oriented development is sometimes just as important as understanding the technology of object-oriented development.

For those of you who have experience with the older NextStep® or Smalltalk systems, I think this book is essential. Much has changed, and the perspective that OpenStep takes will help anyone who is moving forward in any true object-oriented technology.

For those of you who are just curious about leading-edge object-oriented technologies, this book will let you know why customers are migrating to OpenStep: It allows applications to be created faster and with more flexibility. With the increased rate of change confronting business managers and the incredible time-to-market pressures facing information systems managers, this book should be a starting point for your competitive advantage.

>	Dan McCreary
>	President, Integrity Solutions, Inc.
>	St. Paul, Minnesota
>	July 1996

Preface

The nature of business is changing rapidly. What was good enough five years ago, or even five months ago, may not be good enough now. Almost every business is seeing competition growing fiercer and customers more demanding, while also finding opportunities in new channels of marketing, sales, and distribution. Successfully meeting the competition and utilizing these new channels requires having accurate, dependable, up-to-date information at your command.

It's the job of business applications to take in, process, and deliver this information. As the environment of business changes, the information you need to make good decisions changes along with it. Business applications that can cope with both change itself and the pace of change—applications that can be adapted to new conditions quickly—are proving to be strategic advantages for the companies that have them. On the other hand, software systems that are inflexible in the face of change or that take too long to modify soon become liabilities.

Speed and flexibility are today's hot buttons. For some financial firms, software needs to be crafted and deployed in a matter of days to take advantage of new market opportunities. Miss the deadline, and you've missed the market. Other enterprises may need to build a new application every time they prepare a new product, service, or promotion, and building the application is a key part of getting into the marketplace. OpenStep and its predecessor, NextStep, have won accolades as software environments built to address exactly these needs.

Business applications are addressing more issues, becoming bigger and more complex, and hence they take longer to write. This reality drives the need for faster and more flexible applications. However, building GUI-based applications is difficult; building applications that also talk to a database is more complex; and building applications that use both databases and the World Wide Web can be harder still. The only way to make building complex things easier is to package the complexity someplace where you don't have to deal with it. OpenStep does this by taking the complex but well-understood parts of applications and placing them into frameworks. The OpenStep frameworks hide complex issues behind a set of consistent, powerful, easy-to-understand interfaces, letting the development team focus on writing just those parts of the application that are specific to the business problem they're trying to address. Just as important, the frameworks know about and leverage each other. This means that developers often don't need to write much code, if any, to add new capabilities to an existing application when there's a framework available that provides that capability.

OpenStep's frameworks support the rapid construction and evolution of applications. In fact, the term "extemporaneous prototyping" has been used to describe just how fast development takes place in this environment. Building working prototypes in a matter of hours is common, and extending the prototypes into production applications can happen in days or weeks instead of months. The more work the supporting environment does for you, automatically and behind the scenes, the easier and quicker it becomes to build applications. You can then focus on your business problem instead of worrying about your tools. That's really the primary impetus behind OpenStep.

OpenStep itself consists of five basic pieces of technology: the Foundation Framework™, the Application Kit™, the Distributed Objects system, the Enterprise Objects Framework™, and the WebObjects™ framework. Systems compliant with the OpenStep specification include at least the Foundation Framework and Application Kit, which include the Distributed Objects system. The Distributed Objects system is also available on several platforms independent from the rest of OpenStep, allowing you to put some of your object-oriented computing on more powerful servers while still gaining the development benefits of OpenStep on the client platform. The Enterprise Objects Framework supports business objects by handling all the details of storing their state in relational databases and of displaying and editing their values in OpenStep applications. WebObjects makes data available over the World Wide Web, whether on the Internet or inside a corporate intranet, using HTML as a display medium.

These pieces of technology contain over a decade's worth of experience in building object-oriented applications to address business needs. Together they encapsulate much of the complexity of building applications. In this book, we explore what each of them offers and discuss how these technologies apply specifically to designing, building, and adapting applications in the business environment.

Thank you for considering our book. It's the product of two years' work—not only of writing, but of actually taking part in the development of OpenStep itself and applications that use it. We believe that the OpenStep technology and product suites are among the most flexible and powerful applications of object-oriented technology on the market today. However, that technology isn't interesting unless it's useful in the real world. This book explores what OpenStep is, how it fits into the business environment, and the ways it changes the rules of application development. We've found that OpenStep is indeed useful and that it represents a compelling new way of building software; we believe that you will find the same results.

Acknowledgments and Disclaimers

To my parents, Steven and Paulette, who brought me into this world and have taught me much about life, and to all my other teachers.

—Nik Gervae

To my wife, Molly, who's supported me through some long nights. Also to my parents, Terrence and Kathleen, who hoped for a child blessed with curiosity.

—Peter Clark

We Thank...

We couldn't begin to count or name all the people who made this book possible. From the engineers who developed the software, to the writers who documented it, to the quality assurance folks who banged on it, and everybody else, a ton of work has gone into the OpenStep systems from NeXT and SunSoft. However, we both have a few particular groups and individuals to single out for their assistance. Many of them provided particular help in explaining specific parts of OpenStep to us. Despite this, any errors in the retelling are ours alone.

Nik Thanks...

I've bothered my share of people at NeXT, SunSoft, and elsewhere with my incessant questions, often about the most trivial details, and with my requests for them to read a bit of the book here or there or to explain something to me a bit more. The people I bothered most deserve some small acknowledgment, if not cash prizes. Here they are, in alphabetic order so as not to bruise any egos:

Bruce Arthur	Craig Federighi	Ian O'Donnell
Grant Baillie	John Graziano	Bruce Ong
Brian Bias	Ron Hayden	Toby Paterson
Fréderic Bonnard	Lennart Lövstrand	Karin Stroud
Thomas Burkholder	Wendy Mattson	Ken Taylor
Jim DiPalma	Katie McCormick	Kelly Toshach
	Matt Morse	

I'd also like to thank my co-author, Peter Clark, and my editor at Springer-Verlag, Martin Gilchrist, for the seemingly endless delays they put up with. In addition to these people, I'm sure I've forgotten somebody or other. If you think your name should be on this list, just bring your purchased copy to me and I'll be happy to write your name in. ;-)

Peter Thanks...

Credit needs to be given to the OpenStep and NEO development teams at SunSoft, who are some of the most talented engineers I've ever had the pleasure to work alongside. Thanks also go to everyone at Integrity Solutions, who gave me the opportunity to develop NextStep and OpenStep applications and to work with their customers to understand how these technologies apply to day-to-day business operations. Lastly, to my co-author, Nik Gervae, who not only dealt with all the hard issues of writing a book, but also refined my poorly explicated concepts, gave my words cogency, and taught me much about writing.

Disclaimers

Here's the grain of salt you're supposed to take while reading this book. In this section, we admit to the shocking truth of actually being in the employ of our subject's makers, and reveal our utter lack of clairvoyance or other psychic gifts (but especially precognition).

We Worked for These People

We'll be right up front about it: We worked for NeXT and SunSoft while writing this book. After starting the book as an independent contractor, Nik decided to take on a job at NeXT writing documentation for the Enterprise Objects Framework. Balancing a full-time job with this project was interesting, to say the least. He had also worked at NeXT for a few years before. Nik's working at the moment for Pacific Data Images, a computer animation company.

Peter was working at SunSoft when he started on this book. He has since moved on (returned, actually) to Integrity Solutions, a NextStep and OpenStep consulting firm.

In short, we're biased. We've been using NextStep and OpenStep for years, and we like them. Nonetheless, we've done our best to balance our praise with a little criticism where it's deserved. Also, despite our past and present day jobs, the views we express in this book are ours alone and should be attributed neither to NeXT nor to SunSoft, nor to any other employee of those companies.

Caution: Construction Behind

We've done our best to ensure that this book is an accurate description of OpenStep and related technologies. However, both NeXT's and SunSoft's versions of OpenStep are in beta as we finish. We're certain that something will have changed between now and when they ship. We can only plead ignorance of the future, and beg your forgiveness.

Legal Stuff

This section's just for the lawyers. You regular folks can skip it, honest (unless you're like us and want to know who got mentioned in the book). Following is a list of the trademarks we've knowingly used in this book. All other trademarks mentioned belong to their respective owners.

NeXT, NextStep, Objective-C, NetInfo, OpenStep, Foundation Framework, Application Kit, Project Builder, Interface Builder, Enterprise Objects Framework, WebObjects, WebScript, D'OLE, Portable Distributed Objects, PDO, Workspace Manager, Header Viewer, and NeXTmail are trademarks or registered trademarks of NeXT Software, Inc.

Sun, SunSoft, Solaris, SunSoft Workshop, NEO, OpenWindows, Java, and JavaScript are trademarks or registered trademarks of Sun Microsystems, Inc. SPARC, SPARCompiler, and SPARCworks are trademarks or registered trademarks of SPARC International, Inc. UNIX is a registered trademark in the United States and other countries, exclusively licensed through X/Open Company, Ltd. OpenLook is a registered trademark of UNIX Systems Laboratories.

PostScript, Display PostScript, and TIFF are trademarks or registered trademarks of Adobe Systems Incorporated. Apple and Macintosh are registered trademarks of Apple Computer, Inc. VT100 is a trademark of Digital Equipment Corporation. Informix is a registered trademark of Informix Software, Inc. Intel is a registered trademark of Intel Corporation. PowerPC is a registered trademark of International Business Machines Corporation. Microsoft, Windows, Windows 95, Windows NT, and Visual Basic are trademarks or registered trademarks of Microsoft Corporation. Netscape and Netscape Navigator are trademarks of Netscape Communications Corporation. Novell and NetWare are registered trademarks of Novell, Inc. Oracle is a registered trademark of Oracle Corporation. Sybase is a registered trademark of Sybase, Inc. Unicode is a registered trademark of Unicode, Inc. X Window System is a trademark of the X Consortium.

Part One: OpenStep

1 *What Is OpenStep?*

OpenStep is actually three things in one, a characteristic it inherited from its parent, NextStep. Originally, NextStep came as an integral part of a hardware–software system, so there wasn't much need to define its precise nature. It could be regarded on one hand as the user interface, on another hand as the classes used by application programs, and on a third hand as the development tools, such as Interface Builder™, that developers used to create their applications. The name "NextStep" applied equally well to all three.

OpenStep shares the same triune nature, though perhaps better differentiated by virtue of being a multiplatform standard. We have, then, three ways of viewing this thing called "OpenStep":

> **As a run-time, or user, system.** An *OpenStep run-time system*, consisting of libraries and background programs, enables applications based on the OpenStep specification to run on a particular operating system. This system may define its own user interface, as do NeXT's OPENSTEP™ for Mach and SunSoft's Solaris® OpenStep, or it may conform to its host system's standard, as does NeXT's OPENSTEP for Windows NT™.

> **As a programming interface specification.** The *OpenStep specification* is an operating-system–independent, object-oriented programming interface for creating applications. It includes two rich object frameworks and a number of other programming interfaces.

As a development environment. An *OpenStep development environment* is a set of tools for developing applications that conform to the OpenStep specification, for managing projects, and for defining user interfaces.

The run-time system is largely uninteresting, being simply a set of libraries and background programs that sit around until needed by an application created according to the OpenStep specification. We'll have more to say about it when we examine the major implementations in detail. The specification, on the other hand, is a major topic of interest, defining the structure of the applications themselves. It's the one "OpenStep" that remains the same regardless of the operating system. For this reason we cover the specification first.

A great deal of OpenStep's power, however, lies in the development tools, which eliminate the need for most of the code you typically write in developing a graphical application. To show how they work, we've devoted an entire chapter to them at the end of Part One, illustrating their use by developing a simple custom application. We introduce the development tools after the specification, partly to ensure that you understand the concepts behind them, and partly because NeXT and SunSoft have implemented the tools in slightly different ways. All of this will become evident in the following chapters.

With this prologue out of the way, let's examine the more interesting parts of OpenStep.

The OpenStep Specification

The OpenStep specification defines the programming interface you use to create applications that work with a run-time system. It's a big interface, containing over 100 object classes and 2,000 methods (procedures). Fortunately, application developers seldom need to use much of this interface directly, since the development tools described later take care of most of the work. Further, the packaging of elements as object classes allows developers to study particular subsystems as needed.

Before reviewing the specification's components, let's examine the definition of OpenStep given earlier:

> The OpenStep specification is an operating-system–independent, object-oriented programming interface for creating applications.

Each element in this definition summarizes a number of important facts that aren't immediately obvious. They determine OpenStep's applicability to your needs and its relation to other products. The following paragraphs reveal the hidden particulars of each element:

Operating-system–independent. OpenStep programs are fully insulated from the host operating system (and hardware, for that matter). All of a program's essential needs can be met by using the OpenStep API, though programs are free to use host-specific libraries as well. An OpenStep run-time system must be available on the host platform, of course, and this is limited by the features that the host platform provides. OpenStep requires functionality along the lines of the POSIX interface: robust interprocess communication, support for threads, and so on. Given these, an OpenStep program can be ported between systems as different as UNIX® and Microsoft® Windows™ with little effort.

Object-oriented. The bulk of the OpenStep interface is defined in terms of object classes in the Objective-C® language. Casting programmatic elements such as strings, buttons, and windows as objects gives the programmer a uniform, natural model for working with them. Many common paradigms are reused among the classes, making them even easier to learn and use. Though you do have to learn a new programming language, it's actually quite simple.

Programming interface. The OpenStep specification defines only the programmatic interface for applications. It says nothing about what an application's user interface should look or behave like, although it does define many classes that implement common graphical user interface elements, such as buttons and scrollers. It also says nothing about the tools required to create programs. OpenStep development tools are currently not formalized at all, though NeXT's and SunSoft's implementations form a de facto standard. See "User and Development Environments" on page 12 for descriptions of these two implementations.

For creating applications. The primary focus of the OpenStep specification is the development of user applications that display a graphical interface. OpenStep programs—especially business applications—are often clients to a server process running elsewhere. The largest component of the OpenStep specification, the Application Kit, is all about defining functionality for user (client) applications. Depending on how the libraries are packaged, you can use parts of the OpenStep specification to create server programs on non-OpenStep systems; NeXT's WebObjects framework, for example, includes an implementation of the OpenStep Foundation Framework to handle low-level object programming needs. See *Part Two: Business Applications* for more on this topic.

The next section surveys the components of the OpenStep specification. The remaining chapters in Part One delve into the major components in some detail.

Components of the OpenStep Specification

The OpenStep specification includes four major components (Figure 1):

- the Display PostScript® system, which performs all drawing for OpenStep applications;
- the Objective-C programming language, which defines the OpenStep object model;
- the Foundation Framework, which defines low-level object classes;
- the Application Kit, an object framework defining classes that provide standard application behavior.

The two object frameworks are sometimes called "kits," especially by veteran NextStep programmers. The commonly accepted distinction is that a kit defines classes that your application can use (the classical

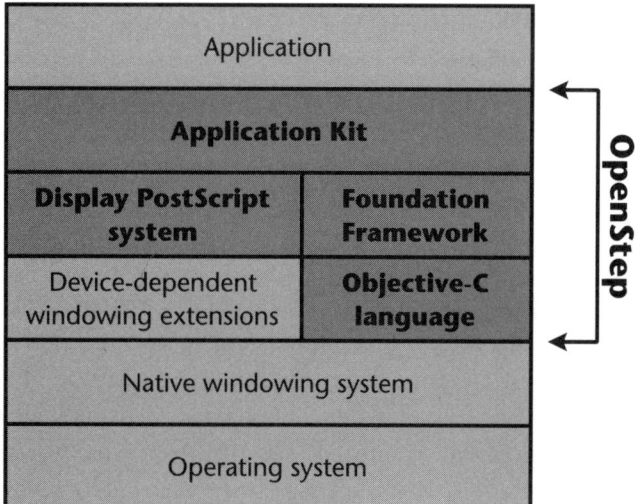

Figure 1. OpenStep Architecture

concept of a library), whereas a framework defines an already functional object system that uses your objects, allowing you to plug in new classes quite easily. In this sense, the Foundation Framework really is just a kit, but the Application Kit is more of a framework, sending messages to your custom objects and running all the logic of display, event handling, and standard services. The term "framework" wasn't in wide use when NeXT named the Application Kit, however, and the name has stuck.

The Display PostScript System

Though perhaps the least important component for many business application developers, the Display PostScript system was a revolutionary feature of the original NextStep system. By unifying the imaging models for screen display and for printing, it simplified the programmer's job and guaranteed true WYSIWYG (what you see is what you get) display for applications. Display PostScript remains integral to OpenStep. Its particular display model does have some impact on OpenStep applications, but it's all at a rather high level, so we don't discuss the subject much beyond this section.

On the up side, the Display PostScript system offers a unified display model for all applications, wherever they may need to draw and on whatever operating system. This can be the computer screen, a PostScript® printer, or a fax machine. Though not really part of the PostScript language, TIFF™ images enjoy a great degree of support from the Application Kit. When you do need it, this level of display integration makes it very easy to get the visual results you want, whatever the final output device may be.

On the down side, OpenStep applications can use only PostScript fonts, and some implementations of OpenStep may be able to print only to PostScript printers. This can be a significant deficiency for sites with a heavy investment in non-PostScript fonts or printers. Fonts can be converted to PostScript format, but they then take up extra disk space. Also, for companies using the X Window System™, the PostScript extensions required by OpenStep aren't always available on X terminals, potentially limiting the use of OpenStep to workstations.

The Objective-C Language and Object Model

Chapter 2: The Object Model presents much of the Objective-C language.

The OpenStep object model is firmly grounded in the Objective-C programming language, a straightforward superset of the ANSI C language that supports a true run-time object system, following the Smalltalk model. Objective-C objects partake of the three classic features of object-oriented programming—encapsulation, inheritance, and polymorphism—and add the feature of dynamism, whereby a number of decisions are deferred from compile time to run time. Classes aren't merely templates for instances; they're true objects and can be sent messages just as instances can. Further, all Objective-C messages are bound to method implementations at run time only, in contrast to C++ messages, which by default are bound at compile time. Dynamism gives Objective-C a huge advantage over C++ for developing flexible high-level systems.

The Objective-C language extensions are simple. A programmer familiar with C programming can learn the basics of using existing classes and objects in just half a day and can be well grounded in the particulars of implementing classes in less than a week. Learning good object design takes a bit longer, of course, but that's true of object-oriented programming in general.

The object model underlying the language closely resembles those of Smalltalk and Java™, as the sidebar indicates. In fact, just as Objective-C is derived from Smalltalk, many aspects of the Java language were derived from both of these languages. All three have true class objects, dynamic messaging by default, and flexible typing.

The Foundation Framework

See *Chapter 3: The Foundation Framework* for a thorough review of Foundation classes.

The Foundation Framework defines classes for the basic features that any program needs, whether a server with no user interface or a client

A Brief Comparison of Object-Oriented Languages

Objective-C lies midway on the scale between barely object-oriented languages (C++) and completely object-oriented languages (Smalltalk):

Feature	C++	Objective-C	Java	Smalltalk
Messaging speed	Fast	Medium	Slow	Slow
Object allocation	Static or dynamic	Dynamic only	Dynamic only	Dynamic only
Type checking	Strict, static	Loose, dynamic	Strict, dynamic	Loose, dynamic
Default method binding	Static	Dynamic	Dynamic	Dynamic
Multiple implementation inheritance	Yes	No	No	Sometimes
Multiple interface inheritance	No	Yes	Yes	No
Operator overloading	Yes	No	No	No
Base classes	Multiple	Single	Single	Single
Class objects	No	Yes	Yes	Yes
Memory management	Manual	Reference counting	Garbage collection	Garbage collection

application with a rich graphical interface. These features fall into four broad groups:

- core run-time and object functionality;
- data storage: values and collections;
- Distributed Objects, including classes for managing concurrent programming;
- environment information.

The Foundation Framework defines the Objective-C root class, NSObject. Nearly all other classes inherit from this class. NSObject's main purpose is to provide the functionality that every other object needs. The root class provides the means for class inheritance and defines methods for object creation and disposal, run-time type inquiry, object identification and comparison, and so on. Other core classes define the features of object archiving, exception handling, message broadcast, and thread handling. One more class, NSRunLoop, automatically establishes a processing loop in which input is read from any of several sources (files, distributed objects, and so on) and dispatched to the appropriate input handler objects.

A number of classes allow you to store simple data values as objects and collect them in various ways. Some classes store numbers and other binary values, some store dates, and others store text strings and raw binary data. Collection classes group objects of any class together in different ways while sharing a common means of enumerating all members of the collection. The Foundation collection classes include array, dictionary, and set. The string, data, array, and dictionary classes also participate in an informal scheme known as *property lists*, which establishes a convenient model for organizing hierarchical data in resource files.

Distributed Objects is a big topic; see Chapter 9: Distributed Applications for a full discussion.

The classes that define the OpenStep Distributed Objects facility also reside in the Foundation Framework. With these classes, a process can connect to another at any time and receive a proxy that represents an object in the other process. This proxy then behaves exactly like a local object as far as the client process is concerned, giving OpenStep programs one of the most elegant distribution models available. We include with Distributed Objects the classes that manage threads and mutexes, as they're often used in the context of distribution.

NeXT has added a number of extra Foundation classes. See the sidebar on page 51 for details.

Finally, the Foundation Framework includes classes that allow your program to determine the arguments it was launched with, to consult the preferences of the user that launched the program, and to retrieve resources stored in the file system such as images and loadable code.

The Application Kit

Chapter 4: The Application Kit describes the individual classes and other elements of the Application Kit.

The Application Kit builds on the Foundation classes to define the features that any user application must provide. Among these are:

- core application behavior, including event handling and display;
- user interface controls, such as buttons and text fields;
- text and fonts;
- drawing support: image and color management classes;
- printing;
- dynamic data links (resembling Microsoft's Object Linking and Embedding or the Macintosh® Publish & Subscribe feature);
- other system services, such as the pasteboard and spell checking.

Interface Builder is formally introduced in Chapter 5: NeXT's OPENSTEP for Windows NT and Chapter 6: SunSoft's Solaris OpenStep.

The best thing about the Application Kit is that you barely have to use it on the programmatic level, especially for business applications that don't need to do much custom event processing and drawing. The OpenStep Interface Builder application, included in the development environment, allows you to graphically build your application's user interface from a palette of standard objects. This allows you to focus on the purpose of your application, not on standard functionality.

The Application Kit is conceptually very rich. Although most of its classes are fairly straightforward, they interact according to powerful models of cooperation and delegation of authority. Again, with the help of Interface Builder, business application developers don't need to worry as much about this as productivity application developers do. However, for those occasions when you do need to understand these models, we survey them in *Chapter 4: The Application Kit.*

User and Development Environments

As essential as a programming interface specification is, it's of no use without concrete implementations and without the tools to build applications. Here there's no specification, but the current development environments from NeXT and SunSoft have a lot in common.

NeXT's OPENSTEP Release 4 for Windows NT

Chapter 5: NeXT's OPENSTEP for Windows NT describes this system in detail.

OpenStep's origins are firmly rooted in the UNIX world, so when NeXT decided to port it to Windows, it took on a big job. With its original UNIX system, NeXT could modify and enhance the operating system and the windowing system to suit its needs. With Windows, it had to make do with what the operating system supported and had to cleanly graft the Display PostScript system onto Microsoft's windowing system. In addition, NeXT decided to modify the user interface presentation of the Application Kit to match the Windows 95® user interface as much as possible. Like we said, a big job.

They've pulled it off fairly well, for what is in many ways a 1.0 release, and are serious about integrating into the Windows environment. OpenStep applications look and largely behave as Windows-native applications, though certain features of Windows, such as combo boxes, multiple-document architecture, and in-place editing of embedded or linked documents, aren't yet supported. Some of these are likely to be added soon, depending on what customers consider most important.

The development environment itself is centered around the Project Builder™ application, which integrates project and file management, code editing, building, and debugging. The Interface Builder application enables rapid development of an application's user interface and ties interface objects into custom objects and other back-end parts of an application. *Chapter 5: NeXT's OPENSTEP for Windows NT* describes these and other development tools.

SunSoft's OpenStep 1.0 for Solaris

Chapter 6: SunSoft's Solaris OpenStep describes this system in detail.

SunSoft's Solaris operating system, now in release 2.5.1, is the planet's most widely deployed commercial UNIX environment. It runs on SPARC®, Intel®, and PowerPC® platforms, scaling from 486-based notebooks to 64-way multiprocessing database servers. Solaris is known for its networking support and was instrumental in building the Internet. Solaris also includes the OpenWindows™ windowing system, which is based on X11R5 with Adobe's Display PostScript extensions and supports both CDE and Sun's OpenLook user interfaces. Several suites of industrial-strength application development and system administration tools are available for Solaris: The system supports over 10,000 applications and can also run Macintosh and Microsoft Windows applications through emulation packages.

Solaris OpenStep builds on these strengths. It's entirely compatible with all existing Solaris and X11-based applications. It supports the same user interface and many of the same applications as NeXT's OPENSTEP for Mach. Third-party applications based on Solaris OpenStep have already been announced, including the productivity suite from Lighthouse Design and the Enterprise Objects Framework from NeXT.

The Solaris OpenStep user environment includes a suite of applications that provide file management, multimedia mail, PostScript previewing, and text editing functions. For the most part, these applications are more useful than the equivalent CDE applications, but you're not required to use them. The CDE and OpenLook applications work within OpenStep as well.

The SunSoft WorkShop® OpenStep development environment includes a suite of application development tools, based both on NeXT's tools and on the award-winning Workshop for SPARC development environment. The OpenStep-specific applications include Project Builder, Interface Builder, and Header Viewer™. However, WorkShop OpenStep also includes SunSoft's C++ compiler, extended to support Objective-C, and a set of tools to support debugging, performance tuning, and multi-threading your applications. If you want to do joint Objective-C and C++ development, the compiler also includes the Rogue Wave Tools++

libraries. *Chapter 6: SunSoft's Solaris OpenStep* discusses both the user and development environments in more detail.

NeXT's OPENSTEP Release 4 for Mach

> See the sidebar on page 83 for more information on the extra goodies you get with Mach.

NeXT's original Mach/UNIX-based system is still available, now truly in release 4. It includes all the features of OPENSTEP for Windows NT, and then some. Notable features include:

- the robust TCP/IP networking and other services offered by Mach and the 4.3BSD UNIX operating system;

- a scalable administrative system, called NetInfo®, that integrates well with NIS (Yellow Pages) networks;

- one of the richest user interfaces available, including nearly photographic-quality icons, true color PostScript support, and full drag-and-drop interaction between all applications;

- the Workspace Manager™ application, which combines file and application management in one very clean interface;

- Mail, the first powerful multimedia electronic mail application, which supports both MIME and the original NeXTmail™ format;

- debugging and performance tools not available on Windows NT;

- an impressive suite of third-party applications that haven't yet been ported to either Windows or Solaris.

NeXT's Mach-based system has been around for a while and is the progenitor of both the Windows and Solaris versions. For these reasons, we haven't bothered with a whole chapter about it, which would repeat what it has in common with its offspring. To see what's unique about OPENSTEP for Mach, see the sidebar on page 83.

2 *The Object Model*

The bulk of the OpenStep specification is an object-oriented programming interface, defined in terms of the Objective-C language and object model. If you're not at all familiar with object-oriented programming, this chapter is required reading. If you're familiar with other object-oriented languages, you should at least skim this chapter to see how Objective-C might differ from the ones you know. You might also want to read the final section of this chapter, which compares Objective-C with the more established C++ language.

This chapter only introduces Objective-C programming, covering the basic principles of object-oriented programming, most of the syntax, which is quite simple, and some of the conventions, where the subtleties of Objective-C lie. It doesn't cover more advanced topics, such as object design, robust class implementation, or taking advantage of run-time features. For those topics, see any general text on object-oriented programming or one on the Objective-C language.

Principles of Object-Oriented Programming

Object-oriented programming arose as a means to simplify the processes of abstraction and modeling. Like procedural programming, which preceded it, object-oriented programming collects lower-level concepts into broader ones, easing the process of mapping real-world entities to programmatic ones. Object-oriented programming does this by introducing the concept of the *object*, which joins data and behavior in a self-contained unit. The abstraction mechanisms resulting from this arrangement are *encapsulation, inheritance, polymorphism,* and *dynamism*. The following subsections explore each of these mechanisms. Of course, you probably know most of the basics; if so, skip ahead to the subsection titled "Dynamism," which may nonetheless contain information new to you.

Encapsulation

Encapsulation is containment, or hiding. An object hides the specifics of its implementation behind a general interface, defining itself in terms of what it *does* rather than what data it contains. This allows the object's implementation to be changed at any time without affecting those using it. For example, an analog clock, whose purpose is to record and tell time, hides the details of its gears and winding mechanism behind a standard dial with hour and minute indicators. The internals can be changed—for example, the gears can be replaced by circuits or the winding mechanism by batteries or a power cord—but the time remains presented by the dial.

An object's interface, then, is defined as a property of the object itself, not as a loose collection of routines to call. Any action must be characterized by both the object performing the action and a specific *message* indicating what to do. This turns around the procedural paradigm, in which the caller of a routine must know the proper arguments, to one in which the user of an object must know what messages it responds to. A clock object, for example, may respond to the messages **hour**, **minute**, and **tick**. A well-designed interface hides the details of an object's implementation, presenting a natural means for using the object according to its purpose.

In programming, the hidden implementation of an object takes the form of private data items, called *instance variables,* and routines tied by the object to the messages it responds to, called *methods*. A clock object might store its time in a single number giving the seconds since midnight, or it might store the time as two numbers, the hour of day and the minutes in the hour. Regardless of this, the interface must remain the same: The **hour** method must return the hour of day; **minute** must return the minutes into the current hour; and **tick** must increment the recorded time by one minute.

Inheritance

Now, in the real world, analog clocks aren't the only kind of time-telling device: There are digital clocks, hourglasses, sundials, and so on. Object-oriented programming accounts for this variety by borrowing a useful technique from taxonomy. Called *classification*, this technique groups similar entities into *classes* according to their similarities. Actual objects—the members of a class—are then referred to as *instances* of that class. In object-oriented programming, object classes that share an interface may be grouped under a parent, creating a more abstract class that describes all the member objects to some useful degree. In some cases, the abstract class can't actually be used to create instances; it just describes the similarities of the subclasses in a formalized way. For instance, clocks of all types—analog clocks, digital clocks, even hourglasses—can be grouped under the single abstract class "Clock," with the messages **hour**, **minute**, and **tick**, even if they individually define their own methods (such as **wind** and **turnOver** for analog clocks and hourglasses).

Turning this bottom-up abstraction over reveals the principle of *inheritance:* Subclasses respond at least to the messages of their superclass. This type of inheritance deals with a class's interface only. Another type of inheritance, that of implementation, applies once we enter into programming. If all types of clocks must be able to report the time of day, we can move the relevant instance variables and methods together into the abstract class, allowing each subclass to use that implementation by default. Subclasses need only define the part of their implementation that makes them different from their superclass: The analog clock can define its **wind** method and hourglass its **turnOver** method, for example. The subclasses can also redefine the behavior of the superclass where that's required, as explored in "Polymorphism."

Polymorphism

Despite their similarities, our three clocks differ in one significant way—the appearance of each type is unique. Analog clocks display hands on a numbered dial, digital clocks present a numeric representation, and hourglasses show varying amounts of sand in their upper and lower chambers. An application simulating these visual features of clocks shouldn't have to know this, of course; it just wants each clock drawn properly. The means for achieving this is called *polymorphism.*

Polymorphism arises from the principle of encapsulation and the messaging metaphor described earlier. A message by itself doesn't define the action that results—the message *and the receiver* do. Objects that share the same message interface may have completely different method implementations. Polymorphism also takes advantage of inheritance, in which a subclass's implementation of a method can differ from that of its superclass. In our example, the abstract Clock class might define a **draw** method that by default simply shows the numeric time. Each subclass then implements its own version to draw the appropriate image. In this case, each subclass inherits the **draw** method but *overrides* the parent class's implementation to do its own thing. AnalogClock draws a dial with hands and Hourglass draws its characteristic figure, while DigitalClock draws a box and then conveniently invokes Clock's implementation to display the numeric representation. The application remains ignorant of this fact; it simply sends a **draw** message to each clock object, and the clock objects execute their own code for drawing.

Dynamism

The final principle of object-oriented programming, though not universally applied, relates to when the application determines the identity, or class membership, of an object. At one extreme, you must know the class membership in advance to send a message, and you may send only messages in the object's interface. At the other, you can send any message you want, even messages that the object might not respond to. These extremes reflect different approaches to the degree of flexibility allowed in dealing with objects. The first approach is called *static typing*, the second *dynamic typing*. Most object-oriented languages fall somewhere between these two.

Another form of dynamism relates to the execution of objects' code. In a *static binding* system, the method implementation for a particular message to a particular object is determined at compile time. Static binding requires some level of static typing, as the language compiler does most of the work. *Dynamic binding*, on the other hand, defers lookup of the implementation to run time—specifically, to the time that the message is actually sent. This requires some support code to be present when the program is running, called a *run-time system*. Dynamic binding is what makes dynamic typing possible, as the run-time system stores the information needed to find the proper implementation for a particular message to a particular object.

Dynamic binding also comes in handy when loading or constructing new classes at run time, as well as when sending messages to objects running in another process. Since the object types don't need to be determined until the time a message is actually sent, messages can be sent to objects that are written by someone else and that exist anywhere in the inheritance hierarchy. As long as the objects respond to the messages you send, you can use any object at all. Later sections and chapters explore these possibilities further.

We've used the terms *message* and *method* somewhat interchangeably up to this point, but there's an important distinction that dynamism introduces. In a procedural language like C, calling a function is a one-step process, involving a simple jump to an address. In a dynamic language like Smalltalk or Objective-C, it's a two-step process, involving the lookup of a method address for a particular message name, and then a jump to that address. The code that wishes an object to do something sends that object a message. The run-time system interprets this message and determines what the proper method is—the method can be defined by the object's own class or by one of the object's superclasses. On finding it, the run-time system then invokes the method. The run-time system can also deal with certain special cases—for example, when the receiver is a null object or a proxy to a remote object accessed through the Distributed Objects machinery.

As a concrete example of dynamism, the OpenStep Foundation Framework defines a number of container classes (such as NSArray) that store other objects—any kind of objects, of the same class or different ones. The single array class, already defined, can store instances of any class in the Foundation and Application frameworks, as well as any class that you define in your application. This is made possible both by dynamic typing, which leaves open the class of object being put in an array, and by dynamic binding, which defers lookup of the messages that the array sends to objects stored in it. All the container knows is that the objects it stores can do the things that all objects do. Nonetheless, because of dynamic typing and binding, the container class can be used to store, retrieve, and send messages to objects of any type.

Without dynamic typing and binding, it would be necessary to define a container class for storing Clocks, one for storing Windows, another for storing Buttons, and so on. With dynamic typing and binding, you need only one kind of container.

Basics of the Objective-C Language

Now that we've covered the principles of object-oriented programming, let's explore how the Objective-C language practices them. As indicated by the name, Objective-C builds on the C language by adding a few simple syntactic elements to define objects and messages, as well as a lot of behind-the-scenes support for dynamic typing and binding. Objective-C is patterned after Smalltalk in many ways, both in terms of the language's syntax and in terms of its behavior. The major goal in the design of the Objective-C language was to extend C to support dynamism as richly as possible.

Objects and Messages

Objective-C objects can be typed either loosely or strictly. They're most simply declared as type **id**, no matter what their actual class membership is. This allows you to write code in which any object can be sent any message, with no complaints from the compiler. You can also declare an object as a pointer to its class type, such as **Clock ***, which brings all the benefits of compile-time type checking for variable assignment and messages.

```
id myClock;
Clock *yourClock;
```

Based on the declarations, **myClock** here could be any kind of object, but **yourClock** must be an instance of Clock or of one of its subclasses (AnalogClock, DigitalClock, and so on). The typical practice in Objective-C programming is to type objects as far down the inheritance hierarchy as needed, but no further.

You construct messages by specifying the receiver and the method name, along with any arguments, all enclosed in square brackets:

```
unsigned int hour = [myClock hour];
```

A method name introduces arguments with a colon, much like Smalltalk. For example, to set the time on **myClock**, you send it a **setHour:minute:** message:

```
[myClock setHour:4 minute:15];
```

Also, because messages are expressions, you can place them anywhere you would place a function call:

```
[yourClock setHour:[myClock hour] minute:[myClock minute]];
```

> This is just like a C++ virtual member function. In Objective-C, all methods are effectively virtual.

Note that because the class of **myClock** isn't even known at compile time, the message expressions can't be bound to implementations until run time. Similarly, even though **yourClock** is statically typed as a Clock, the **setHour:minute:** message isn't bound until run time. It's possible for both **myClock** and **yourClock** to be an instance of Clock or of any subclass of Clock—or of different subclasses. At run time, the appropriate class's implementation for each message is dynamically determined and executed.

Implementing Objects: Classes and Protocols

Every Objective-C object is an instance of some class. The class defines instance variables and methods for all of its instances and ties the instances to inherited variables and methods through its superclass. An Objective-C class definition consists of two components: the interface declaration and the implementation. An additional mechanism, called the *protocol,* allows you to bundle interfaces into meaningful groups distinct from class membership.

Class Interface Declaration

An Objective-C class interface describes the class in terms of its superclass and the methods it adds to or overrides from its superclass. This template shows the basic syntax for a class interface:

```
@interface Class : Superclass
{
    instance variable declarations
}

method prototypes

@end
```

@interface is an Objective-C directive that announces a new class (all Objective-C directives begin with an @-sign). *Class* is the name of the class being defined, and *Superclass* is that of the class it inherits from. The class's instance variables are listed between a pair of braces and declared as in any other block of C code. Finally, the prototypes for the class's methods are listed, followed by **@end** to wrap up the interface declaration.

A method prototype serves the same purpose as a function prototype, but its form is somewhat different. Class and instance methods are distinguished by a tag character: + for class methods; − for instance methods (class methods are described later). Also, because the syntax for messages indicates arguments with colons rather than parentheses, the data type for each method parameter and for the return value must be enclosed in parentheses, as for a type cast. So, a generic method prototype looks like this:

```
- (returnType)methodName:(argType)argument;
```

This class interface shows how we might present the Clock class to the world:

```
@interface Clock : NSObject
{
    unsigned long minutes;
}

- (id)initWithHour:(unsigned short)hour
    minute:(unsigned short)minute;
- (unsigned short)hour;     /* military time (0-23) */
- (unsigned short)minute;   /* 0-59 */
- (void)tick;               /* increments minutes & wraps */
 (void)setHour:(unsigned short)hour
    minute:(unsigned short)minute;

@end /* Clock */
```

Instance Variables: Interface or Implementation?

Instance variables are really part of a class's implementation; however, the compiler needs to calculate how much room a class's data requires in order to properly accommodate subclasses. So in today's world, instance variables remain visible in the interface declaration. The Objective-C language does what it can by providing a set of directives to protect instance variables (just like C++ does).

@protected is the default status for instance variables. It means that the class itself and any subclasses can access the instance variables, but no other class is able to. **@public** opens instance variables to direct access, so that you can read them by pointer dereferencing. **@private** seals instance variables into their class; not even subclasses can access private instance variables.

Class Implementation

<aside>To distinguish them from C code, class implementation files use a **.m** extension (for *method*).</aside>

A class's implementation looks much like the interface declaration:

```
@implementation Class

method definitions

@end
```

All that's needed here, though, are the name of the class and its method definitions. Here's the implementation for the Clock class:

```
@implementation Clock

- (id)initWithHour:(unsigned short)hour
    minute:(unsigned short)minute
{
    self = [super init];
    [self setHour:hour minute:minute];
    return self;
}

- (unsigned short)hour   { return minutes / 60; }

- (unsigned short)minute  { return minutes % 60; }

- (void)tick
{
    minutes++;
    minutes = minutes % (24 * 60);
    return;
}

- (void)setHour:(unsigned short)hour
    minute:(unsigned short)minute
{
    /* Check for bounds error omitted. */
    minutes = (60 * hour) + minute;
    return;
}

@end /* Clock */
```

Method definitions are essentially function definitions, with only a few differences. First is the format for the method name and arguments, which is the same as for method prototypes. Second, within the body of a method implementation, a number of names are predefined for the object's use: all of its instance variables, including those inherited (but not those declared **@private** by superclasses), and the special names **self** and **super**.

Self and Super

self is like the C++ **this** keyword: It refers to the instance currently executing the method. Objects often use it to send messages to themselves. Here's a Clock method that uses **self** to invoke another of its own methods:

```
- (void)synchronizeWith:(Clock *)otherClock
{
    [self setHour:[otherClock hour]
           minute:[otherClock minute]];
    return;
}
```

> **super** simply pushes method lookup outside of the object's class. Unlike in C++, you can't invoke a specific superclass's implementation of a method.

super allows an object to skip its own class's implementation of a method, instead invoking that of an ancestor. This allows overridden methods to be invoked. An AlarmClock subclass of Clock provides a good example of using **super**. Each time the AlarmClock is told to **tick**, it must check whether it should start its alarm. So AlarmClock has to override Clock's **tick** method but still advance the minutes. It could do so explicitly by incrementing the **minutes** instance variable defined by Clock, but Clock's implementation also wraps the time from 23:59 to 00:00, so this would be an error. AlarmClock could duplicate that bit of code too, but if Clock's implementation then changes, AlarmClock won't exhibit the new behavior. Rather than having to duplicate code from Clock and track changes to Clock's implementation, AlarmClock can simply invoke the superclass's implementation:

```
- (void)tick
{
    [super tick];
    if (minutes > alarmTime) [self startAlarm];
    return;
}
```

Protocols

Classes provide a useful mechanism for inheritance of both interface and implementation, but they inherently package both together. If you

> For readers familiar with Java, this is the same as the Java notion of an *interface*. In fact, Java borrowed this concept from Objective-C.

simply want inheritance of interface, you use Objective-C *protocols*. A protocol is a named collection of method prototypes, unattached to any class and without implementations. A class can *adopt* a protocol by including the protocol in its interface declaration, and the compiler can perform type checking based on that declaration. Protocols are defined according to this template:

```
@protocol ProtocolName

method prototypes

@end
```

A class adopts protocols by including their names after its superclass, enclosed in angle brackets. Suppose you wish to create a number of classes for drawing various shapes, but don't want to restrict them to a single parent class. You can define protocols for different graphical attributes, such as one named ColorSetting (with methods **setColor:** and **color**), another named BordersAndShadows (**setBorderThickness:**, **borderThickness**, **setDropShadowDepth:**, **dropShadowDepth**), and so on. A Polygon class then adopts these protocols like this:

```
@interface Polygon : Graphic <ColorSetting, BordersAndShadows>
{
  unsigned int numberOfSides;
}

- (void)setNumberOfSides:(unsigned int)anInt;
- (unsigned int)numberOfSides;

other methods

@end
```

You can declare objects of anonymous classes, but specify their protocols so that the compiler can perform type checking based strictly on formal interface:

```
id <ColorSetting> myColoredObject;
```

Classes can adopt any number of protocols, and protocols themselves can incorporate other protocols by naming them in their declarations:

```
@protocol GraphicObject <ColorSetting, BordersAndShadows>
method prototypes common to graphic objects
@end
```

Objective-C supports only single inheritance of implementation (class), but by allowing classes to adopt any number of protocols, and protocols to incorporate any number of other protocols, it does support multiple inheritance of interface. This brings Objective-C the benefits of multiple inheritance without the problems that multiple implementation inheritance can cause.

Run-Time Features

Essential though the syntax is, the real action in Objective-C programming happens when the program runs. The Objective-C object model pushes as many decisions as possible from compile time to run time, which requires a fair amount of extra information (interface-to-implementation binding, argument types, class membership, and so on), but pays back in power and flexibility. In addition to the run-time system itself, programs rely on the conventions established by the root object class. This section covers interesting aspects of the run-time system and conventions you need to know when programming with Objective-C. *Chapter 3: The Foundation Framework* reviews the actual classes that implement these features.

Class Objects

Objective-C's dynamism is supported largely by the existence of special objects that represent classes at run time. These class objects maintain the method dispatch tables linking interface to implementation and provide a central point for run-time management of their instances. Every Objective-C object has an instance variable called **isa**, which identifies the class that the object is a member of. The run-time system uses this variable to access the method dispatch tables for every message sent to the object.

In its role as a manager of its instances, a class object can itself respond to messages. The messaging system treats any message to a defined class name as a message to the class object. Class methods can perform any kind of operation, but they're typically used for creation of instances, inquiries about the capabilities of instances and about the class inheritance hierarchy, and so on. Class methods differ from instance methods in only one respect—because a class method isn't executed by an instance, it can't refer to any instance variables.

The Root Class

The Objective-C class hierarchy has a single root class, NSObject, from which all others inherit (there are exceptions to this rule, for reasons presented later). The root class defines the functionality needed by all object classes, such as lifetime management, run-time inquiry of an object's interface (including individual methods, protocols, and superclass), and dynamic construction of messages at run time (as opposed to writing them in code).

The methods of the root class are outside the definition of the Objective-C language, in the same way that the standard C library functions aren't strictly a part of the C language. Nonetheless, they play an essential role in Objective-C programming. In a very real way, Objective-C programming is more about learning to use specific classes than it is about the language itself. The root class is the programmer's starting point in this task.

Object Lifetime

Objective-C objects are always created dynamically, most often with the **alloc** class method and some variant of the **init** instance method defined by NSObject:

```
Clock *myClock = [[Clock alloc] initWithHour:3 minute:15];
```

alloc returns a new, blank instance of the class. This instance must immediately be sent an initialization message to establish a valid state, after which it's a usable object. (Allocation and initialization are separated to allow for different allocation mechanisms.) When the object is no longer needed, a **release** message disposes of it.

Objects are often shared or passed among other objects, of course, so just who is responsible for sending that **release** message isn't always clear. When objects are shared, there must be a convention for deciding who is responsible for disposing of them, so that they aren't freed more than once and so that they're not leaked. In Objective-C programming the convention is simple: If you own an object, you alone are responsible for releasing it. If you don't own it, you shouldn't release it. Owning an object means one of three things:

- You allocated the object using the **alloc** method.
- The object is a copy you made with a variant of the **copy** method.
- You added a reference to the object using the **retain** method.

As indicated by the last point, what makes the releasing convention possible is that Objective-C objects are reference-counted. New objects and copies have an implicit reference count of 1, and **retain** increments the reference count. **release**, then, simply decrements the reference count; when the count reaches zero, the object sends itself a **dealloc** message, which each class must override to free any allocated memory and to send **release** messages to any objects it owns (you never send **dealloc** directly to an object).

Reference counting allows objects to be kept valid for as long as any other object needs them. The original creator can release its reference according to the rule without invalidating others' references. The only context where this doesn't work is when a method must return a created object. After all, the method can't release the object before passing it to the invoker, since then the object is immediately deallocated. Objective-C sidesteps this problem by defining a delayed-release method, called **autorelease**.

autorelease marks the receiver to be sent an actual **release** message "sometime later." This allows the object to be returned from a method and used by the invoker without requiring the invoker to explicitly retain and release the returned object—though it can still do so if it needs to keep the object around for a while. The "sometime later" when the object is actually released depends on how you structure your program. By default, all autoreleased objects are released at the top of a program's run loop (defined by the Foundation Framework's NSRunLoop class). This means that you can continue returning objects that you don't own right up the call stack to the run loop object itself. If you need to keep an object beyond that, you must retain it. You can also define tighter contexts for autoreleasing using the NSAutoreleasePool class, as described in *Chapter 3: The Foundation Framework* and *Chapter 16: Performance*.

The Objective-C reference-counting mechanism makes it possible to:

- share values without copying, which saves memory usage;
- share objects with assurance that the objects will remain as long as needed (especially important in distributed applications);
- use objects simply and naturally—the recipient of an object never needs to worry about disposing of it, but explicitly retains it to hang on to it.

It also has its costs, of course. Although the ownership convention makes less likely the possibility of an object being destroyed early or leaked, it is still possible—and when this happens, it can be difficult to track down. *Chapter 15: Testing and Debugging* discusses this problem in more detail. Also, the reference counts and autorelease pools do take up a small amount of extra memory, which can affect performance. Proper use of the autorelease feature and pool management are covered in *Chapter 16: Performance*.

Archiving

A critically important feature of Objective-C for OpenStep is that of archiving, whereby objects can write their state out to a data stream and reconstitute themselves from it later. Archiving is the basis for the Interface Builder application, which allows you to edit live objects and save them as an archive that's loaded into an application when it runs. The OpenStep Foundation Framework defines a handful of classes to direct the archiving process and to archive individual data items. This allows entire object graphs to be archived, collapsing multiple references, properly recording mutual references between objects, and even optionally including nonessential objects, so that references to them are made only if another object actually archives them.

Objective-C and C++

At the time OpenStep's predecessor, NextStep, was being designed, C++ and Objective-C had fairly equal market acceptance. NeXT chose Objective-C because it was clearly more suited to high-level, rapid application development. Despite C++ having overtaken Objective-C in the market, Objective-C remains a better language for application development.

Although both Objective-C and C++ derive from C, C++ is a systems-level language, whereas Objective-C is an applications-level language. The distinction can be summarized by saying that C++ was designed with *program* efficiency in mind, while Objective-C is geared more toward *programmer* efficiency. The difference is substantial—C++ is driven by a philosophy of efficiency and compatibility with existing C which, while necessary for a low-level language, proves quite restrictive in other contexts.

The most important features of C++ in this arena are strong typing and static method binding. Object methods can't be overridden unless the parent class explicitly allows it by using the **virtual** keyword, and such use still carries strict compile-time typing constraints. The compiler does a great deal of checking at compile time, postponing as few decisions as possible. If a method invocation can be resolved to a specific piece of code at compile time, even one declared to be virtual, the compiler resolves it. This forces detailed decisions by engineers early in the design cycle and makes C++ programs brittle—minor changes in one area, or even extensions and subclassing, can cause the program to break or behave in unintended ways. It also makes software development slow; changing part of an object's private data structure requires the recompilation of every bit of code that uses that object. Memory usage must be carefully and manually tracked by the developer, and different toolkits often have different memory management rules. When building low-level software such as an operating system or device drivers, this is all arguably the proper behavior. However, when building applications, where time-to-market and flexibility are crucial issues, these qualities of C++ become damning flaws.

Objective-C takes exactly the opposite tack, being driven by a philosophy of simplicity, reuse, and support for "interchangeable parts" with well-defined interfaces. The Objective-C model postpones as many decisions as possible until run time—both its strengths and its weaknesses as a language derive from this heritage of flexible typing and dynamic binding. In essence, Objective-C is C with as much Smalltalk thrown in as could reasonably be fit, given the constraints of C as a base language.

As discussed previously, most of the utility of the Objective-C model is in the run-time system, not in the compiler. Any method can be overridden—in fact, it's impossible to disallow overriding of methods. Because of run-time binding, though, changes to class data structures and implementations have no impact on clients, which need not even be recompiled to make use of the changes. Objective-C has simple memory management rules, and OpenStep extends these rules to provide a consistent policy throughout its frameworks. Dynamic binding makes Objective-C messages a bit slower than C++ messages, but the tradeoff in flexibility, speed of development, and maintainability more than makes up for this small penalty. Again, the language is designed to facilitate programmer efficiency rather than program efficiency; raw speed is usually less important for applications than it is for system code. In any case, where raw speed is needed, it can be obtained (as *Chapter 16: Performance* describes).

The experiences of companies like Taligent point to the difficulty of building flexible application-level systems in C++. It's telling that C++ started out with no dynamic binding at all; C++ proponents argued that it was dangerous and inefficient. Dynamic binding was then added in special cases, with the **virtual** keyword. The latest attempt to add a form of dynamic binding takes the form of the Run-Time Type Information proposal (RTTI), which is usable only for C++ objects that define virtual functions. While C++ has been undergoing various retrofitting efforts to remedy the lack of dynamic typing and binding, and not all compilers support all the different techniques, Objective-C has had it available, in a well-supported and predictable way, from the very beginning. And, since Objective-C and C++ can be fairly easily integrated, it makes sense to write the parts of the application in C++ that need to integrate with C++ libraries, or that need to be particularly efficient, and write the bulk of the application in Objective-C.

Mixing Objective-C and C++

As the C++ language is essentially an expansion of C, it makes sense to add the Objective-C run-time system and language extensions to C++, allowing the use of both object models from within the same program. The programmer gains the use of C++-style comments, stronger type checking, and the use of both kinds of objects in a single source file. Since the object models are quite different, the models retain their individual characteristics, features, and problems, but they do coexist and interoperate quite well. However, the languages exist in separate name and type spaces. You typically can't interchange the different kinds of objects—Objective-C objects are always Objective-C objects and can't be passed to things that expect C++ data types, and vice versa. There are some tricks that clever programmers can play to cause C++ objects to look like Objective-C objects, but these tricks can cause problems as well.

Most implementations of OpenStep support mixing Objective-C and C++ (this mixed language is often referred to as Objective-C++). As of this writing, both NeXT's GNU-based compiler and SunSoft's WorkShop compiler support Objective-C++.

Although use of the mixed language is supported in both of the above-mentioned environments, the level of support varies. C++ is a second-class citizen in the OpenStep world. NeXT's OpenStep development tools have either limited or no support for manipulating C++ objects. NeXT's implementation of Objective-C, based on the GNU compiler, requires the use of the **extern** linkage directive when mixing languages. For mixed C++/Objective-C source code, any references to external Objective-C symbols must be bracketed by this directive. For example:

```
extern "Objective-C" {
#import <Foundation/NSObject.h>
}
```

As SunSoft's compiler is based on the C++ compiler, there's no need for linkage specification when mixing Objective-C and C++ code in the Solaris environment.

Another pitfall is that statically declared C++ objects are initialized before the Objective-C language run-time system. Referring to Objective-C objects or even calling Objective-C run-time functions fails if performed in the constructors of static C++ objects, and the program typically crashes on being launched. These problems are often difficult to debug, as the order of instantiation of static C++ objects is implementation-dependent but always happens before the program's **main**() function is invoked.

3 *The Foundation Framework*

OpenStep's object classes are divided into two frameworks. The higher-level framework, the Application Kit, contains classes specifically for running an application with a graphical user interface. It builds on the classes of the Foundation Framework, a more general framework that defines core object functionality, basic data and collection types, a distributed object system, and other general program functionality.

The goals of the Foundation Framework are straightforward:

- provide a small set of basic utility classes;
- make software development easier by introducing consistent conventions for things such as memory management and collections of objects;
- support transparent object distribution;
- support internationalization through the Unicode® character encoding;
- support object persistence through archiving;
- provide a level of platform independence to enhance portability.

Although the Foundation Framework has a few dozen classes, many of them operate behind the scenes. Several groups of classes also share similar interfaces, making them quite easy to learn and use. In this, the design meets the goal of utility fairly well.

The second goal, of consistent conventions, is also realized to a fair degree. Foundation classes that do similar things do them in similar ways, with a similar interface. Also, where they can hide the details of operations, they do so (Distributed Objects is a prime example of this).

These means of easing development cover the 80 percent or more of the things you want to do as a developer, making that part of your job much simpler. The remaining things, where you're pushing the bounds of what the classes can do or squeezing out that last bit of performance, do reintroduce some complexity and pitfalls, but this is true of programming in general. Coding in assembly language to boost performance, for example, is inherently more difficult, error-prone, and limiting than coding in higher-level languages.

Transparent object distribution is one of the hallmarks of the Foundation Framework and of OpenStep in general. In fact, its Distributed Objects facility works so well in many ways that it can lull developers into application designs that don't work well due to unanticipated bottlenecks and networking problems. *Chapter 9: Distributed Applications* goes into great detail about distributed objects and their pitfalls, so this chapter only briefly surveys the topic.

The Foundation Framework meets the remaining goals—internationalization, object archiving, and platform independence—only partially. Additional facilities for implementing these features weren't solidly designed at the time NeXT and SunSoft put the OpenStep specification together. The Foundation Framework's string classes fully support Unicode internally, for example, but they provide only basic means of manipulating the characters themselves. Further, the Application Kit's text object doesn't support the full range of Unicode characters. NeXT includes a suite of Unicode-ready text classes in its implementation, but this system wasn't ready in time for the OpenStep specification. Object archiving is currently hampered by an unpublished format for the archives, leaving open the possibility of incompatibilities between implementations. NeXT and SunSoft have worked together to make sure this doesn't happen between the classes in their implementations, but it's still a formal gap to be aware of. Finally, the degree of support for platform independence in the Foundation Framework has turned out to be not quite enough in some respects. NeXT has added a few classes to its implementation to address this problem, mostly in the realm of file management. This isn't a big gap, but again it may be an area where you have to write different code for different platforms.

NeXT and SunSoft are well aware of these limitations of the OpenStep specification and are working to resolve them. Expect a revised version of the specification that includes some new classes to fill in the gaps—eventually. For now, you'll have to accept the fact that if you want to do certain things, you must resort to platform-dependent or incompatible coding strategies for certain parts of your application.

Keeping in mind the purposes of the Foundation Framework, let's quickly examine the classes it comprises. We'll do this in functional groups, describing each class quite briefly and telling where it fits in with other classes.

The Classes

Figure 1 shows the inheritance hierarchy of the Foundation Framework. At the root is NSObject; nearly all other classes in both the Foundation Framework and the Application Kit inherit from it. The other classes fall into about four functional groups, described in the following sections:

- core run-time and object functionality;
- data storage: values and collections;
- Distributed Objects, including classes for managing concurrent programming;
- environment information.

Core Run-Time Classes

Much of the run-time functionality described in the previous chapter is defined by Foundation classes. The root class, NSObject, defines basic functionality needed by all Objective-C objects. Other classes help objects to coordinate their actions, handle assertions and exceptions, and manage the archiving of objects. The following sections describe

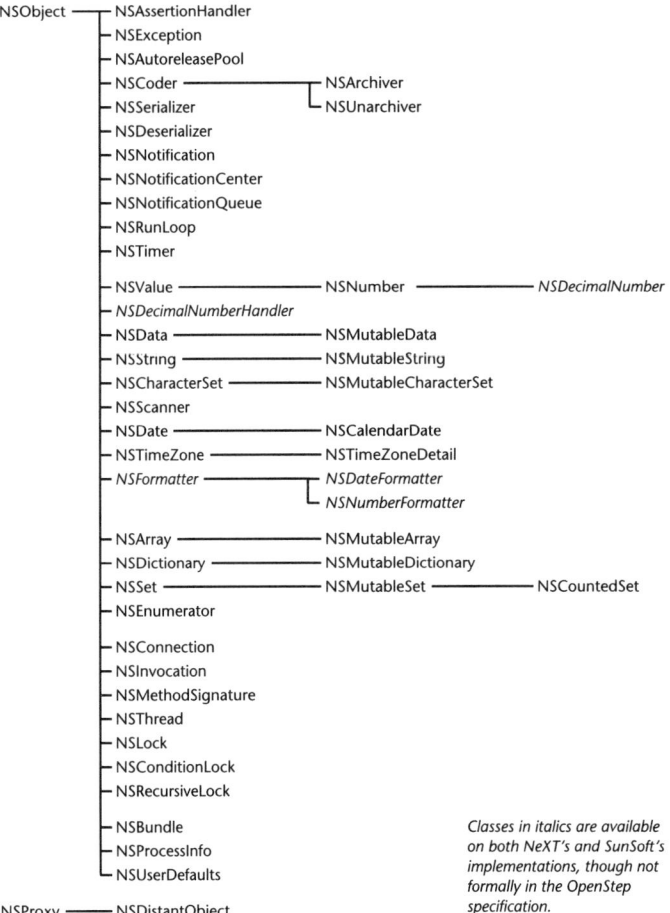

Figure 1. The Foundation Framework Class Inheritance Hierarchy

such areas as the coordination of multiple objects, object lifetime, and error handling.

Object Coordination

Programs and objects alike are driven by input. Without incoming requests and data, most programs, and most objects, are inert pieces of code. Client applications are typically structured around an event loop, which queues keyboard and mouse events for input to the application components that handle the events. Programs can also generate their own input, triggering other components to perform certain actions.

The basic processing loop of an OpenStep program is defined by the NSRunLoop class. Client objects can ask it to monitor input sources and provide input data as it becomes available. Its interface is quite small, consisting mostly of a few variants on the **run** message with time-outs and special modes. The Application Kit uses NSRunLoop to gather keyboard and mouse events, and the Foundation Framework's NSConnection class (described in *Chapter 9: Distributed Applications*) uses it to coordinate Distributed Objects messages between different processes or threads. Specific implementations add special input sources, such as NeXT's NSFileHandle and SunSoft's NSPosixFileDescriptor objects, which allow programs to monitor data availability from a file.

NSRunLoop defines the basic input channel for OpenStep programs but hides most of the details of external input sources. Programs can generate their own input through two major mechanisms: timers and notifications. NSTimer works intimately with NSRunLoop itself to define a delayed message to a single object. You create an NSTimer with a target object, a method to invoke, information to present on invoking the method, and a time to invoke (or "fire") the method. NSTimers can also be configured to repeat with a delay between each firing. This code, for example, sets up a timer to send a **noteAppointment:** message to **myCalendar** after a delay of one hour:

```
[NSTimer scheduledTimerWithTimeInterval:(60 * 60)
        target:myCalendar
        selector:@selector(noteAppointment:)
        userInfo:theAppointment
        repeats:NO];
```

When the timer fires, the argument to the **noteAppointment:** message is the NSTimer itself, from which **myCalendar** can receive the appointment object using NSTimer's **userInfo** method:

```
- (void)noteAppointment:(NSTimer *)theTimer
{
    Appointment *theAppointment = [theTimer userInfo];
    [appointments addObject:theAppointment];
    return;
}
```

This implementation simply gets the Appointment object and adds it to an existing array of Appointments using the NSMutableArray method **addObject:** (arrays are described ahead under "Collection Classes"). The timer created above doesn't repeat, but if it did, the message would be sent every hour until the appointment object (or some other object) sent the timer an **invalidate** message.

NSNotifications are broadcast notices, receivable by any object that registers its interest. NSNotification defines the broadcast notice, which includes the object posting it, the name of the notification, and any additional data included with it. NSNotificationCenter is the coordinator of activity. Objects that want to listen to notifications register themselves with the notification center, specifying the notification name

---

File Input Through NSRunLoop

The lack of a standard file-processing class is one of the OpenStep specification's more serious flaws. Though you can use standard C functions such as **fopen()**, **fread()**, and so on, these don't tie in to NSRunLoop at all. Thus, if you want to multiplex several files or check for input waiting on a file, you must use different classes: NSFileHandle on NeXT's version of OPENSTEP and NSPosixFileDescriptor on Solaris.

To set up an NSFileHandle for automatic reading as the run loop progresses, create a custom object to handle input and register it as an observer of the file handle:

```
[[NSNotificationCenter defaultCenter]
    addObserver:myFileReader
    selector:@selector(getFileData:)
    name:NSFileHandleReadCompletionNotification
    object:myFileHandle];

[myFileHandle readInBackgroundAndNotify];
```

myFileReader then implements **getFileData:** like this:

```
- (void)getFileData:(NSFileHandle *)fHandle
{
    NSData *newData = [fHandle availableData];
    [self doSomethingWithData:newData];
    return;
}
```

NSPosixFileDescriptor works in a similar manner but explicitly provides for a single object that it automatically messages when data is ready.

they're interested in, and objects that post notifications do so through the notification center. The NSNotificationQueue class provides finer-grain control for posting a notification, allowing the poster to specify the urgency of the notification (such as posting immediately or on the next cycle of the run loop), as well as whether it can be combined with similar pending notifications.

The following code fragments show how to set up an object that watches a document's size, possibly to display it in a status bar. **sizeMonitor** is the object that observes **theDocument**; it's registered with a notification center like this:

_{The @"..." compiler directive creates a string object.}

```
#define DocumentDidChangeNotification @"Document changed"

[[NSNotificationCenter defaultCenter] addObserver:sizeMonitor
    selector:@selector(sizeChanged:)
    name:DocumentDidChangeNotification
    object:theDocument];
```

The **defaultCenter** message returns the NSNotificationCenter used by most objects; you can create your own, but you should rarely need to. **addObserver:selector:name:object:** registers **sizeMonitor** so that it receives a **sizeChanged:** message when **theDocument** posts a notification named DocumentDidChangeNotification. When **theDocument** changes, it posts the notification like this:

```
[[NSNotificationCenter defaultCenter]
    postNotificationName:DocumentDidChangeNotification
    object:self];
```

And every object observing it gets sent the message it registered, in this case, **sizeChanged:**.

Object Lifetime

The last chapter described how the **autorelease** method causes an object to release itself after a delay. This behavior is made possible by the NSAutoreleasePool class, which is a simple container that, when deallocated, releases all of its objects. NSRunLoop automatically creates and destroys autorelease pools on each pass through the loop. You can also use them explicitly to bracket loops that create many temporary objects. Here's a typical example:

```
    BOOL keepGoing = YES;

    while (keepGoing) {
        NSAutoreleasePool *pool = [[NSAutoreleasePool alloc]
            init];

        keepGoing = [myObject doSomethingReallyExpensive];

        [pool release];
    }
```

In this loop, **myObject** is sent a message that causes it to autorelease many objects, which would normally accumulate in the default pool until the loop was broken and control returned to the top-level loop. This would have a disastrous effect on memory usage, so the loop brackets the expensive message with its own autorelease pool. Any object sent an autorelease message during **doSomethingReallyExpensive** is released at the end of the loop, cleaning things up on each pass.

Error Handling

Neither the C nor the Objective-C language provides much in the way of error handling. The Foundation Framework fills in some of the gaps by defining error-handling classes and macros for using them. The first class, NSException, represents various exceptional conditions, such as an invalid argument to a method, a timeout on a remote method invocation, or an internal error of some sort. Each exception object has a name that identifies it, a reason that can be logged, and a user dictionary of key-value pairs that allows the code raising an exception to provide additional information about the nature of the exception. Companion to NSException are three macros for defining an exception-handling context. NS_DURING begins a section of code where an exception can be caught. NS_HANDLER begins the code that's invoked if any exception is raised. This code can examine the exception and take appropriate action. NS_ENDHANDLER closes the exception-handling code.

The **riskyAction** method below, for example, sends a message to an object that sometimes raises an exception when poked. If the object raises an exception named "Don't touch me!", this method catches it and returns NO. If the object raises some other exception, this method throws it back up, not knowing how to handle it at this level. If no exception occurs, this method returns YES.

```
- (BOOL)riskyAction
{

NS_DURING
    [myFragileObject poke];

NS_HANDLER

    if ([[localException name]
            isEqualToString:@"Don't touch me!"]) {

        /* Handle error. */
        return NO;
    } else {
        /* Unrecognized exception. */
        [localException raise];
    }

NS_ENDHANDLER
    return YES;
}
```

The second error-handling class, NSAssertionHandler, provides macros for testing conditions during program execution. If a macro condition evaluates false, the NSAssertionHandler object is called upon to handle the failure. The default behavior is to log a message and raise an exception. NSAssertionHandler offers a richer assertion-handling mechanism than the standard C library's **assert()** macro, being able to handle both functions and methods and being customizable by the standard object-oriented technique of creating subclasses.

Archiving and Serialization

To support storing objects in files and transmitting them between processes, the Foundation Framework defines the NSCoding protocol, consisting of two methods, **encodeWithCoder:** and **initWithCoder:**. Objects that adopt this protocol use these methods to store and retrieve their state, along with the coder classes, NSCoder, NSArchiver, and NSUnarchiver. NSCoder defines the abstract interface for coding, with general archiving methods such as **encodeValueOfObjCType:at:** and

decodeValueOfObjCType:at:, along with others for managing networks of objects that contain obligatory and optional members.

An additional archival mechanism—*serialization*—is based on the value and collection classes described in the next section. The NSSerializer and NSDeserializer classes write data to and read it from structures called *property lists*, which are nested groupings of information created from the array, dictionary, string, and data classes as described in the "Property Lists" subsection ahead.

Value and Collection Classes

Among the Foundation classes used most often by application programs are those that represent simple values and those that handle collections of other objects. Because these classes are used so much, they define a rich set of methods for many operations, including numerous different methods for constructing values or collections of one class from those of another. Value and collection objects also cooperate with the Distributed Objects system to prevent unnecessary network traffic; this topic is discussed in "Transferring Data and Objects" in *Chapter 9: Distributed Applications.*

Most of the value and collection classes distinguish themselves into immutable versions, which can't be changed, and mutable subclasses, which can be changed. Immutable classes offer protection in type declarations, which allows errors to be detected at compile time, and in actual behavior, which prevents illegal modifications at run time. Immutable objects can also be copied very cheaply, simply by retaining themselves, and cheap subsets can be taken by referencing the contents of the immutable collection. Mutable objects must of course produce actual copies. The **copy** and **mutableCopy** methods allow you to create immutable or mutable copies of either type of object.

Value Classes

The various value classes represent character strings, dates and times, raw binary data, and atomic and structured C data types. NSString and

NSMutableString store series of Unicode characters, can convert their values to and from a number of other character encodings, and provide a raft of methods for searching, extracting, and combining strings. An auxiliary class, NSScanner, allows you to search for and extract numeric and substring values from a string. Both the string classes and NSScanner use the NSCharacterSet and NSMutableCharacterSet classes to group characters together for search operations.

Dates (including time of day) are represented by the NSDate and NSCalendarDate classes. NSDate defines the basic storage and calculation of dates, while NSCalendarDate adds methods to access calendar components such as year, day of week, and so on. The date classes also make use of the NSTimeZone and NSTimeZoneDetail classes, which allow them to represent their times in local terms and to adjust their values for daylight savings time.

NSData and NSMutableData store arbitrary binary data, from any source. NSMutableData in particular can be used as an open-ended memory stream, which can be written to in order to build an archive of

Formatters

Though they weren't created in time for formal inclusion in the OpenStep specification, NSFormatter, NSDateFormatter, and NSNumberFormatter are available with both NeXT's and SunSoft's Foundation Frameworks. These classes format values into human-readable strings, parse strings into appropriate values, and validate partial strings according to the expected format.

NSFormatter is an abstract class that defines the two methods that do this, **stringForObjectValue:** and **getObjectValue:forString:**. Its two subclasses, NSDateFormatter and NSNumberFormatter, handle formatting of NSDates and NSNumbers, respectively. NSDateFormatter produces and interprets the various date formats defined by NSCalendarDate and also does some heuristic interpretation of natural language expressions, such as *May 27th 96* and *27th of May '96*. NSNumberFormatter uses different format templates for positive, negative, zero, and null values; rounding modes for floating-point values; thousands and decimal separators; and a few other NeXT-specific format settings.

data as it's constructed. The archiving classes described earlier use exactly this technique.

The remaining value classes, NSValue and NSNumber, store atomic and structured C data types—**char**, **unsigned int**, program-defined **struct**s, and so on. Both classes are immutable; since their contents are so simple, it's easier to simply create a new object with the changed value than to spend the code required for all possible changes. NSValue is essentially a byte bucket that also stores type information. NSNumber, a subclass of NSValue, restricts its possible values to the C numeric types and adds a number of methods, such as **intValue**, **unsignedIntValue**, and **floatValue**, for accessing the numeric value as any of these types. NSDecimalNumber, an additional class not formally in the OpenStep specification, handles extra-high-precision fractional values, with up to 38 significant digits.

Collection Classes

The Foundation Framework defines three basic kinds of collection: array, dictionary, and set. The collection classes are NSArray and NSMutableArray; NSDictionary and NSMutableDictionary; and NSSet, NSMutableSet, and NSCountedSet. NSCountedSet represents what is commonly called a *bag;* it allows objects to be entered more than once.

A collection object contains other objects, and only other objects; to put an integer value into an NSArray, for example, you must encapsulate it in an NSNumber object. An array object offers access to its contents by index, a dictionary by arbitrary object key (usually strings), and a set by identity of object **id** pointer or equality via the standard **isEqual:** method. The different collection classes support a common means for enumerating their contents with the **objectEnumerator** method. The dictionary classes also provide the **keyEnumerator** method to iterate over keys.

An important feature of the collection classes, stemming directly from Objective-C dynamism, is that a collection can accommodate objects of any type. There's no need to define a template and generate a collection class dedicated to one particular type of contents. An NSArray can contain NSStrings, or NSTimers, or other NSArrays; it can even contain a mixture of object types. This may seem dangerous to those used to strong type checking, but in practice it turns out to be more convenient, more compact, and more powerful. In this limited domain, type checking can be handled by means other than the compiler.

Property Lists

As mentioned earlier, some value and collection classes participate in an informal arrangement called the *property list*. A property list is any object composed only of string, data, array, and dictionary objects. A string object alone is a valid property list; as is an NSArray of string objects; an NSDictionary whose values are data, string, and array objects is also a valid property list. Property lists are useful for grouping related data in a well-known and easily readable format, especially complex structures of key-value pairs (dictionaries) and simple value lists (arrays).

Property lists can be stored to ASCII or more compact binary files using NSArchiver and NSUnarchiver objects and can be used to store application resources such as localizable strings and user preferences. The ASCII files can even be edited by hand, making both debugging and customization by expert users more convenient.

This code fragment builds a small dictionary as a property list containing a string, a chunk of data, and an array of strings:

```
NSMutableDictionary *myPropertyList;

NSData *scratchData;
NSArray *scratchArray;

myPropertyList = [[NSMutableDictionary alloc] init];
[myPropertyList setObject:@"Nik Gervae" forKey:@"name"];

scratchData = [NSData dataWithContentsOfFile:@"MyFace.tiff"];
[myPropertyList setObject:scratchData forKey:@"picture"];

scratchArray = [NSArray arrayWithObjects:@"reading",
    @"science fiction", @"surfing the net", @"snowboarding",
    nil];
[myPropertyList setObject:scratchArray forKey:@"hobbies"];
```

There are several things to note in this example. First, note that you can pass any kind of object as the argument to NSMutableDictionary's **setObject:forKey:** method. Also, note that the NSData and NSArray objects are created with special methods—not **alloc**—so they don't have to be released explicitly.

The ASCII representation of this property list can be retrieved with a **description** message. It looks like this:

```
{
    name = "Nik Gervae";
    hobbies = (reading, "science fiction", "surfing the net",
        snowboarding);
    picture = <4d4d002a 000025a4 803fd2e9 repeats... fc800000
        2710>;
}
```

This is the standard format for ASCII property lists. Dictionaries are enclosed in braces, with each key-value pair terminated by a semicolon. Strings with whitespace are enclosed in quotation marks. Arrays are enclosed within parentheses, and their items are separated by commas. Data blocks are enclosed with angle brackets, and their contents are rendered as hexadecimal text in eight-digit sets. This clear representation makes debugging output easier to read.

Due to their convenient recursive structure, OpenStep uses property lists extensively in many areas. Since there's just one paradigm—and one set of classes for accessing them—storing and retrieving information is a simple task, performed the same throughout OpenStep.

Classes for Distributed Objects and Concurrency

Chapter 9: Distributed Applications delves much further into the various distributed object models that OpenStep programs can work with.

As mentioned before, the Foundation Framework includes an object distribution facility that operates transparently at the level of the language. This facility makes the syntax for messaging a remote object look exactly the same as that for messaging a local one. The Foundation classes that make this possible do so by exploiting some fairly esoteric (but fundamental) features of the Objective-C object model, especially message forwarding. The OpenStep Distributed Objects facility works by defining a proxy object class, which stands in for a real object in another process (or in another thread within the same process). Proxies implement almost no methods of their own, so any time a proxy receives a message the forwarding mechanism traps it, sends it to the real object, and returns the result.

The Foundation Framework actually defines an abstract proxy class, NSProxy, which allows other kinds of proxies to be created under a common parent. Note that NSProxy is not a subclass of NSObject. It's a root class in its own right, but it defines only enough functionality to fulfill its role as a proxy. Subclasses must implement functionality that characterizes the particular proxy mechanism needed. The proxy subclass used for distributed objects is called NSDistantObject. Most messages sent to it are forwarded to its real counterpart, a descendant of NSObject in another process or thread.

Although an NSDistantObject represents its real counterpart, it does very little work itself. Most of the processing for remote messages is performed by NSConnection objects. Each NSDistantObject belongs to exactly one NSConnection, which communicates with a peer connection object in a remote process. The NSConnection makes objects available remotely by vending proxies to them, and it also keeps track of which ones have been vended where. When an NSDistantObject forwards a message, it does so by passing the message to its connection object, which does the work of packaging up the arguments and such for transmission. A pair of auxiliary classes called NSMethodSignature and NSInvocation represent method argument and return types, and an actual message with arguments, respectively.

Distributed objects run concurrently in separate processes or threads, so the Foundation Framework defines a few classes for managing concurrent access to shared resources. NSThread represents a running thread within a process. NSConnection objects coordinate their handling of messages within threads to avoid deadlock conditions. Three mutex or lock classes allow you to protect your own data explicitly. NSLock defines a simple lock–unlock mechanism. NSConditionLock allows you to set a state attribute upon unlocking it, which another client can use as a condition for attempting to acquire the lock. NSRecursiveLock allows the same thread to be acquired multiple times by the same thread, so that it needn't keep track of this fact to prevent deadlock.

Process Environment Classes

The last group of classes in the Foundation Framework provides information about a process's run-time environment. NSProcessInfo contains the arguments used to start the process, including the executable file's name; environment variables defining system parameters; and the host name and application name for the process.

NSUserDefaults gives applications access to user preferences, storing this information on disk so that the preferences are read each time the application starts and are saved when it exits. The defaults are stored as a big nested property list, so applications can examine the values using string, data, array, and dictionary objects.

The NSBundle class allows applications to load disk-based resources, such as images, sounds, and interface files, in a uniform manner. It also handles dynamic loading of new classes, making it possible to update or extend an application piecemeal. Bundles organize their on-disk resources into localizable and custom subdirectories and determine the user's language through the user defaults system, automatically retrieving the proper resource for that language.

Other Additions to the Foundation Framework

Besides the added classes already mentioned, NeXT has implemented about a dozen more classes for its own purposes, several of which may well end up in a future version of the OpenStep specification. Among these are:

- NSAttributedString. This class associates arbitrary user-defined attributes with specific ranges in an NSString. NeXT's Unicode text system uses it extensively for recording fonts, color, kerning, and other string formatting information.

- NSPPL. This class handles incremental reading and writing of property list files on disk, whether in ASCII or in a more compact binary representation.

- NSFileManager and NSFileHandle. A file manager object checks for the existence and access rights of files; moves, copies, links, and deletes files; and performs other standard file system operations. An NSFileHandle represents a single file as an object.

- NSPort, NSPortCoder, and other Distributed Objects support classes. These classes represent features of the Mach operating system that NeXT duplicated in porting Distributed Objects to other platforms. They can be useful for some customizations of Distributed Objects functionality.

- NSProtocolChecker. A protocol checker acts as a gatekeeper to another object, forwarding messages in its protocol and raising an exception for any other message. Protocol checkers are typically used to restrict the messages that can be sent to an object vended through the Distributed Objects facility.

- NSDistributedLock. A distributed lock uses a file as a mutex shared among tasks, otherwise behaving much like a regular NSLock.

- NSHost. A host object records the names and Internet addresses of a machine.

- NSPipe. A two-way communication channel between a parent and child process pair.

- NSTask. An NSTask records the arguments for a process, records input and output objects as NSFileHandles or NSPipes, and posts a notification before exiting that allows observers to clean things up.

4 *The Application Kit*

The Foundation Framework is quite low-level and general purpose, defining classes that any program can use, from server programs with little or no interface to user applications with highly graphical interfaces. For the latter type of program, the OpenStep specification also offers the Application Kit, a rich, sophisticated framework of object classes that implement nearly all of the common functionality of event handling, display management, and standard panels and controls, into which you graft your custom objects for application-specific behavior. Additional Application Kit classes provide such amenities as spell checking, data linking between documents, and offering of application functionality to other applications.

Rich as the Application Kit is, as a business application developer you may well find you don't have to program much with its classes at all. The Interface Builder application, a development tool described in following chapters, allows you to construct your application's interface in the manner of a drawing or diagramming program. With it, you drag user interface elements such as windows, buttons, and text fields onto the screen from palettes, arrange and connect them as needed, and declare the interfaces for whatever custom classes you define that must interact with the user interface objects. If you're simply using the predefined graphical objects and not creating classes that handle events and perform drawing, constructing the interface itself can be as simple as dragging and dropping.

That said, the fact remains that even applications constructed through drag and drop in Interface Builder require some programming to achieve any level of sophistication and unique behavior. The purpose of

NeXT's Enterprise Objects Framework handles even more interface coding for you. See Chapter 10: Database Applications.

the Application Kit is to minimize this burden with regard to the application's interface, allowing you to concentrate on the logic unique to your application. This chapter, then, describes what the Application Kit does for you, thereby showing some of what you *don't* need to do when creating an OpenStep application. Unlike the description of the Foundation Framework in the last chapter, this description reviews functional areas of the Application Kit and doesn't describe every individual class.

Preliminaries

The Application Kit works by a model of guided cooperation. The usher and traffic cop is the NSApplication object, which connects the application to the windowing system and coordinates the efforts of the most basic user interface elements: windows and views. The remaining Application Kit classes work in concert to handle the events brought in through the basic elements, recast the events as meaningful input to your custom objects, and display the results that your objects produce from those inputs.

The Application Kit uses a few basic cooperation strategies that color its entire design. An early acquaintance with these strategies will help you better appreciate that design, as well as simply make things clearer when we describe the details later. Some of these strategies are quite simple; some require additional explanation later on, after relevant classes have been formally introduced.

See "Driving the Application" on page 60 for a more thorough description of the responder chain and target–action paradigm.

The *responder chain* characterizes the Application Kit's event-handling system. In an application with many windows, each of which contains many objects that can receive an event, this mechanism determines which of those objects actually gets the event. The responder chain begins with the "active" object in a window, which gets first crack at all events. If it doesn't handle a particular event, its containing objects are given a chance, right up to the window containing them, through a few other objects, and ultimately to the NSApplication object itself.

The *target–action* paradigm, used by control objects and a few others, translates raw events, especially mouse events, into more meaningful requests to perform specific actions. The target–action system uses the responder chain but passes special *action messages* up the chain instead of events.

The more complicated Application Kit objects, which don't accommodate subclasses easily, allow you to customize their behavior by appointing a custom object as a *delegate*. A delegate is informed of certain operations that the object is about to perform or has performed; can approve or refuse a pending operation; can modify the parameters used for the operation; and receives a message telling it the operation has been performed. (Delegation is actually a generic strategy of object-oriented programming, but since it doesn't play a visible role in the Foundation Framework, we put it off until this chapter.)

Another type of customization-by-appointee is handled by objects that serve as *data sources* to others. In this strategy, an object that displays a large amount of variable data asks another object for what to display as it's needed. This allows you to hook the display object up to any underlying data set without having to actually create a subclass. A data source is sometimes the same object as the delegate in the Application Kit, but this need not always be true.

The final strategy is that of an *owner*, or an object responsible for managing or providing data in a looser way than a data source. A data source continually interacts with, and is more or less a permanent partner of, its client. An owner, on the other hand, can change quite frequently, or isn't linked directly to the object using its services, or is asked to perform only occasionally. This is the least formalized strategy, with little API referring explicitly to the role; we'll highlight it as needed.

Core Application Functionality

The OpenStep application architecture (Figure 1) is defined by a number of core classes and by the interactions among them. The

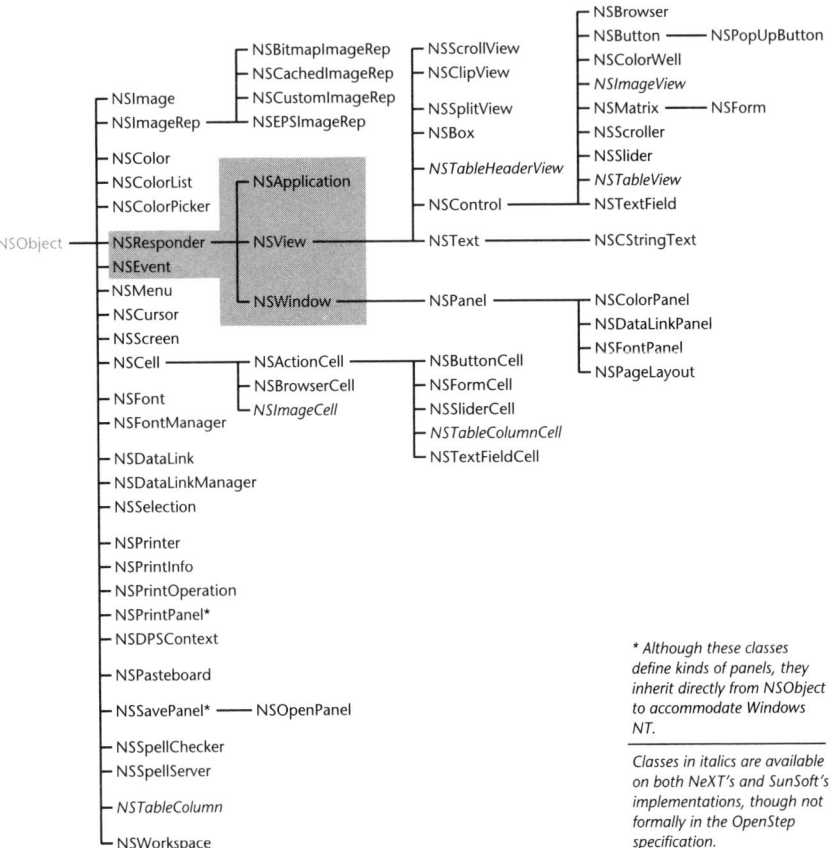

Figure 1. The Application Kit Inheritance Hierarchy

NSWindow and NSView classes define the fundamental graphical structure of the application, while the NSApplication object coordinates event handling and display. These three classes also participate in the responder chain, by which events and dynamic messages are distributed through the application.

Graphical Structure

An OpenStep application presents itself as a number of independent windows, each containing a nested hierarchy of view objects that define visual items such as buttons, scrollers, and text fields. Views can contain other views, allowing applications to display highly structured interfaces. All display and drawing is performed automatically by views, which handle the problems of display order, clipping, and coordinate transformation. Each view subclass implements just one drawing method to perform its own unique kind of drawing, and the display machinery invokes it at the right time.

Windows and Panels

The NSWindow class defines the basic behavior for all standard windows: placement on the screen and ordering back-to-front, distribution and handling of events sent to them, and coordination with other parts of the application. A standard window is one that presents significant content: a document of some sort, or the primary interface to the application. Other types of windows are represented by NSWindow's one subclass, NSPanel. Panels typically present auxiliary information, such as user preferences, a palette of options (such as colors), attributes of a selected object, error messages, and so on.

In an OpenStep application all windows are free-standing; there is no nesting of windows in the manner of Microsoft Windows. A window object allows for several border elements: a title bar, a close button, a miniaturize (minimize) button, and a resize bar or border. Within the frame defined by these elements, the window places its *content view*, an NSView object representing the canvas on which the window's contents are drawn.

A window object can be assigned a delegate, which is informed of such things as the window moving, closing, resizing, and so on. The delegate can modify the parameters of some of these operations or prohibit them altogether. Window objects also broadcast the same notifications to any interested object using NSNotification objects.

NSPanel alters some of the default behaviors of NSWindow and adds a few convenience methods for commonly altered attributes. Panels disappear from the screen when their application isn't active, unlike windows, which typically remain visible unless the user explicitly closes or miniaturizes them. Some panels also float above standard windows so that they're never obscured. They can also be brought on screen in a modal manner, blocking other windows and panels in the application from receiving events until they're dismissed.

Views

When it comes to drawing, a window simply represents the virtual device in which drawing instructions are interpreted. The objects that actually perform drawing and display in an OpenStep application are NSViews. An NSView stakes out a rectangular area in its window and maintains the graphic state for its image, handling coordinate transformation from other views, clipping, and other such things. A few other Application Kit classes draw, but always within a host view. See "Display and Drawing" just ahead for details on drawing.

Event handling is described in detail under "Message Routing in the Responder Chain" on page 60.

An NSView's other major responsibility is the handling of events. While NSApplication and NSWindow primarily act as distributors of events, view objects are the typical recipients and interpreters of events. Mouse events are always targeted at a view, for example, as are most key events. The Application Kit defines abstract methods for events, such as **mouseDown:**, **mouseUp:**, and **keyDown:**, which subclasses of NSView can override to catch the events and interpret them as needed. Subclasses don't need to worry about retrieving most events; they simply implement the appropriate event-handling methods, which are automatically invoked by the Application Kit.

NSViews also offer the features of image dragging, whereby the user can drag an icon or other graphic element from one view to another; cursor-update rectangles, which change the cursor automatically as the user moves the mouse in and out of them; scrolling primitives, which are used by the Application Kit's scrolling classes; and support for custom pagination and PostScript output when printing.

The View Hierarchy

All view objects in an NSWindow are arranged in a hierarchy whereby every view, except for the window's top-level view, is contained in another view, called its *superview*. A view's contained views are called its *subviews*. The top-level view is the NSWindow's content view. The view hierarchy plays a fundamental role in the display of a window and the distribution of events, as described in various sections of this chapter.

Views are often arranged so that a larger view contains a number of smaller subviews to group them together; the content view is a ubiquitous example of this. The NSBox class groups its subviews visually as well as programmatically, by drawing a border and title around its subviews. Another arrangement involves placing a very large view inside a smaller superview. This arrangement is used for scrolling large document views by the Application Kit's scrolling classes, NSScrollView, NSClipView, and NSScroller.

Display and Drawing

NSViews use a highly structured display mechanism, whose machinery operates automatically to draw all NSViews in a window. The drawing act itself is all that an NSView subclass need handle; the Application Kit takes care of the rest. Every time the event loop completes, all NSViews are told to redisplay themselves if necessary using a method called **displayIfNeeded**. You can mark a view as needing display in its entirety or in a particular region with methods like **setNeedsDisplay:**. You can also simply display a view unconditionally using the **display** method or one of its variants, or turn off automatic display altogether in a particular NSWindow.

The display methods all set up the proper coordinate transformations for the view and invoke the **drawRect:** method. NSView's implementation of **drawRect:** does nothing. Subclasses override this method to send PostScript instructions to the Window Server for interpretation. In **drawRect:** the view subclass can call just about any PostScript operator, invoke other Objective-C methods that in turn produce PostScript instructions, and even send messages to objects that draw within views, such as NSImages, NSStrings, and NSCells.

After a view draws itself, the display mechanism goes on to display all of its subviews in the rectangle drawn. In this manner a group of views always displays itself properly, from back to front, relieving the programmer of nearly the entire burden of managing display.

Driving the Application

The motor of an OpenStep application is the NSApplication object itself. This object's job is to run the event loop and other periodic mechanisms and to send incoming events and internally generated action messages to their appropriate destinations. Any operation involving events that affects the entire application is typically defined by NSApplication. The application object also maintains the application's connection to the Window Server and to other system services such as the pasteboard server.

Message Routing in the Responder Chain

The application object distributes events and action messages through a series of objects called the *responder chain*, which was introduced briefly earlier. The responder chain comprises objects that descend from the abstract class NSResponder. NSApplication, NSWindow, and NSView all inherit directly from NSResponder, and all of their subclasses therefore participate in the responder chain. NSResponder defines the event-handling methods mentioned earlier, such as **mouseDown:** and **keyDown:**, to do nothing but pass the event to another object, called

> ### SunSoft's Thread-Safe Application Kit
>
> The Application Kit as defined in the OpenStep specification isn't thread-safe; multiple threads competing for the single connection to the Window Server can cause all sorts of nasty problems. Though you can get around this problem in various ad-hoc ways, SunSoft decided to include a special subclass of NSApplication to make creating multi-threaded applications easier.
>
> The LockingApp class adds the methods **lockAppkit** and **unlockAppkit** to NSApplication's interface. All a background thread need do to ensure safe operation is bracket event-handling or drawing code with these methods.
>
> Code in the foreground (Application Kit) thread must also use these methods if it sends messages to objects in background threads. Because the Application Kit is locked during the event loop, any method invoked in the main thread must release the lock before messaging a background thread and reacquire it after sending the message.

the *next responder*. In this way an event is passed along until some object handles it.

At any time, exactly one object in a window is its *first responder*, the object that defines the beginning of the responder chain. This object may be a text field that the user is typing in, a drawing program's canvas, or the window itself. The first responder is typically established by the user clicking on the object with the mouse, but it can be established programmatically by sending the window a **makeFirstResponder:** message.

The responder chain varies from moment to moment. It always begins with the currently selected responder in the foremost window, called the application's *key window*. Every window has its own tree of responders defined by its views, whereby each view's next responder is its superview. The sole exception is the window's content view, whose next responder is the window itself. A window also passes all of its responder chain messages to its delegate, though the delegate needn't descend from NSResponder.

The active responder chain, then, is defined by the key window's first responder and successors, up to the window and its delegate. An application may also have a secondary window, called the *main window*, which is included in the responder chain for action messages (when there's no separate main window, the key window plays both roles). The main/key window distinction usually arises between a document window and an auxiliary panel such as a Find panel. When the Find panel isn't being used, it isn't in the responder chain at all and the document window is both the key and the main window; when the Find panel is being used, it becomes the key window and the document window gets demoted to main window status. In this case, the Find panel receives action messages before the document window, but since the Find panel is searching the document, the window is offered a chance at action methods after the Find panel.

At the end of the responder chain is the application object itself, which forwards responder chain messages to its delegate in the same way that a window does. The full responder chain in an application thus consists of the key window's first responder and successors, up to the key window and its delegate, the main window's first responder and successors, and the application object and its delegate. Various kinds of messages are passed up and down different parts of the responder chain, depending on the dispatch method used and the type of message being sent.

Event Messages

Events are user inputs such as keystrokes and mouse actions, as well as automatically generated occurrences like periodic events and mouse-tracking notifications. Events arrive in an application from the windowing system and are distributed by the application object's **sendEvent:** method. **sendEvent:** handles a few special events, such as key equivalents, and passes others along to the key window using NSWindow's **sendEvent:** method. Event messages are distributed only to responders in the key window (or the window clicked on for mouse-down and mouse-up events). NSWindow's implementation of **sendEvent:** directs key events to the first responder and mouse events to the NSView containing the cursor (which may change the first responder). A few other kinds of events are handled specially.

As described earlier, an NSView need only implement an event message to receive it and handle a particular event. If the first responder implements **keyDown:**, then as the user types, it receives **keyDown:** messages for each keystroke. The receiver of the **keyDown:** messages can then interpret the characters of each key event as appropriate, inserting text or deleting it, moving the insertion point, and so on. When the user clicks in a view, it's sent a **mouseDown:** message. The view clicked on can then track the movements of the mouse until the user releases it, send a message to another object letting it know the view was clicked on, or do whatever else it needs to handle the mouse event.

If no view wants a particular event, the event proceeds up the window's responder chain to the window object itself. NSWindow ignores mouse events that come back its way. It does handle some kinds of key events, such as those for handling keyboard accelerators and for navigating among controls with the Tab and other keys. For other key events, the window simply beeps.

Action Messages

A number of the standard OpenStep user interface objects handle mouse events merely by sending a message to another object, thus acting as simple triggers. This is the essence of what an NSButton does, for example. The messages sent by these and other objects are called *action messages*. An action message names only the action to be taken and has a single argument, the sender of the message. An action message can be sent directly to an object that's known in advance, but for targets that can vary, such as "the selected item" or "the current document," NSApplication offers a mechanism to dispatch an action message to whatever object in the full responder chain cares to handle it.

NSApplication's **sendAction:to:from:** takes an identifier for the action method to invoke, the intended receiver of the action message (called the *target*), and the sender, and finds an appropriate receiver for the message. If the target is an actual object, **sendAction:to:from:** simply invokes the action method. If the target is **nil**, however, the NSApplication object searches the full responder chain for an object that responds to the action method, only sending the message if it finds one. If no responder wants the action, it simply falls off the top of the responder chain.

Using the responder chain to distribute untargeted actions allows for very simple structuring of code based on variable targets, such as the selected object, the active document, and so on. A **delete:** action message, for example, can cause a text field to delete the character before its insertion point, or a drawing canvas object to delete the selected graphic, while a **close:** action message (if not intercepted earlier) causes the key window or the main window to close. Both messages are distributed via the same mechanism, and none of the target objects needs to be aware of this. The messages simply arrive at the appropriate objects in the chain, based on which object is interested in each action message.

Standard User Interface Controls

The Application Kit includes a number of classes that define common controls such as buttons, sliders, scroll bars, and so on. These classes all use the responder chain's target–action paradigm to interact with other objects in the application. The abstract superclass, NSControl, defines the interface and general mechanism used by the concrete subclasses. Among these are methods for accessing the target and action, for accessing a stored value as a number of data types (**int**, **float**, NSString, and so on), and for transferring the stored value from one object to another.

Among the Application Kit's control subclasses are:

- NSButton, which can behave in a number of different manners. It can be a simple push button that sends its action on a mouse-up event or a toggle button that changes its image or title on a mouse click, in either mode highlighting itself in a number of ways.

- NSSlider, which displays a knob that the user can drag within a bar to set its value. It sends its action as the user drags the knob and when the user releases the mouse.

- NSTextField, which displays its value as a formatted string and which sends its action when the user presses the Enter (or Return) key.

> ### NeXT Additions: Rulers and Keyboard Interface Control
>
> NeXT has made two particularly useful additions to the Application Kit's user interface controls. The first is NSRulerView, which interacts with the document inside an NSScrollView to display markers for such things as margins, text indents and tabs, and guidelines. The document view is notified by the ruler view whenever the user drags or removes a marker, and it can update the elements that the markers represent appropriately.
>
> The other addition is keyboard interface control, which allows the user to navigate among controls using the Tab and arrow keys, and manipulate them using the space bar and Enter key. The lack of such a facility was long a rather annoying quality of NextStep, and though it isn't yet formally part of OpenStep, it's certainly a welcome development.

- NSBrowser, which gets hierarchically arranged data from a data source object and displays it in a multicolumn view. Each item in a column is either a leaf or a branch; branches display small arrows and, when selected, cause the column to the right to be filled with their subnodes. Browsers can send different action messages on single-click and double-click events.

- NSTableView, an unofficial member of the OpenStep Application Kit, which displays tabular data from a data source object in a series of labeled columns.

Other control subclasses include NSColorWell, a color selection object, NSPopUpButton, which implements pull-down and pop-up menus, and NSScroller, used to control an NSScrollView.

Most controls handle an initial mouse-down event but pass further event processing to an associated object, called its *cell*. Each NSControl subclass that uses a cell uses a subclass of NSCell designed specifically for it. NSButton, for example, has NSButtonCell, while NSTextField has NSTextFieldCell. A cell performs most of the actual drawing of its control, allowing controls to be customized in some ways by making a subclass of the cell only. In addition, the NSMatrix control class can arrange nearly any kind of cell in a row, column, or matrix and can track the entire group as a unit.

Other Functional Areas

Outside of the general functionality defined by the core classes, the Application Kit supplies a number of other features in more specialized areas.

Text and Fonts

The OpenStep text classes provide for editing of either plain or rich text and can display images within the text as well. Nearly all the text drawn in an OpenStep application, in fact, is drawn by an NSText object: the titles of buttons, the text in text fields, menu items, and of course larger text documents. NSText is the abstract superclass defining the general text-handling interface; the NSCStringText subclass offers a concrete implementation. The text classes are unique among Application Kit classes in the breadth of features they offer and in their complexity. Besides supporting multiple fonts and text color, each cooperates with the font system (described ahead), participates in interapplication services, uses the Application Kit's spell checker, and can copy and paste font and ruler information as well as the text itself.

Unfortunately, although NSText's interface is defined in terms of NSString objects, the OpenStep implementation currently doesn't support the Unicode character encoding. NeXT was still working on its implementation of such a text system when the specification was developed, and SunSoft and NeXT agreed to support the existing text class, which was based on an 8-bit extended ASCII encoding. International support is a major goal of the OpenStep specification, however, so we can expect that NeXT's text system, or one as capable, will be adopted into the OpenStep specification in the future.

In addition to the classes that handle text, three classes manage fonts and font conversion: NSFont, NSFontPanel, and NSFontManager. The font class simply provides an object-oriented wrapper for a PostScript font. It can find PostScript font resources by name and allows you to retrieve various attributes of the font through method invocations. The Font panel is OpenStep's standard mechanism for displaying the font of the selection, for previewing fonts, and for changing the font of the selection. The font manager works with the font panel and the text-drawing object to convert fonts, adding and removing traits such as weight (plain, light, bold), angle (normal, italic, oblique), size, and so on. The font classes are tightly integrated into the Application Kit's text-handling classes and are quite reusable by any such classes you might create.

Drawing Aids

As suggested in the description of NSViews, objects other than views can invoke PostScript operators, so long as they do so under the aegis of a view. Cells and fonts, described earlier, are examples of such classes. The two others in the Application Kit are NSImage and NSColor. Image objects are more analogous to cells, in that they produce marks in the view using them, while colors behave more like fonts, merely affecting the results of further drawing.

> ### NeXT's Unicode Text System
>
> For its own implementation of OpenStep, NeXT decided to pursue a true international and customizable text system. This is a huge job, so it's little wonder that this system is not yet part of the OpenStep specification; it supports only Latin and Japanese scripts fully, with others still in development. Still, it's likely to be incorporated into the OpenStep canon in time.
>
> The text system uses a three-layer architecture. At the bottom, NSTextStorage objects store the raw Unicode characters and associate various attributes with them, such as font, color, kerning and ligature settings, and so on. The characters and attributes form the pure content, separate from their appearance when rendered.
>
> The middle layer is represented primarily by the NSLayoutManager class, which uses rulebooks for various world scripts to generate *glyphs* for the Unicode characters in the text storage object, based on their font, script system, and neighboring characters. The layout manager also arranges the glyphs as appropriate in a shape defined by an NSTextContainer object. A text container can define any shape, and the layout manager adjusts its lines to fit inside that shape.
>
> At the top is the NSTextView class, which draws the glyphs generated and placed by the layout manager and handles user input such as keystrokes and mouse events. Each text view has its own text container, and a series of text views can be linked together to form pages, columns, or other arrangements of text.
>
> There's also a comprehensive input management system, which allows for input of many kinds of text from standard Latin keyboards. The input manager is most apparent on the Japanese version of NeXT's OpenStep system but can be seen in action even when typing accented characters in English.

The NSImage class is based on a multirepresentation architecture. A single NSImage object can hold any number of image representations as instances of the NSImageRep classes. An image representation can be an Encapsulated PostScript image, which is device-independent, or a bitmap of any resolution and depth. For example, an NSImage can contain a 2-bit image that's used on grayscale screens, a 12-bit color image used when the screen supports that depth, and a 24-bit true color image used on high-end screens. The Application Kit's standard bitmap format is TIFF, but you can create a subclass of NSImageRep that handles other formats (or you can use the Services facility to filter other types to TIFF, as described later in this chapter under "Interapplication Services").

Color is handled in the Application Kit by the NSColor class, with its associated management classes NSColorWell and NSColorPanel. An NSColor object represents a single color value, expressed in any of a number of models: red-green-blue, hue-saturation-brightness, gray level, and so on. NSColorWell objects display color selections made by the user in the color panel; both allow the user to drag colors around as small swatches and drop them into other color wells, palettes, and even directly onto graphical objects. Dragging a color onto selected text, for example, changes the color of the text, as long as it allows that operation.

Printing

Because OpenStep uses the PostScript language for all drawing, most of the work involved in printing is done for you. Other aspects of printing—pagination, page layout, generation of PostScript document structuring comments, and coordination of the components of the printing machinery—all work according to a default scheme that you can customize to suit your needs. NSView objects handle their own pagination and the generation of PostScript document structuring comments when printed. You can override a number of methods defined by NSView to alter the default pagination or add PostScript comments. Page layout information, such as paper size and orientation, margins, and pagination method, is recorded in an NSPrintInfo object, which the user accesses through an NSPageLayout panel. When the time comes to print, the whole process is managed by an NSPrintOperation object, which displays the print panel and instructs the views being printed to draw their images. An NSView can modify its output based on whether it's drawing to the screen or to a printer by checking with its NSDPSContext object; for example, it can omit the highlighting of selected text when drawing to a printer.

System Services

The remaining functional areas involve sharing of data and services among applications. NSPasteboard defines the medium by which the Cut, Copy, and Paste commands, among several other data-transfer mechanisms, work. Object Links allow objects that can be transferred over the pasteboard to be pasted as links instead of static data and to be updated automatically according to the user's preferences. Finally, a variety of interapplication services allow any application to export its functionality to others through the pasteboard. Interapplication services form the basis for cooperating tools, automatic filtering of imported or pasted data, spell checking, and print output filtering.

Data Transfer: Pasteboards

The Application Kit's general data-transfer mechanism, for use both within and between applications, is called the *pasteboard*. Pasteboards are used both to store data temporarily, as in the standard Cut, Copy, and Paste commands, and to transfer data between applications, as in image dragging and interapplication services (described ahead). An application can create and use any number of pasteboard objects, giving each a unique name. Predefined pasteboards include the general pasteboard, used for Cut, Copy, and Paste; the font and ruler pasteboards, used for text settings; the find pasteboard, used to share search strings among applications; and the drag pasteboard, used to pass dragged data between the source and destination applications.

Pasteboards allow you to provide your data lazily, so that you only have to export the data if another object or application requests it. This avoids delays in transferring large amounts of data unnecessarily. You indicate that you have data to provide by declaring to the pasteboard what types you have and which object is responsible for providing the data (called the *owner*). Types are data formats such as ASCII, RTF, TIFF image data, and so on, as well as any custom formats defined by your application. After you've declared the data types, another object can ask the pasteboard what types it has available and request data for a given type. At this point the pasteboard asks the owner for the data of that type, and the data transfer is actually performed.

Dynamic Data Links

The Application Kit's data link classes allow the user to copy items from one document and paste them "live" into any cooperating application. Then, when the originally copied item changes, the linked copy can be updated automatically or manually. This feature compares in some ways with Microsoft's Object Linking and Embedding (OLE) and Apple's Publish and Subscribe facilities. Both the source and destination applications for linking must support links in general and the specific data formats of linked items in particular.

Objects that support being linked must work with the link management classes: NSSelection, NSDataLink, NSDataLinkManager, and NSDataLinkPanel. When a linkable object is copied to the pasteboard, it must create an NSSelection to describe just what is being copied and also create an NSDataLink to implement the link. The NSSelection object allows the pasted link to find its source material when it updates later. The user can paste the copied data as normal, or choose the special menu command Paste and Link to paste the link instead. The source and destination applications use NSDataLinkManager objects to monitor changes to links, updating them according to the user's preferences. Links can be set to update continually, only when the source is saved, manually, or never. The NSDataLinkPanel class allows the user to examine the selected link, set its update frequency, open its source document, and break the link, rendering it into static data.

Interapplication Services

Every OpenStep application has the potential to export its functionality to other applications and to take advantage of functionality exported by others, through the Application Kit's Services facility. A special Services menu in the application lists all services exported by other applications. When the user chooses a command from the Services menu, the selection is placed on a special pasteboard object, if necessary, and the other application is sent a message to perform the service, being launched if it isn't already running. The service provider operates on the data sent and returns the result (if any) to the application that requested the service using the same pasteboard. Many Application Kit objects support sending and returning data for service requests; all you need to do is add the Services menu to your application for it to be a consumer of other applications' services. You can also export services from your application, or enable a custom object class to use services, by implementing a few standard methods.

The Application Kit uses the Services facility architecture for three other kinds of services: filter services, which simply transform data from one format to another; print filter services, which transform the PostScript output of printing operations; and spell-checking services, which allow an application to connect to different spell-checking server programs. You request filter services programmatically through the pasteboard, which automatically contacts the filter service provider to transform the data you provide—a GIF image, for example—into a type that your application can use, such as TIFF. Print filter services typically modify PostScript output to take advantage of special features of the selected printer, to include extra data in the PostScript code such as special fonts or images, and so on. Spell-checking services handle searching a stream of text for misspellings, as well as suggesting corrections and storing new words in user dictionaries.

5 *NeXT's OPENSTEP for Windows NT*

Microsoft's Windows operating systems are the undisputed standard on the PC platform. When NeXT started work on the OpenStep specification, it was clear that porting their existing frameworks and tools from NeXT's native Mach operating system to Windows would make it available to a huge number of customers. Essential differences between the two operating systems and user interfaces made this a hefty challenge, but NeXT has risen to the occasion, producing an OpenStep system that looks and feels very much like Windows itself. The most noticeable differences are cosmetic, such as a lack of certain interface controls, and the fact that every window in an OPENSTEP application is freestanding. Beyond that, however, everything behaves pretty much like you would expect.

This chapter reviews the salient features of OPENSTEP for Windows NT, including how the user interface departs from the Windows 95 standard and which programs and development tools are included with the user and developer versions. Chapter 7, immediately following the next chapter, shows how you use the developer tools to create a simple OpenStep application on either Windows or Solaris.

> **OPENSTEP Spelling Reform**
>
> NeXT calls its product OPENSTEP, putting it in all capital letters to distinguish it from the OpenStep specification. Though not particularly helpful, it's in fine keeping with NeXT's history of changing the case of letters in the name of OPENSTEP's predecessor. First there was NextStep, then NeXTstep, NeXTSTEP, and finally NEXTSTEP. The press ignored all of these spellings, generally sticking to NextStep, which we also use.

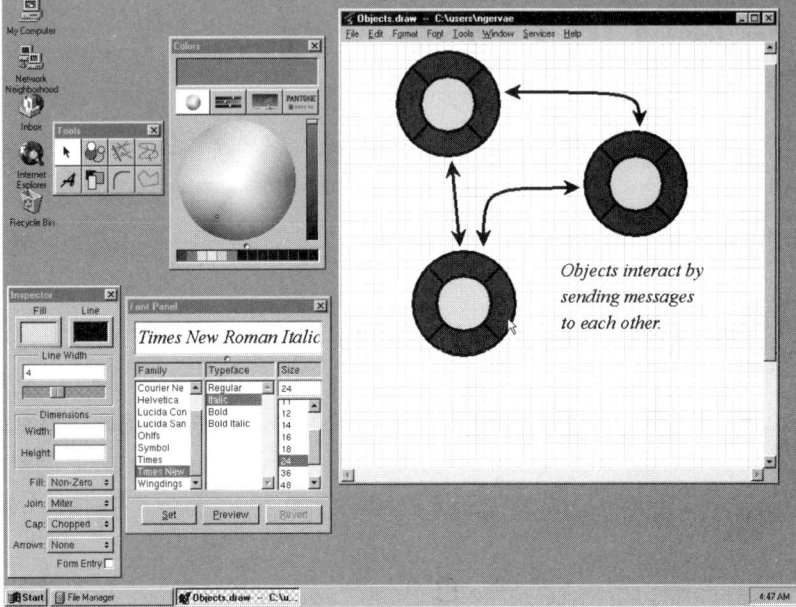

Figure 1. The Draw Demo Application

The User Interface

The user interface of an OpenStep application running on Windows has two notable features. It looks and behaves almost exactly like any other Windows application, rendering its controls and other graphical elements in the Windows 95 style. However, it adds some controls of its own, such as table views, color wells, and the Colors and Font Panels, while lacking several controls available to native Windows applications, notably combo boxes, multiple-document architecture, and OLE containers.

Figure 1 shows a demo included with the OPENSTEP user package, a simple drawing application. Note the Colors and Font Panels, which are standard objects available to any OpenStep application. You can select colors using a color wheel (shown in the figure), a grayscale slider, and RGB, HSB, and CMYK sliders. When you find a color you like, you can simply drag it into a color well (visible at the top of the Inspector panel) or in some cases right onto an object that supports color. The

Font Panel displays the general font families available, along with their specific typefaces. You can select any size, since PostScript fonts are inherently scalable, and preview your selection in the area at the top of the panel.

As for interaction with native Windows applications, you can cut and paste most things between OPENSTEP and Windows, as long as the receiving application understands the format, of course. You can also drag and drop files between the two. One notable incompatibility is OPENSTEP's current lack of support for OLE linking and embedding. Except for this, things pretty much just work.

User System Programs

More interesting than the look and feel of OPENSTEP applications on Windows NT are the actual application programs that come with the system. The user system consists basically of the run-time libraries and background programs needed by OpenStep applications. Windows already has its standard applications for such things as file management, electronic mail, and word processing, but OPENSTEP includes several demos. The really cool applications are in the developer package, described right after this section.

Background Programs

OPENSTEP includes four programs that run in the background and provide various interapplication services. These programs must exist in your Startup group or be launched manually before you can run any OPENSTEP application:

- The Mach interprocess communication server, **machd**. The Distributed Objects system uses this for messaging between processes on the same machine.

- The network message server, **nmserver**. The Distributed Objects system uses this for messaging across the network.

- The Window Server, which runs the Display PostScript system.

- The pasteboard server, **pbs**, which holds data copied or cut and performs other resource management tasks.

An additional background program, the NeXT ORB, allows Objective-C objects to communicate with OLE Automation objects, as described on page 149 in *Chapter 9: Distributed Applications*. The ORB needn't be launched at startup time, but must be running in order for Objective-C objects to interact with OLE Automation objects.

Demo Applications

Although the OPENSTEP user system is essentially just the run-time libraries, it includes a few demos to show off the system. Among them are:

- Preview, a PostScript document and TIFF image viewer.

- Draw, a simple drawing program (shown in Figure 1).

- TextEdit, a text-editing application that supports multiple fonts and images in documents.

Preview is perhaps the neatest demo to have, as it allows you to view just about any PostScript or EPS file right on your computer, without having to print it to a PostScript printer. If you don't have Adobe Acrobat, or if you need to proof PostScript output, this is quite handy.

The Development Environment

Rapid development of custom applications is OpenStep's main purpose, and for this you need more than class libraries or frameworks—you need good tools. The primary tools in OPENSTEP Developer are the Project

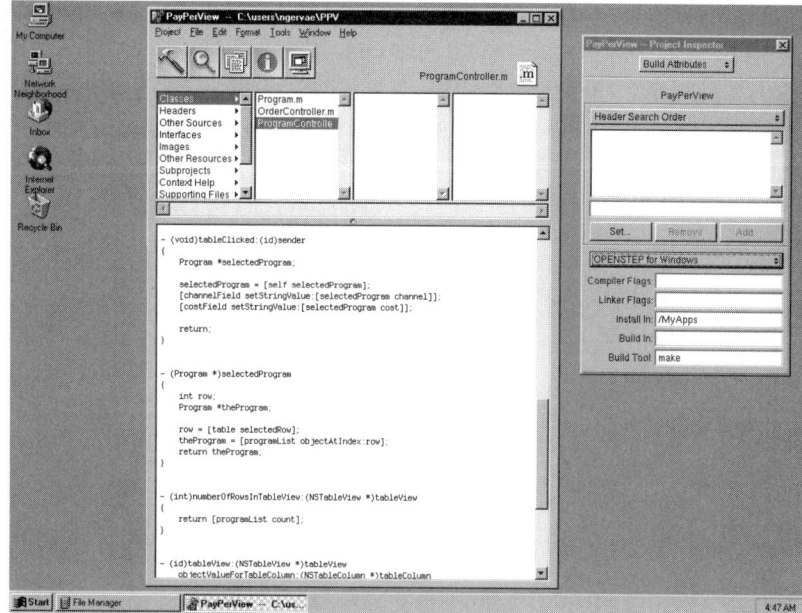

Figure 2. The Project Builder Application

Builder and Interface Builder applications. Project Builder manages source files and edits code, while Interface Builder handles the creation of an application's user interface in the manner of a drawing or diagramming package.

This section summarizes the tools, describing what they do without going into much detail of how they do it. *Chapter 7: Building an Application* leads you through many features of Project Builder and Interface Builder, showing how you use these tools to build a simple OpenStep application.

Project Builder

Project Builder (Figure 2) is the hub of OPENSTEP application development. With it you create applications, command-line programs, libraries, and other types of code packages; manage the source files and other resources in the project; edit source code; and build and debug your programs. Project Builder packages reusable class libraries into *frameworks*, which contain the compiled code, header files, resources, and documentation in one directory, thus giving concrete form to the abstract notion of a framework.

Project and File Management

A project's main window (the large window in Figure 2) contains a browser that categorizes header files, class implementation files, other source files, and general resources. It also displays the individual classes and methods defined in the files. The Inspector panel on the right allows you to set attributes for the whole project, such as its name, default language, and document icons; for building, such as where to look for header files and where to install the compiled project; and for individual files selected in the browser, such as the file's name and whether it's a localizable resource.

Project Builder can manage several different kinds of development efforts, from graphical applications to command-line programs, to libraries, to frameworks. It can even group them together as *subprojects* under a more general project, maintaining the dependencies between them so that subprojects are updated as needed to rebuild the main project.

Code Editing

Project Builder's built-in code editor has all the standard functionality of any text editor but adds a raft of power-user features:

- auto-indent of code;
- block selection by double-clicking delimiters (braces, parentheses, and so on);
- name completion, which finishes a partially typed word when you press the Escape key (really handy with some of OpenStep's longer class and method names);
- split views of code, allowing you to view two distant parts of a file simultaneously;
- the ability to edit rich text, with graphics.

The editor is also integrated with Project Builder's Build panel and debugger. When a build error occurs, you can click the error message in the Build panel, and the code editor opens the file and selects the offending line. Similarly, when debugging the project, the code editor displays breakpoints and highlights the code being executed.

Frameworks

A Project Builder framework packages a library of classes together with their header files, supporting resources, and documentation. For example, the OpenStep frameworks exist on the system in these directories:

    C:\NeXT\NextLibrary\Frameworks\Foundation.framework
    C:\NeXT\NextLibrary\Frameworks\AppKit.framework

Each of these directories contains the library for the framework, header files, reference documentation for every class, and resources used by the framework such as images and user interface definitions (nib files, which you'll learn about soon). Project Builder knows how to navigate the structure of a framework directory, making the header files available in its browser, and presenting the documentation in its Project Find panel (described ahead).

Indexing and Searching

Many of Project Builder's powerful editing abilities come through its indexing facility, which examines a project when it's opened and records the symbols in each source file. The indexing facility is aware of Objective-C syntax, so it does the right thing when faced with complex expressions.

The Project Find panel uses the index to provide project-wide searching for tokens based on where they're defined and where they're used or referenced. It also allows for plain text or regular expression search. Looking for a particular item results in a list of all occurrences of that item in the project's source code, in the framework header files, and in the framework documentation. Clicking any list entry opens the source file in the code-editing area of the project window. There are also a number of shortcuts and accelerators for performing different kinds of searches.

In addition to this, the Project Find panel allows you to perform global replacement throughout your project source files. After finding a list of matches, you can select one or more of the items and click the replace button, and they're all changed to the text you specify.

Building and Debugging

Chapter 7: Building an Application shows the Build and Launch panels in action.

Apart from editing code, most development time is spent compiling the project and debugging it. Project Builder includes an integrated Build panel, which allows you to specify how the project should be built, which computer architecture and operating system (Windows NT or Mach) it should be built for, and even which host to perform the compilation on—a handy feature when you have a powerful server. When errors and warnings occur during compilation, they're listed on the build panel, where a simple click brings up the code editor with the erroneous line selected.

Debugging is similarly integrated with Project Builder through the Launch panel, which allows you to simply launch the application without having to fish for it on the disk, or to start the debugger, **gdb**. This is a command-line debugger originally developed on UNIX systems, but the Launch panel and code editor add a number of graphical controls for managing the debugging process. When you start the debugger, a column appears to the left of the code editor, where you can double-click to set breakpoints, and move, enable, disable, or delete them by manipulating the markers. The build panel itself contains buttons for starting and suspending the application being debugged, for single-stepping across and into functions and methods, and for printing the values of expressions (variables, function calls, and messages) selected in the code editor. When the application is suspended, a program counter indicator appears in the breakpoint area, which you can drag down to skip past ranges of code visually.

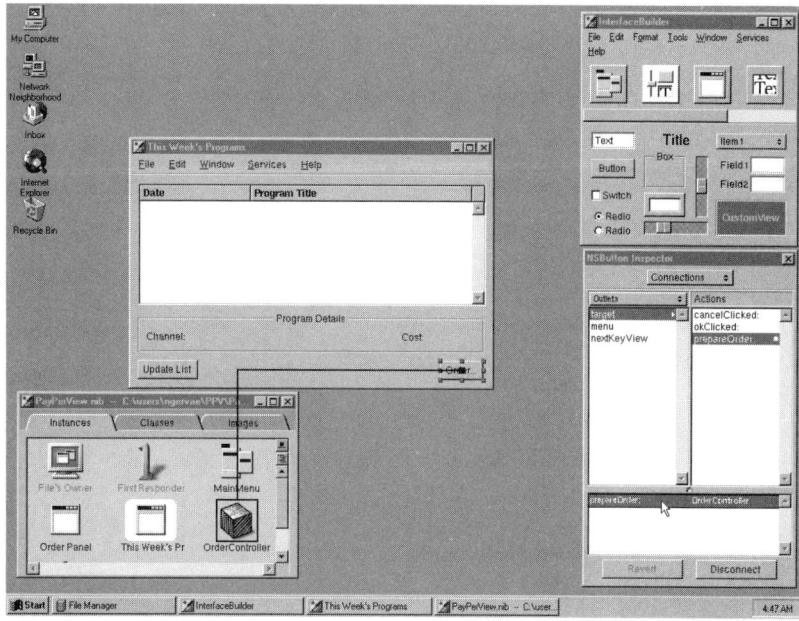

Figure 3. The Interface Builder Application

Interface Builder

Chapter 7: Building an Application shows Interface Builder at work.

Although Project Builder does much to ease the task of writing code, it's far better not to have to write code at all. This is where Interface Builder (Figure 3) comes in. This application allows you to define the user interface of your application, along with parts of the engine, as an archive of objects. Using Interface Builder, you drag live interface objects from palettes into a resource file, arrange and configure them by direct manipulation, and save the lot into a resource file that your application loads at run time.

Interface Builder is a real object editor, not just a screen-painter. The objects you set up are real. You can examine their behavior by entering a special test mode, where sliders slide and text fields edit their text. This allows you to prototype your application's user interface and see how it might work, before even writing any code. And when you do write code, you write less.

82 Developing Business Applications with OpenStep

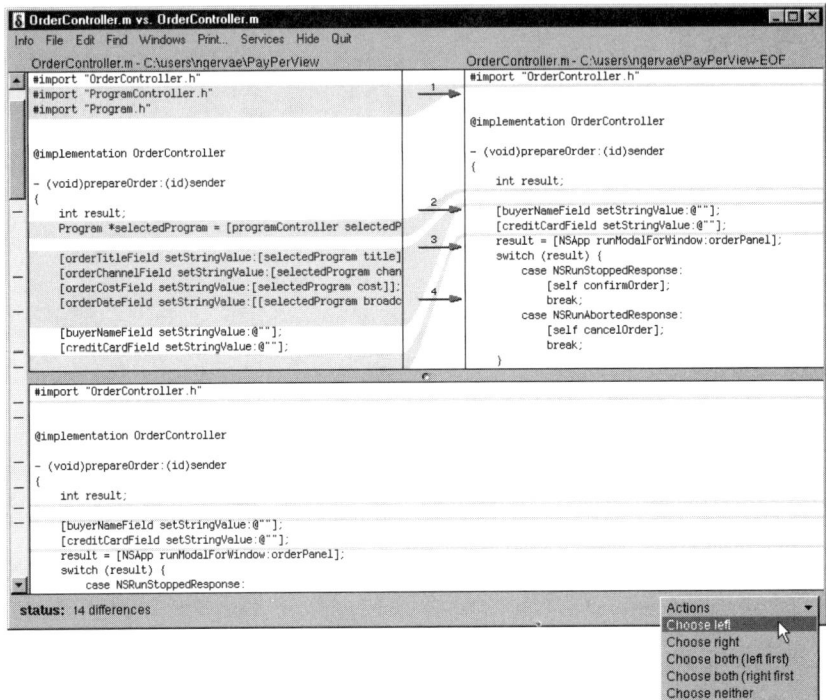

Figure 4. The File Merge Application

Interface Builder is also an object archiver, rather than a code generator. It does generate files for custom classes that you define, but the interface objects that you wire together are archived in their entirety into the nib file. There's no generated C or Objective-C code to tweak, which thereafter can't be read back into Interface Builder. In fact, you *can* alter the custom class header files and read them back into Interface Builder to update their definitions.

Other Tools

OPENSTEP Developer comes with several other tools, the most interesting of which are Yap, an interactive PostScript previewer, the Bourne shell, a command shell used by Project Builder, and File Merge, a file comparison and merging utility. With Yap, you can type PostScript commands into an editor and execute them in a preview window to see the effect they have. This comes in handy when writing drawing code for the Application Kit. The Bourne shell is used mostly by Project Builder for running its various internal utilities, but you can also use it to run some command-line tools, such as the user defaults editor or the ORB registration tool.

File Merge, though, is the most useful of the remaining development tools. Using this application, you can take two versions of a file or an entire directory of files and compare them for changes. The results of a file comparison are shown in a side-by-side view (Figure 4), with differences highlighted and correlated. You can use this comparison to merge the files into a new version, taking specific differences from the left or the right file, as shown in the figure. This application is a big help in projects that get copied and modified by several different programmers, as it allows you to quickly coordinate the divergent copies into a single new master copy.

OPENSTEP for Mach

OPENSTEP began as NextStep on a Mach/4.3BSD UNIX system and is still available on that operating system. Along with the standard UNIX features of strong TCP/IP networking and SMTP mail support, NeXT's Mach OS includes a highly scalable administrative system called NetInfo, which interoperates with NIS (Yellow Pages) and also supports Novell® NetWare® networking protocols.

This version of OpenStep is primarily of interest to two groups:

- Companies that already use NextStep on Mach. These companies can continue to use OPENSTEP on Mach, porting their applications to the OpenStep specification, or use it as a stepping stone to port their applications to the Windows version.

- Companies that want NeXT's development tools on UNIX (regardless of where they ultimately deploy applications). NeXT's Mach system has some debugging and performance tools not available for Windows, for example.

(continues)

User Applications

OPENSTEP for Mach includes several applications not available for the Windows version, including:

- Workspace Manager, a sleek file and application manager with a powerful browser, shelves to put frequently accessed documents on, and an application dock that acts like a permanent task bar on the screen.
- Mail, a multimedia electronic mail application that supports MIME and the more compact NeXTmail formats.
- Terminal, a UNIX terminal emulator that works with any standard shell.

In addition, there's a fair number of existing third-party applications that continue to run on OPENSTEP for Mach or are being ported to the OpenStep specification.

The Development Environment

Mach is the original home of OPENSTEP, so it should be no surprise that it hosts a number of specific development tools not yet available for Windows. These include several command-line debugging and performance analysis tools, and some graphical ones. Even if you're doing your development on Windows, you may want to get a copy of OPENSTEP for Mach just to have these tools. Contact NeXT for more information on using OPENSTEP for Mach.

6 SunSoft's Solaris OpenStep

Solaris OpenStep is the result of two years of joint effort by SunSoft and NeXT. It's implemented as a set of standard Solaris libraries and applications that work within the Solaris operating system and the X Window system to present the classic NextStep look and feel. The Application Kit uses the Display PostScript system for drawing within windows and uses X11 for window management and event handling. Solaris OpenStep is tightly integrated with the native windowing system; to other applications running on the system, an OpenStep application appears as a normal X11-based application. The development environment, WorkShop OpenStep, also includes parts of SunSoft's Workshop SPARCompiler™ language system, which aren't available in other vendors' OpenStep offerings.

This chapter reviews the interface and applications of Solaris OpenStep, including how they behave with different X Window managers. It also covers a few issues particular to OpenStep applications running on Solaris. *Chapter 7: Building an Application* shows how you use the development tools to create a simple OpenStep application on either Windows or Solaris.

The User Interface

With OpenStep Solaris running (Figure 1), the user's workspace is defined by an application dock on the right side of the screen, which

86 *Developing Business Applications with OpenStep*

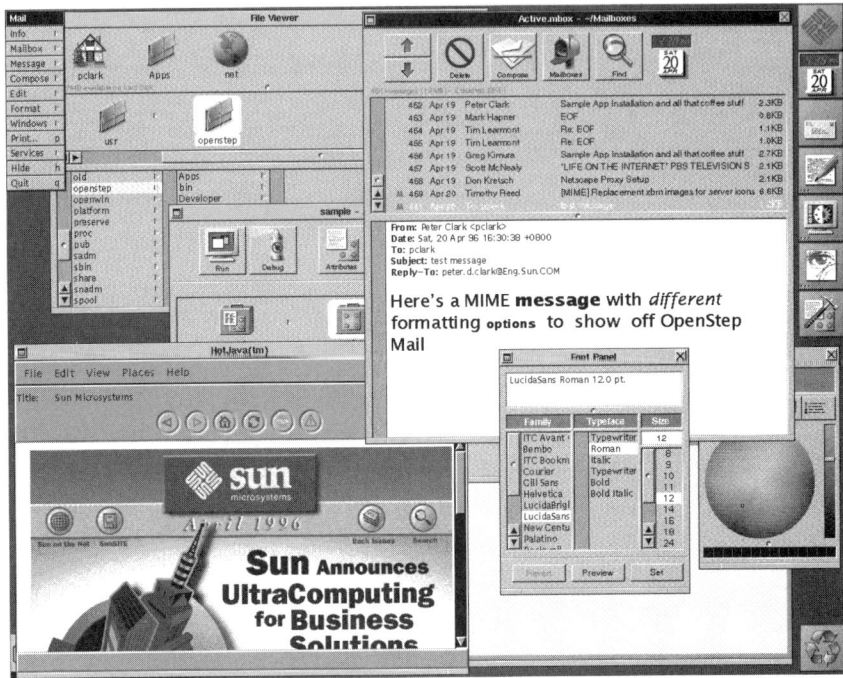

Figure 1. Solaris OpenStep with the OpenStep Window Manager

puts both OpenStep and other executables in prominent view for the user to launch or activate. Elsewhere, applications run in freestanding windows. Menus typically sit at the upper left corner as floating panels of command items.

In the X11 environment, the look and feel of an application is determined partly by the toolkit used to develop the application and partly by the window manager. The window manager determines how the outside frame of a window looks, where its close and miniaturize buttons are, where the resize handles are, and several other traits. OpenStep includes an ICCCM-compliant window manager, called **oswm**, that gives all windows on the system the original NextStep look and feel. However, other window managers can be used, such as the CDE window manager **dtwm**, which gives all applications running on the system, including OpenStep applications, the CDE look and feel (Figure 2). Although the **oswm** window manager is the preferred

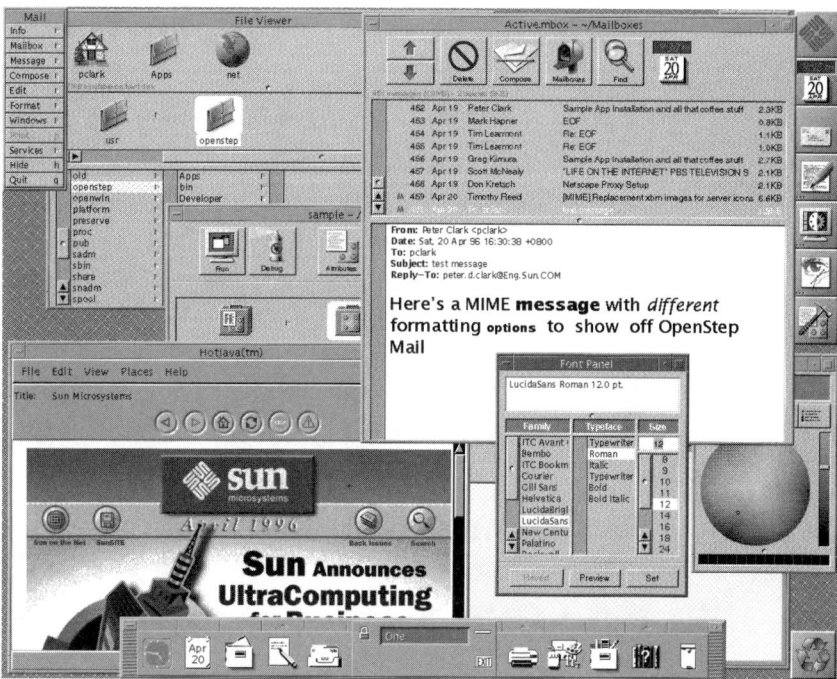
Figure 2. Solaris OpenStep with the CDE Window Manager

window manager for OpenStep applications, other window managers work just fine with them.

The Solaris OpenStep pasteboard interacts with X11 selections, so users can cut and paste between OpenStep and X11 applications. Drag and drop between OpenStep applications and non-OpenStep applications isn't currently supported, but is planned for a future release.

Because Solaris OpenStep is based on the X11 Window system, applications can be displayed remotely on X terminals, provided they include the Display PostScript extensions required by OpenStep. As we write this book, only Sun's X terminals have these extensions, so OpenStep applications can't be displayed yet on other vendor's terminals. As other vendors of X11-based display systems include Display PostScript with the OpenStep extensions, though, you should be able to display OpenStep applications remotely on their X terminals as well.

User System Programs

Like the Windows version, Solaris OpenStep has a few background programs that provide services to user applications. They're basically the same as those listed in the previous chapter, and since every UNIX system has dozens of these things nibbling at the CPU anyway, we won't bother to list them here. Unlike the Windows version, though, Solaris OpenStep includes a number of handy user applications ported from NextStep's original suite, including a powerful file manager and a multimedia electronic mail application.

Workspace Manager

Workspace Manager is most users' first look at Solaris OpenStep. This application is a file manager unparallelled in its ability to handle huge directory trees, making navigation across an entire networked file system seem trivial. It displays multiple file viewer windows, each containing an independent view of the file system. You can choose between a hierarchical browser for quick navigation (as shown in the back of Figures 1 and 2), a flat list view to see file attributes and permissions, or an icon view to see the pretty pictures. Each view is accompanied by an *icon path* that shows the path to the directory displayed in the main file view. Above the icon path is a shelf, where you can drop icons for frequently used files.

Many operations in Workspace Manager are based on the drag-and-drop metaphor. You can move, copy, and delete files by dragging icons from one window to another, differentiating the operations by holding down a modifier key while dragging. You can also drag files between a file viewer and any OpenStep application that accepts files, especially Mail (described next). Workspace Manager allows you to format storage devices, view the applications registered for file extensions and choose which application opens a given extension, set permissions, and perform all the other tasks that file managers in general facilitate.

Mail

OpenStep Mail (in the foreground of Figures 1 and 2) is a MIME-compliant electronic mail agent that supports formatted multifont text, attached files, and voice clips. It's fully integrated with both OpenStep and the rest of Solaris and can read mail and attachments sent using CDE or OpenLook® mail. OpenStep Mail checks for new mail automatically and stores messages in multiple mailboxes, including an Active box for incoming mail and an Outgoing box for mail you send. There's also a Drafts box where you can save messages you haven't finished composing.

OpenStep Mail sports a hierarchical address book that automatically reads in system mail aliases for individuals and groups and allows you to define your own private aliases. Pressing the Escape key while typing an address in a compose window completes the address based on the aliases. Most of the basic **emacs** key bindings work in every text area in Mail, making life easy for those not stuck on **vi**.

Lastly, OpenStep Mail also supports receiving, but not sending, NeXTmail-formatted messages for backward compatibility with NextStep.

Edit

Edit is a multidocument text editor that supports plain ASCII and rich (RTF) text, as well as graphic and other file attachments. Like Mail, it supports **emacs** key bindings, though only inside document windows. One of Edit's most interesting features is "contracted" editing (Figure 3)—similar to an outline mode, it allows you to hide all the text indented more than a given number of tab stops, which makes it easy to work with and reorganize a document at a higher level.

Edit can also apply shell commands and filters to its document or to the selection. You define the command to apply, such as **wc** or **grep**, with an argument variable of **$file** for the file's name or **$selection** for the selection, and Edit forks off the command with the appropriate arguments.

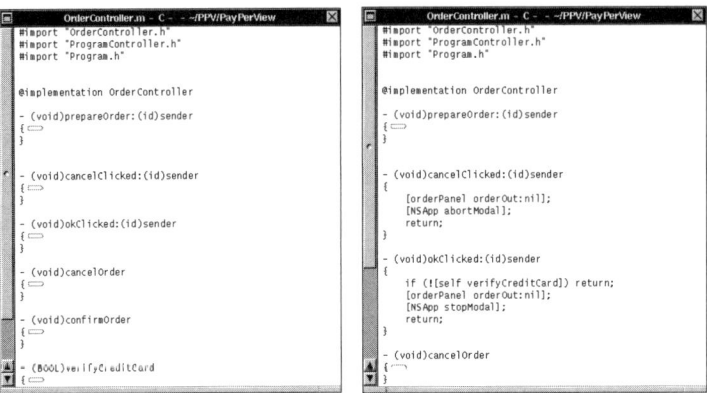

Figure 3. Contracted Editing

The output is presented in a new window. Filters, also called pipes, automatically apply to the selected text, replacing it with the filter's standard output (and error) streams. You can use standard commands such as **sort** to sort the selected lines and **date** to insert a timestamp.

On top of all this, Edit is integrated with the OpenStep Project Builder and debugger, as we describe ahead in the "The Development Environment."

Terminal

Terminal is a VT100™ terminal emulator similar to **xterm**, **shelltool**, and other terminal emulators available on most UNIX platforms. It lets you access the command-line interface to Solaris using one of several shells (**sh**, **csh**, **tcsh**, **zsh**, and **bash**, to name the most popular). You can open as many terminal windows as you want and use the shells to run other command-line tools as you would on any UNIX platform. Terminal offers some special features that these other emulators don't, such as access to Application Kit Services. It also lets you construct Services out of UNIX programs, similar to Edit's commands and pipes, but which Terminal makes available to any application through the Services menu.

One of Terminal's really nifty features is that it accepts dragged files, pasting the full path of the file into the shell. Among other things, this allows you to change to a directory by typing "cd" followed by a space and then dragging the directory icon from Workspace Manager into the Terminal window.

Preview

Preview is a viewer application for multipage PostScript documents, Encapsulated PostScript images, and TIFF images. Like most other OpenStep applications, it can display any number of separate files, so you can look at more than one document or image at a time. You can zoom in and out when viewing both PostScript and TIFF images and print them to any PostScript printer. Preview also has special logic to deal with PostScript files that don't conform to the Adobe Document Structuring conventions, so it can often display files that other viewers can't.

Preferences

The Preferences application controls the user's system defaults, such as mouse acceleration, standard application fonts, date and time, password, and file permission mask. While running, it also displays the time in its application icon in one of several styles, making it a handy on-screen clock.

The Development Environment

Although the user applications are some of the most usable tools on the Solaris platform, the real action is in the development tools included with Workshop OpenStep. Like OPENSTEP Developer on Windows, the primary tools are Project Builder and Interface Builder. The Solaris version of Project Builder is quite different from NeXT's, however.

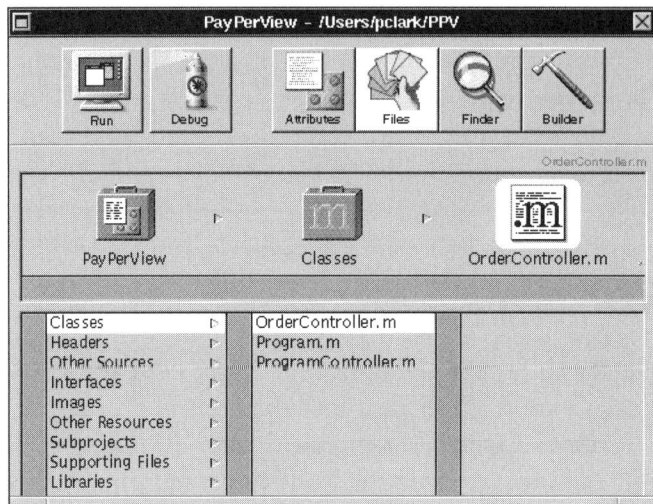

Figure 4. A Project's File Listing

Workshop OpenStep also includes a separate browser for the object frameworks, called Header Viewer.

This section summarizes the tools, describing what they do without going into much detail of how they do it. *Chapter 7: Building an Application* leads you through many features of Project Builder and Interface Builder, showing how you use these tools to build a simple OpenStep application.

Project Builder

Project Builder is the focal point of most OpenStep development, being used to construct applications, libraries, command-line tools, and bundles (dynamically loadable groups of object classes and resources). Project Builder manages the source files and other resources in the project, launches appropriate tools to edit source code and other resources, maintains a makefile for you, and drives the compiler and debugger. Each of these functions is managed in the same window, by switching between different views using the buttons at the top of the window. Project Builder performs some of these functions by itself, but

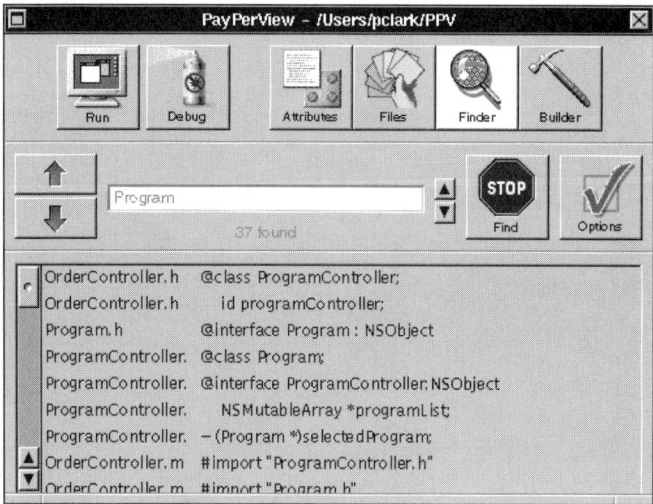

Figure 5. Searching in the Project

it delegates many of them to other tools, such as Edit, Terminal, and Interface Builder.

Project and File Management

A project's main view (Figure 4) contains a browser that categorizes header files, class implementation files, other source files, and general resources. Selecting a file displays an icon on the right side of the window, which you can double-click to launch an appropriate editor and which you can drag out of the window to other applications, such as Interface Builder.

Like NeXT's version, the Solaris Project Builder can manage several different kinds of development efforts, from graphical applications to command-line programs, to libraries. It too supports subprojects for grouping commonly used sets of code and resources.

Searching

In Project Find mode (Figure 5), Project Builder can recursively search through all the files in all the directories that make up a project, looking for specific information. It allows for plain text or regular expression

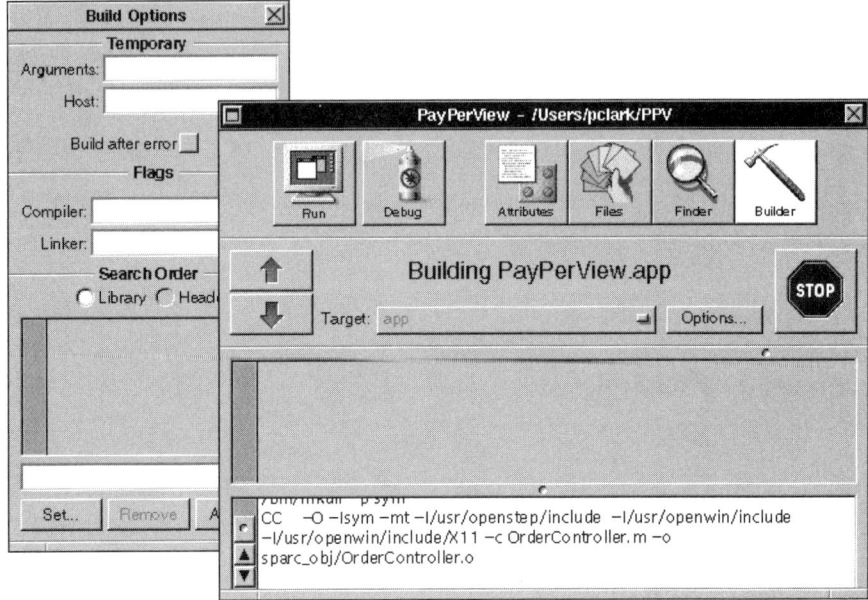

Figure 6. Building a Project

search. Looking for a particular item quickly results in a list of all occurrences of that item in any file in the project's code base. Clicking a list entry opens the source file in Edit.

Building and Debugging

Project Builder on Solaris drives building and debugging as its cousin on Windows does, but in a slightly less integrated manner. Its Build view (Figure 6) is a mode of the same project window that displays files, but it behaves just like the Build panel in the Windows version. When you build a project, errors and warnings from the compiler appear in two forms, as formatted, clear messages in the top pane and as raw compiler output in the bottom. Clicking a message in the top pane opens the problem file in Edit with the line that caused the error selected.

The Run and Debug buttons at the top of the window immediately launch the application or start the debugger if it's up to date, otherwise initiating a build first.

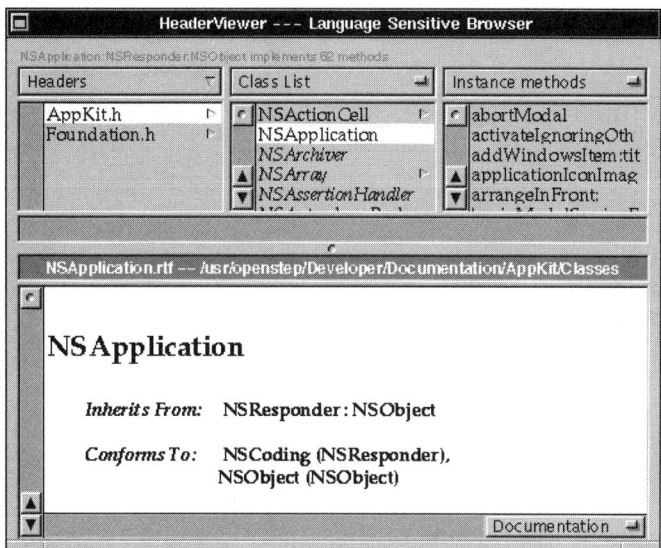

Figure 7. Header Viewer's Browse Mode

Debugging is likewise driven by Project Builder through the Edit application. The Workshop OpenStep debugger is based on **dbx**, which has been extended to understand Objective-C constructs and to send Objective-C messages during debugging. When you start a debugging session from Project Builder, a Terminal window appears with **dbx** running inside it, and both your source code and a special control panel appear in Edit. The panel displays a set of buttons for managing breakpoints, stopping, starting, and single-stepping through your code, and evaluating expressions. Most of the debugging work is done by selecting lines of source code and clicking on a button—to set a breakpoint, for instance, you select a line of code and click the "stopat" button. To inspect the contents of a variable, you select it in Edit and click the Print button.

Edit also contains a stack browser that allows you to inspect, though not modify, the contents of the entire call stack. The browser displays all the stack variables and breaks out structures and pointers into their constituent elements so that they can be seen as a group.

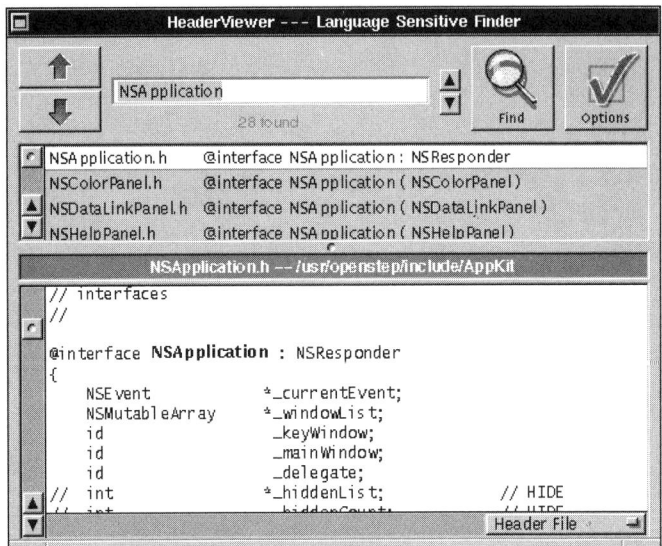

Figure 8. Header Viewer's Find Mode

Interface Builder

Interface Builder on Solaris is functionally identical to the Windows version. See the brief description on page 81, as well as the tour in the next chapter.

Header Viewer

The OpenStep frameworks contain a lot of interfaces, which can make it difficult to find the appropriate class or method needed to achieve a specific goal. Workshop Solaris includes a program called Header Viewer, which allows you to scan through all the classes in the system. Header Viewer operates in two modes, browsing and searching. In either mode you can view both the class's textual documentation and the header file in which it's defined.

In browse mode (Figure 7), Header Viewer displays the class tree in a browser window. You can organize the class tree by which header file the class is first defined in, by name, or by other attributes. When you select a class, you can display a list of instance methods, class methods, instance variables, or all of the above. This mode is most useful when you want to explore the inheritance relationships in the frameworks or look at several related classes.

In find mode (Figure 8), HeaderViewer allows you to search the class tree for any string or regular expression. All the matches for the search string appear in a listing, with documentation for the selected one in the lower pane of the window. This mode is most useful when you want to know which classes define a named method or when you need to find the specific argument ordering for a given method.

7 *Building an Application*

This example only presents highlights of the application. See *Appendix A: PayPerView Source* for a full source listing.

The previous chapters described the OpenStep development frameworks and tools. This chapter shows how they work by leading you through the process of developing a simple application, which shows a list of pay-per-view shows that the user can select, examine, and purchase with a credit card. The PayPerView application highlights several major classes of the Foundation Framework and Application Kit, showing how to write code that:

- creates an NSArray;
- interacts with user interface objects;
- provides data to an NSTableView;
- runs a modal panel.

Perhaps more significant is what you don't have to write code for. Because Interface Builder makes nearly all interface setup as simple as dragging windows and controls around, you don't have to write a single line of code for creating windows, placing elements in the windows, or setting up menus. You also establish connections between these graphical elements using Interface Builder, so that your custom code is automatically invoked as needed by interface objects. The Application Kit handles event dispatch and display for you, as well as pasteboard interaction for standard objects. This all comes for free in OpenStep development.

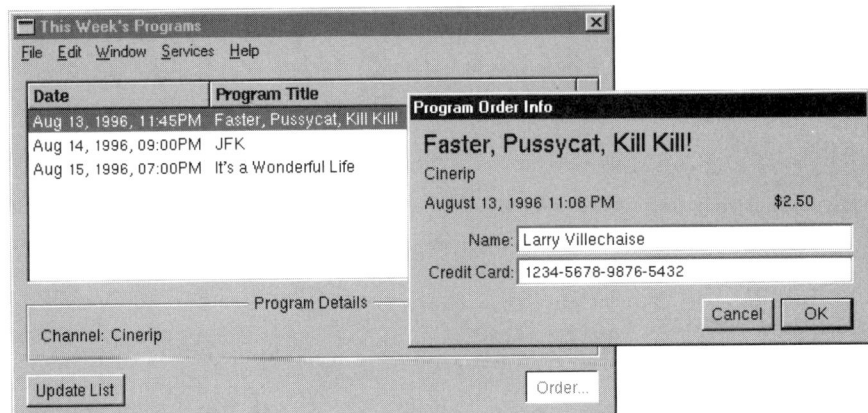

Figure 1. Placing an Order in PayPerView

PayPerView: The Design

The basic idea of the PayPerView application is to show a list of programs in a window, with their broadcast times and titles (Figure 1, shown in the Windows 95 interface). When the user selects a program, its channel and cost appear below the list. There's also an Order button on the window, which opens a panel showing the program information and two fields for the user's name and credit card.

One of the tenets of object-oriented design is to model the real world. This application has several real-world entities that the system needs to deal with, so they should be represented by objects. PayPerView's design suggests at least three custom object classes to define the functionality of this application. First, it needs Program objects to represent the programs available for purchase. Since there are also a window and a panel with nontrivial behavior, it should have a class to manage each of these. Several other classes are necessary for real functionality, such as one for checking credit cards and one for maintaining a record of orders placed. This example shows only the first stages of development, however, so we leave these extra classes as likely future steps and don't pursue them here.

The Program class can be fairly simple. All it needs to do is record the program's title, broadcast date and time, channel, and cost. Since these attributes should be accessible, the Program class must also define *accessor methods* to return their values.

The second class controls the window that lists the programs. Its first job is obviously to keep a list of programs, so a good name for it is ProgramController. In addition to keeping the programs, it interacts with the interface objects in the main window to display values and respond to user actions.

The third class is in chage of placing an order and so is called OrderController. It defines methods that open the order panel, verify the user's name and credit card, and present a message to the user indicating the status of an order.

Creating the Project

To create the project for the application, launch Project Builder and choose New... from the Project menu. A panel opens prompting for the

Keeping the Model and Interface Separate

A classic problem in application design is that the logic of the problem being solved often gets tied up in the logic for the user interface. Smalltalk solved this problem by defining the Model–View–Controller paradigm, in which model objects—in this case, Programs—deal indirectly with the user interface through special controller objects.

With this arrangement, Programs don't need to know how to draw, and the interface objects don't need to know the structure of the data they display. This clearly reduces dependencies, but it increases the programming burden by adding a new class for each interaction between model objects and the user interface. As we'll see in *Chapter 10: Database Applications*, however, the Enterprise Objects Framework solves this problem rather neatly by defining generic controller classes that can be applied to many kinds of model objects.

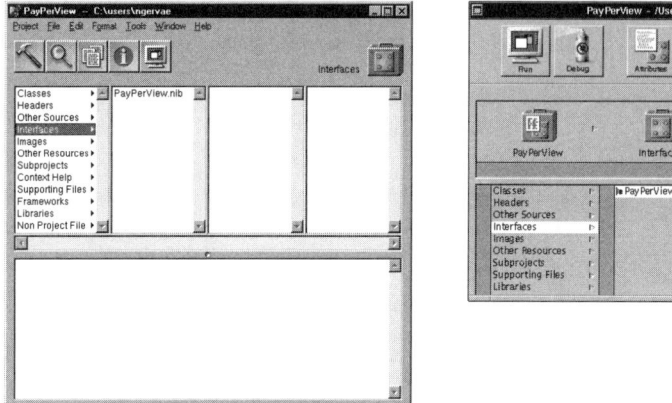

Figure 2. The New PayPerView Project (Windows and Solaris)

name of the project. There's also a pop-up list for the type of project; Project Builder can manage graphical applications, command-line tools, libraries, and several other kinds of compiled programs or modules. You're building an application, so you can leave the pop-up list at the default setting; type "PayPerView" as the project name, and a project window appears (Figure 2).

The top of this window contains buttons for various tools, such as building the project, searching, inspecting file attributes, and debugging. You'll be using most of these in building PayPerView.

Right below the buttons is the resource browser. This series of lists shows the general resource categories at the left. Selecting one of these in most cases lists the individual source files, such as the interface file **PayPerView.nib**, or class header and implementation files like **Project.h** and **Project.m** (which you'll create later). NeXT's version of Project Builder includes a Frameworks category, which allows you to browse the header files of the Foundation Framework and Application Kit (along with whatever other frameworks your project uses).

When you select a file, an icon appears on the far right of the window. You can drag this icon out of the project window for some operations and double-click it to open the file in another application. NeXT's version adds an extra section at the bottom of the project window,

Chapter 7: Building an Application   103

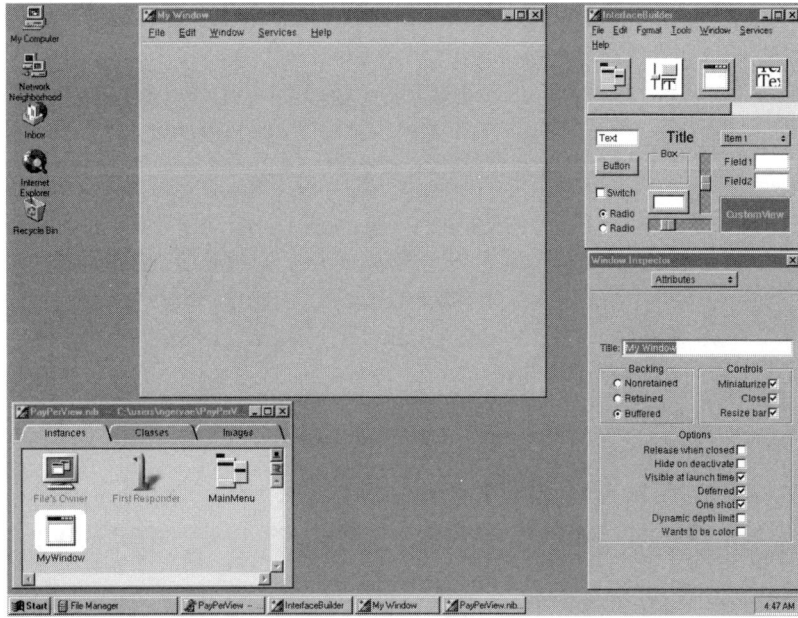

Figure 3. PayPerView's Blank Slate

which is devoted to editing source code and other text files. When you select a text file in the browser, its contents appear in this area.

For a project as simple as PayPerView, it's easiest to prototype the user interface first. To do this, choose the Interfaces category in the resource browser, select **PayPerView.nib**, which is the main interface file for the application, and double-click the icon. This launches Interface Builder.

Building the Interface

For the sake of continuity, all of the illustrations show the Windows version of Interface Builder. The Solaris version behaves identically.

When Interface Builder opens the nib file, four windows appear (Figure 3). At the center of the screen is an empty default window, which is where the main interface will go. At the lower left is the file window, which shows nongraphical components of the user interface: background and helper objects, icons for closed windows, and other objects that don't draw on the screen. By way of orientation:

- The first icon, File's Owner, represents the object that loads the nib file into the application at run time. File's Owner is the bridge through which the application can get at the other objects in the nib file. In this case, File's Owner will be the NSApplication object.

- First Responder is used to set up untargeted action messages (as described in *Chapter 4: The Application Kit*, "Message Routing in the Responder Chain"), which make their way up the responder chain from whatever object happens to be the first responder at the time.

- MainMenu is, of course, the main menu used by the application.

- MyWindow represents the big, empty window on the screen. If you close the window, you can open it again by double-clicking this icon.

On the right side of the screen reside the Palettes window, which contains interface items you can drag and drop onto your application's interface, and an Inspector panel that displays the attributes of the selected object (in this case, the default window).

Laying Out the Window

Interface Builder is based on the drag-and-drop technique, whereby you grab copies of the interface objects you want off the Palettes window and arrange them on the windows of your application. The Palettes window contains several palettes: one for menu items; one for controls such as text fields and buttons; one for new windows and panels; one for a text editor and image view; and one for tables and browsers.

Adding a Table View

The whole point of PayPerView is to display a list of programs, so a table seems a good choice for this. To put it on the window, choose the tables

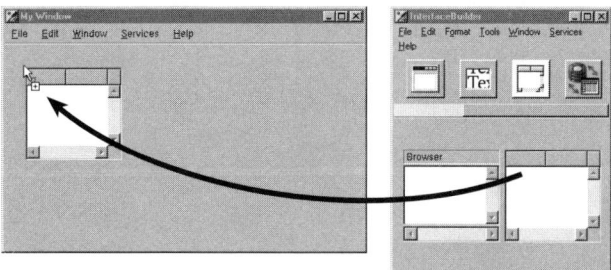

Figure 4. Dragging a Table View from the Palette

palette and drag a table view right onto the empty window, as in Figure 4. After this, resize both it and the window to something reasonable. The idea is to make this window look like the one in Figure 1 (minus the programs in the table, of course).

Next, edit each column in the table view by double-clicking and typing the headings "Broadcast Date" and "Title." While each column is selected, the Inspector displays some attributes, among them the Column Identifier. These will be needed later to distinguish the columns, so enter values there: "broadcastDate" and "title", formatting them as variable names to differentiate them from labels.

Adding Other Controls

The table will show the date and title of every program, with text fields below showing the channel and cost of the selected program. These objects live in the controls palette, so choose that and drag four text fields onto the window. Two will be labels, and two will change to show the channel and cost. To set the label fields' titles, simply double-click them and type the new text.

You should also configure the text fields to be uneditable, since they only display values to the user. Using the Inspector panel (Figure 5), uncheck the editable and selectable boxes for each one, and also remove the border and background colors.

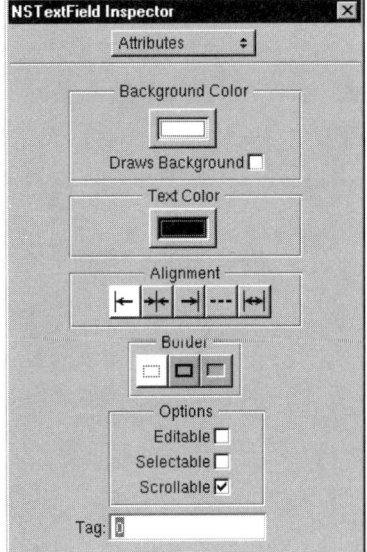

Figure 5. The Text Field Inspector Panel

A box around the text fields might be nice, so choose the Group in Box command from the Arrange menu and change the title to "Program Details." The window will also need a button for ordering a program and one for updating the list of programs, so drag two buttons out and set them up appropriately.

Finishing Touches

To finish up this window, you need to use the Inspector panel. First, select the window itself. The Inspector changes to show attributes you can set for the window. Among these are the title, and whether the window has a close button, a resize border, and a miniaturize button. Edit the title to say "This Week's Programs," and uncheck the close button option—it wouldn't do to allow the user to remove the only window this application puts up.

Use these same techniques to create the order panel, dragging a blank panel from the windows palette and populating it with text fields, a

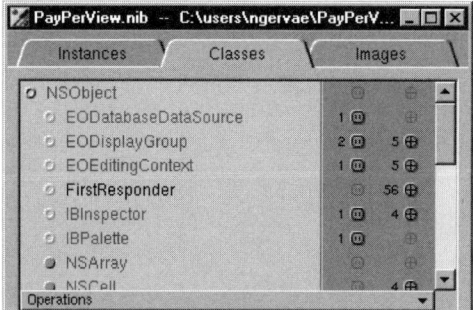

Figure 6. Interface Builder's Class Listing

Cancel button, and an OK button. You'll soon be hooking all this up to the controller objects.

Creating the Controller Objects

Now you're ready to create the classes that interact with the user interface. You do this by prototyping the classes in Interface Builder and then generating source files to edit later. The end result will be placeholders for the custom objects in the nib file, which are replaced when the application runs by real objects created from the compiled source files. This differs from the standard objects in the nib file, which are "live" objects that actually work inside Interface Builder as well as when the application runs.

Since you're defining new classes, switch views in the Interface Builder file window by clicking the "Classes" tab (Figure 6). This shows an indented listing of all the classes Interface Builder knows about, starting with NSObject at the top. Small dots to the left of each class indicate whether it has hidden subclasses (solid) or whether its subclasses, if any, are shown (hollow).

The ProgramController class can inherit directly from NSObject, so select it and choose Subclass from the Operations pull-down list at the bottom of the window. This adds a new class named MyNSObject,

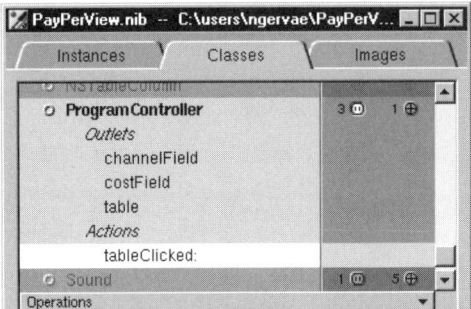

Figure 7. Defining the ProgramController Class

which you should rename to ProgramController. Now you must define the class's *outlets* and *actions*. Outlets are instance variables that refer to other objects, while actions are target–action methods, as described in *Chapter 4: The Application Kit*. Defining these allows you to hook up the ProgramController to other interface objects, as you'll see ahead.

To display the outlets, click the little electrical socket button on the right side of the window (an outlet, get it?). The ProgramController needs to send messages to the table view and to the two text fields, to set the values they display. To create these outlets, press the Enter key to create a new entry and type the new name for each one (Figure 7). Similarly, the

> ### Other Ways to Define a Custom Class
>
> Interface Builder provides for three different ways of defining a custom class. The first, shown in the example, is to define its outlets and actions in the Classes listing and generate a header and implementation file. The second involves reviersing this process: You create a header file and have Interface Builder read it in, upon which it determines the superclass, outlets, and actions by parsing the class declaration. You can even make incremental changes to the header file and reload it into Interface Builder, or rename outlets and actions by hand. The implementation file, once generated, never comes into play again as far as Interface Builder is concerned.
>
> The third way of defining a custom class involves creating it via either of these two methods and then packaging it in a loadable palette, from which you can then drag instances directly into your nib file. This is a somewhat advanced option, which we explore no further in this book.

Chapter 7: Building an Application   109

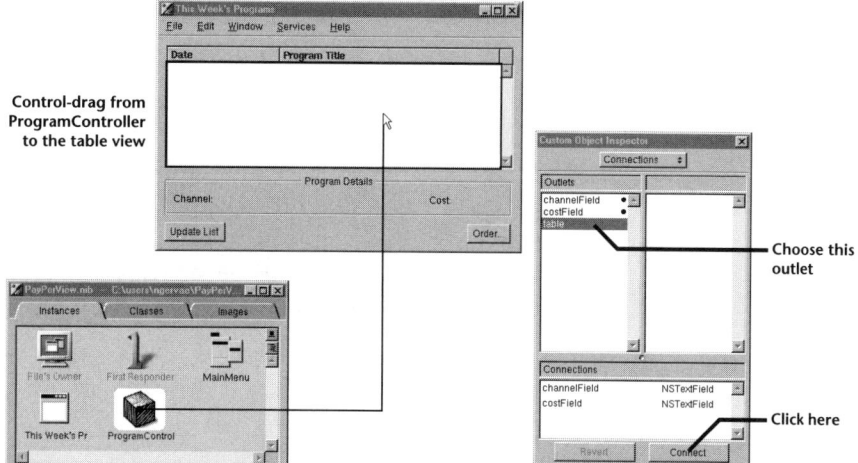

Figure 8. Connecting the ProgramController to the Interface

ProgramController needs to respond when the table view or Update List button is clicked, so add the action methods **tableClicked:** and **updateList:** in the same way.

Once you've defined the outlets and actions for the ProgramController class, choose Create Files from the Operations pull-down list. This causes Interface Builder to create the header file for ProgramController, along with an implementation file containing empty method definitions for the actions. You'll be editing this file shortly.

Connecting Interface Objects

Once the ProgramController class is defined, you can create an instance by choosing the Instantiate operation from the pull-down list. This returns you to the Instances view of the file window, where you're immediately ready to hook up the new object to the user interface. You hook up outlets by holding down the Control key and dragging from the source object to the intended outlet. When you release the mouse, the Inspector panel presents its Connections list, which shows all the outlets of the source object and what they're connected to. Figure 8 shows the

table outlet being connected. You connect the **channelField** and **costField** outlets in exactly the same way.

For the action methods, you perform this process in the other direction, Control-dragging from the object that sends the message, in this case the table view, to the ProgramController. Action messages are always sent to the **target** outlet, so select this and find the ProgramController's **tableClicked:** action method in the Inspector panel. Choose it and make the connection. Now, when a row in the table view is clicked, it will send a **tableClicked:** message to the ProgramController. Do the same for the Update List button and the **updateList:** action. Table views also have a **dataSource** outlet with no action; hook this up to the ProgramController in anticipation of its role as the holder of Program objects.

See Appendix A: PayPerView Source, page 255, for diagrams of all the connections.

You define the OrderController class and instantiate it in the same way. It has outlets to the ProgramController, the order panel, and the various text fields on the panel. Its action methods are **prepareOrder:**, **okClicked:**, and **cancelClicked:**. Hook up these actions from the Order button on the main window and the OK and Cancel buttons on the order panel.

The Program class, not being involved in the user interface at all, must be created from scratch in Project Builder.

Fleshing Out the Classes

Now it's time to write code, so return to Project Builder. Here you add non-outlet instance variables and non-action methods to the class interfaces, and you implement all of the classes' methods. Note that the changes you make to the header files don't affect Interface Builder's ability to reload them; it simply ignores elements that don't apply to nib files.

The ProgramController Class

See Appendix A: PayPerView Source, page 256, for ProgramController's source code.

The ProgramController class has outlets to the table view and to two text fields, as you specified in Interface Builder. It must also store an array of Program objects. Declare this as an NSMutableArray, since the ProgramController will need to alter it, and call it **programList**.

```
@interface ProgramController : NSObject
{
    id  table;

    id  channelField;
    id  costField;

    NSMutableArray *programList;
}
```

Creating the Program List

For this simple example, the ProgramController creates its list of Programs when initialized, in its **init** method. Custom objects in nib files automatically get initialized with this method, so it's a reasonable place to set up the Programs. In a real-world application, the ProgramController would gets its list from some external source; we'll explore some options in Part Two of the book. Here, then, is the **init** method:

```
- (id)init
{
    NSCalendarDate *aDate;
    Program *aProgram;

    self = [super init];

    programList = [[NSMutableArray alloc] init];

    aDate = [NSCalendarDate dateWithString:@"8/13/1996 23:45"
        calendarFormat:@"%m/%d/%Y %H:%M"];
    aProgram = [[Program alloc]
        initWithTitle:@"Faster, Pussycat, Kill Kill!"
        channel:@"Cinerip" broadcastDate:aDate
        cost:@"$2.50"];
```

```
        [programList addObject:aProgram];
        [aProgram release];

        /* Make a few other programs the same way. */

        return self;
    }
```

Note that it first invokes **super**'s implementation and reassigns **self** to the return value. Any initialization method can return an object different from the receiver, so this guarantees that the custom class works appropriately with its superclass. Following this, **init** creates an NSMutableArray.

The next few lines create a Program object and add it to the array. The ProgramController first creates an NSCalendarDate from a string representation (there's a much longer method that takes each date component as a separate argument). Then it creates the Program object itself, using a method not yet written: **initWithTitle:channel:broadcastDate:cost:**. Once the Program is created, the ProgramController adds it to the array with an **addObject:** message, which retains it for safe keeping. The ProgramController can then release it.

Providing Data to the Table View

The ProgramController works in a reciprocal relationship with the table view in the main window. It provides data to the table view and reacts when the table is clicked by displaying the channel and cost of the Program selected in the table view. The first method it uses to provide data to the table view is **numberOfRowsInTableView:**. This method lets the table view know how many rows it needs to display, corresponding directly to the number of items in the data source. ProgramController's implementations simply returns the result of a **count** message sent to the **programList** array.

Once the table view knows the number of rows, it sends the data source a **tableView:objectValueForTableColumn:row:** message for each cell, passing an NSTableColumn object and a row index to identify the cell. This method must return an object that can be formatted for display, such as an NSString or NSNumber. Here's ProgramController's implementation:

```
- (id)tableView:(NSTableView *)tableView
    objectValueForTableColumn:(NSTableColumn *)tableColumn
    row:(int)row
{
    Program *theProgram = [programList objectAtIndex:row];
    id colID = [tableColumn identifier];

    if (!theProgram) return nil;
    if ([colID isEqual:@"title"]) return [theProgram title];
    else if ([colID isEqual:@"broadcastDate"]) {
        return [theProgram broadcastDate];
    }
    else return nil;
}
```

This method first gets the Program for the row specified and then retrieves an *identifier* from the table column. This is the very string you entered earlier in Interface Builder's Inspector panel when setting the titles of the table columns. After checking for an actual program, this method compares the identifier with the two labels expected, returning the appropriate attribute of the Program as the value to display.

You could make the table view editable by also implementing a **setObjectValue:forTableColumn:row:** method. If you did, the table view would allow the user to edit cells and would pass the changes back to the data source using this method. That's all there is to putting data on the screen in a table view.

Handling User Actions in the Table View

The ProgramController's other responsibility is to update the display when the user chooses a program. For this, the ProgramController must act as the target of the table view, which sends an action set up in Interface Builder, in this case, **tableClicked:**. This straightforward method figures out which Program is selected, then gets the channel and cost from it, and displays them in the text fields inside the Program Details box:

```
- (void)tableClicked:(id)sender
{
    Program *selectedProgram;

    selectedProgram = [self selectedProgram];
    [channelField setStringValue:[selectedProgram channel]];
    [costField setStringValue:[selectedProgram cost]];

    return;
}
```

We've cheated a bit by assuming a **selectedProgram** method, which returns the currently selected program. This information is actually available from the table view, so to avoid duplication from storing it in the ProgramController, this method determines the selected program from the selected row in the table view:

```
- (Program *)selectedProgram
{
    int row;
    Program *theProgram;

    row = [table selectedRow];
    theProgram = [programList objectAtIndex:row];
    return theProgram;
}
```

And that's the most complex code in ProgramController.

The Program Class

See *Appendix A: PayPerView Source*, page 259, for Program's source code.

After ProgramController, the Program class is quite simple. Create its files in Project Builder using the New in Project command from the File menu, and define its instance variables:

```
@interface Program : NSObject
{
    NSString *title;
    NSString *channel;
    NSCalendarDate *broadcastDate;
    NSString *cost;
}

/* Initialization and accessor methods. */

@end
```

In addition, declare the initialization method used above in ProgramController, **initWithTitle:channel:broadcastDate:cost:**, and a pair of *accessor methods* for each instance variable, of the form **set***Attribute***:** and *attribute*. The set methods autorelease the old value (to avoid its being deallocated in the local context, where someone might be using it) and copy the new one provided for storage, as shown here:

```
- (void)setBroadcastDate:(NSCalendarDate *)value
{
    [broadcastDate autorelease];
    broadcastDate = [value copy];
    [broadcastDate setCalendarFormat:@"%B %d, %Y %I:%m %p"];
    return;
}
```

This particular method also sets the format used to display the date as a string. The other methods, taking strings already, don't need this. The methods that return attribute values simply return the appropriate instance variable.

The OrderController Class

OrderController's principal job is to handle the process of placing an order, whereby a modal panel appears for the user to enter his or her name and credit card number. A modal panel appears above all other windows in an application and blocks events to those windows, monopolizing all input. The Application Kit accomplishes all the work of reducing the scope of events with only a handful of methods, making it easy for applications to create modal panels.

See *Appendix A: PayPerView Source*, page 261, for OrderController's source code.

The OrderController object is the target of the Order button in PayPerView's main window, with **prepareOrder:** as the action sent. This method sets up the order panel, runs it modally, and takes an action based on the outcome of the modal session:

```
- (void)prepareOrder:(id)sender
{
    int result;
    Program *selectedProgram = [programController
        selectedProgram];
```

```
            [orderTitleField setStringValue:[selectedProgram title]];
            [orderChannelField setStringValue:[selectedProgram
                channel]];
            [orderCostField setStringValue:[selectedProgram cost]];
            [orderDateField setStringValue:[[selectedProgram
                broadcastDate] description]];

            [buyerNameField setStringValue:@""];
            [creditCardField setStringValue:@""];

            result = [NSApp runModalForWindow:orderPanel];
            switch (result) {
                case NSRunStoppedResponse:
                    [self confirmOrder];
                    break;

                case NSRunAbortedResponse:
                    [self cancelOrder];
                    break;
            }
            return;
        }
```

The first part of **prepareOrder:** gets the selected Program and puts its various attributes into fields on the order panel, to identify the Program being ordered. It then empties the name and credit card fields and sends the global NSApplication object, NSApp, a **runModalForWindow:** message with the order panel as the argument. The result of the modal session is saved and compared against the standard modal return values NSRunStoppedResponse and NSRunAbortedResponse, invoking the appropriate method in either case.

runModalForWindow: brings the specified window on-screen and confines event input to that window until the NSApplication object receives either a **stopModal** or an **abortModal** message. The first causes **runModalForWindow:** to return a value of NSRunStoppedResponse, the second a value of NSRunAbortedResponse. In PayPerView, these methods are invoked as part of action methods triggered by the OK and Cancel buttons on the panel itself. When the user clicks the OK button, it sends an **okClicked:** message to the OrderController:

```
- (void)okClicked:(id)sender
{
    if (![self verifyCreditCard]) return;
    [orderPanel orderOut:nil];
    [NSApp stopModal];
    return;
}
```

okClicked: verifies the credit card information, refusing to stop the modal session if it isn't valid. In this example, **verifyCreditCard** merely checks for nonempty strings in the name and card number fields. A real application, of course, needs to check with an actual card verification service. If the information is valid, **okClicked:** removes the panel from the screen with an **orderOut:** message and invokes **stopModal**. **cancelClicked:** behaves similarly.

If **runModalForWindow:** returns NSRunStoppedResponse, the Order-Controller invokes its own **confirmOrder** method, which simply presents an alert panel indicating that a Program was ordered:

```
- (void)confirmOrder
{
    NSString *status = [NSString
        stringWithFormat:@"%@ ordered %@ using card #%@\n",
        [buyerNameField stringValue],
        [orderTitleField stringValue],
        [creditCardField stringValue]];

    NSRunAlertPanel(@"Order Placed", status, nil, nil, nil);
    return;
}
```

This method first constructs a message to present using NSString's **stringWithFormat:**, which inserts relevant strings into a template much the way the standard C function **printf()** does. **NSRunAlertPanel()** presents a predefined panel with a title, a message, and up to three buttons. The method invoked when the Cancel button is clicked presents a similar message stating that the order was canceled.

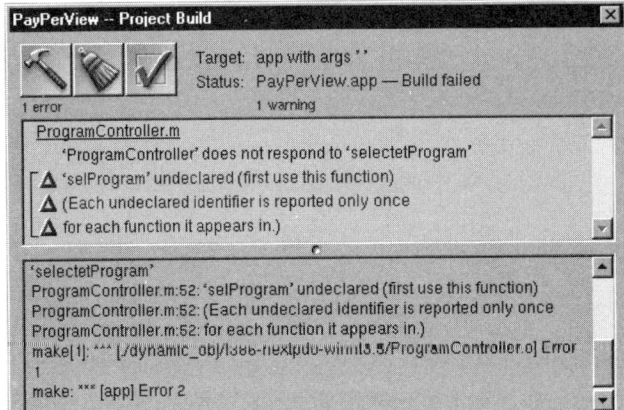

Figure 9. Windows Project Builder Build Panel Catching an Error

Building and Debugging

Now that you've defined the interface and written code for the custom classes, you can build the application and launch or debug it. How you do this depends on which system you're using. NeXT's version has separate build and launch panels for managing these processes. SunSoft's version uses the project window to build the application and starts a debugger in a terminal window.

NeXT's Way

To build PayPerView on Windows or Mach, open the Build panel, which has three buttons: one for building the application; one for cleaning up derived files; and one for setting options (Figure 9). The options you can choose include how to build (for debugging, for installation, and so on), additional arguments to provide to the **gnumake** utility used to perform the build, a host to perform the build on, and which computer architecture to build for.

As the project builds, the top portion of the status area lists errors and warnings as they occur, while the bottom portion shows every command

Chapter 7: Building an Application 119

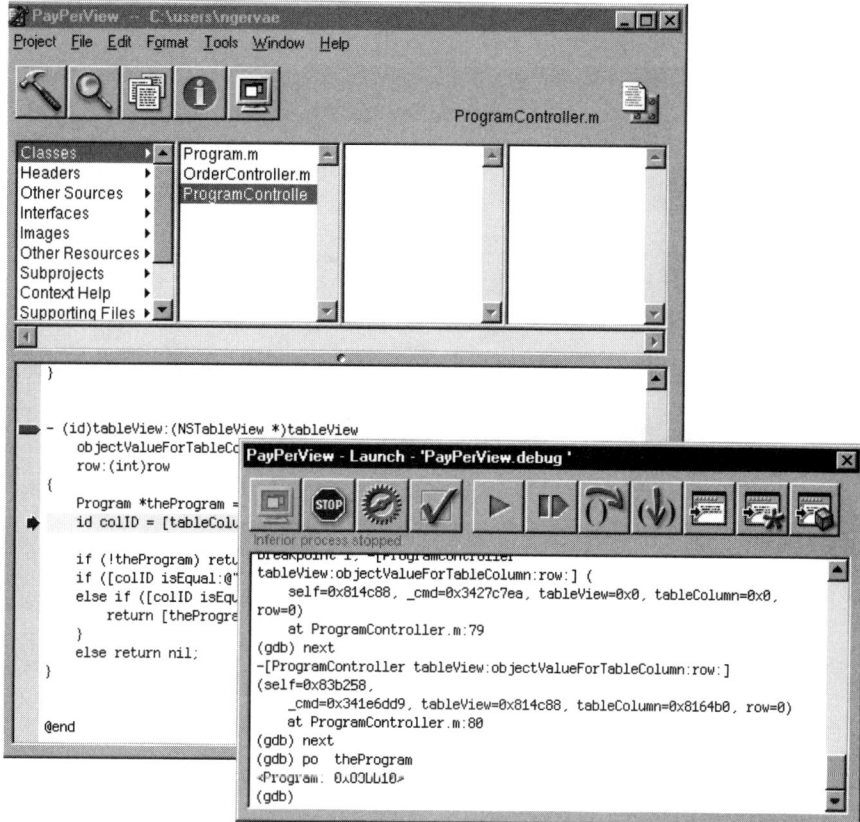

Figure 10. Windows Project Builder Launch Panel with Debugger

line executed by the **gnumake** utility. If any errors or warnings do occur, you can click on them, which causes Project Builder to open the source file in its code viewer and select the offending line. This makes debugging compile-time errors that much faster.

Once the application is built, you can use the launch panel to run or debug it (Figure 10). The launch panel contains buttons for running the application, starting the debugger, examining the environment of the process as it runs (including stack frames), and setting options. It also contains buttons that control the debugger, starting, pausing or continuing the program, single-stepping across or into subroutines, and printing values selected in the code editor.

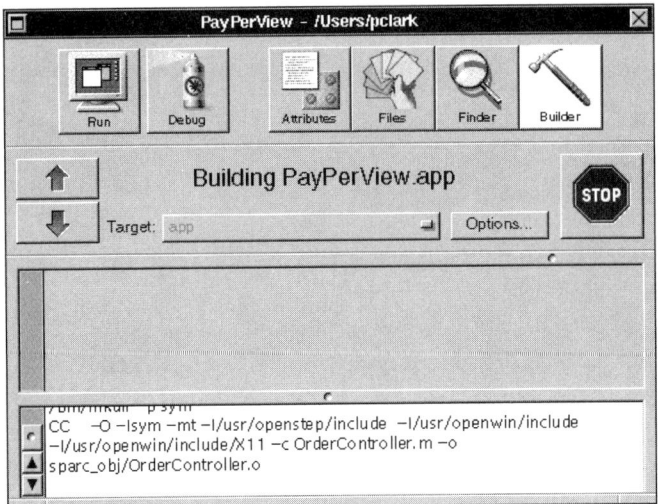

Figure 11. Solaris Project Builder Build Mode

The bottom part of the launch panel is the interactive debugger console. Project Builder uses the GNU debugger, **gdb**, which originated as a UNIX command-line source debugger. You can still run **gdb** from this console by typing commands, though the buttons and interactive tracking of the program counter in the code editor make things considerably easier. When the debugger is running, a strip appears down the edge of the code editor, in which you can place breakpoints by double-clicking and alter them by manipulating the breakpoint markers, disabling them, moving them, and so on. When the application hits a breakpoint, a small arrow also appears in this strip, which advances with the program counter and which you can actually drag down to skip past some lines of code.

SunSoft's Way

To build PayPerView on Solaris, click the Builder button, which puts Project Builder into build mode (Figure 11). The controls are slightly different from NeXT's version, but they act in basically the same way. Note that SunSoft's version of Project Builder uses **make** by default, not **gnumake**.

You can also click the Run or Debug button, which builds the application if necessary, then starts either it or the debugger. On Solaris, the debugger runs in a terminal window and communicates with the Edit application to show the code being examined. While the debugger is running, the Edit application displays a debug panel with buttons for starting the application, examining the environment of the process as it runs (including stack frames), and setting options. It also contains buttons that control the debugger, starting, pausing or continuing the program, single-stepping across or into subroutines, and printing values selected in the window.

Part Two: Business Applications

8 *The Character of a Business Application*

At first blush, OpenStep is the Foundation and Application frameworks and the tools you use to build graphical applications. The real power and significance of OpenStep, however, is in its object model, which is powerful enough to extend across processes and networks, to transform the static content of databases into live objects with logic built in, and to support the presentation of data in a variety of media. These abilities address many of the significant needs of business applications: support for multitier client/server architectures; access to relational databases; swift development and straightforward maintenance; and deployment on heterogeneous networks.

This second part of the book covers the more significant uses of this broader view of OpenStep in a business environment. These uses are enabled by the built-in Distributed Objects facility as well as by the add-on frameworks: the Enterprise Objects Framework and WebObjects. These two products are both made by NeXT, but they're available on all OpenStep platforms. Parts of all three of these systems are also available on several other UNIX platforms, enabling server development and deployment on a wider variety of systems.

The Business Environment

Business use of software generally falls into two categories, that of standard productivity applications and that of custom business applications. Productivity applications, such as spreadsheets and word processors, assist individuals in creating documents, reports, and other concrete things. The generic nature of these tools allows businesses to buy them off the shelf and use them as they come.

Custom business applications, on the other hand, move the business's data through processes unique to the business, embodying its policies in a system that coordinates the work of its users. As such, business applications must be developed specifically with the business's practices in mind, whether by an outside party or by the business itself. To develop these applications, businesses require technologies that support their particular practices.

Data, Process, and Policy

Every business manages its own unique system of processes that create, modify, and redistribute data among the parts of the business. These processes are governed by policies that determine what operations are meaningful and legal for specific kinds of data, such as inventory and payroll. More importantly, though, both the data and policies must be shared throughout the business, with the processes based on them being distributed appropriately and made accessible to every part of the business.

Consider a shipping company that must deal with the processes of receiving inventory, cataloguing and storing it, and then shipping it to its final destination. The company's data records the nature of the inventory, the costs to transport and store that inventory, where it came from, and where it's going. This information must be made available in the proper form to many different people in the company, who all have their separate tasks to perform with regard to both the inventory and the data about the inventory. These tasks in turn are governed by the company's policies, such as what can be received and processed, payment types accepted, credit limits, and so on.

The Elements of a Business Application

Unlike productivity applications, which handle a single task in a single program, business applications often handle many separate tasks using many programs, typically taking the form of client/server systems or suites of related programs. To support such architectures and to address business needs with regard to data, process, and policy, a business application needs four things:

- access to the business's data, usually in the form of a database server that provides a structured set of data to business applications;

- well-defined business components that implement general processes and that can take advantage of computing power wherever it may be;

- a programmatic business model that embodies the business's entities, giving them the power to enforce the policies defined for them;

- a means for allowing the people running the business to view and edit the information contained in the entities.

The first three elements seem well defined as representatives of data, process, and policy, respectively, but in fact all four combine them to some extent. The following sections explain how they do this.

Databases

All businesses use and share data among their members. The most common means of doing this is with a relational database management system. A database's schema records what kinds of values may be stored, along with limits on those values based on business policy. Databases are thus major representatives of both data and policy, in that order.

However, being relatively passive repositories, they don't embody processes very much. This quality is reserved for the other elements.

Business Components

Business components embody pure processes that consume quantities of data, such as payroll calculation, recording of transactions, and report generation. A business component can be a functional module within a single program or a program in its own right with a dedicated function. A component often functions as a server in a client/server system, making its resources available to many other applications. In this way, cooperating groups of components encompass complex processes distributed throughout the business.

A business component typically defines no lasting state of its own. Instead, it simply operates on the data and entities that come its way, examining them and using their values as input to its process. In this sense, components are the interchangeable parts of a business application: When you need a particular service, any component that provides it will do.

Business Entities

Unlike components, business entities represent the unique, individual elements of a business. By tightly binding the three aspects of data, process, and policy, entities have lasting identity based on internal state as well as consistent behavior. Whereas a component acts on whatever data it's presented with, an entity's role is to cultivate its own private data and relationships to other entities, interacting with those entities to execute its processes, and enforcing its own policy in those interactions.

Entities typically represent real assets and resources of the business, such as inventory, employees, and equipment. Their processes define how they interact with each other, and their policies limit how they may interact in specific situations. For example, employees may requisition equipment (process), but if the equipment is valued over a certain amount, the manager must approve the requisition (policy constraint).

Presentation of Information

Data is of no use if it can't be viewed and manipulated by real people. To this end, the data from business components and in business entities must be made available for presentation in any number of forms: as printed reports, as editable forms on interactive screens, and so on. Ideally, the means of presentation should be handled by special elements tailored to the task, relieving the entities from dependence on external data formats and presentation mechanisms.

Elements as Objects

The latter three elements listed above—business components, business entities, and presentation elements—all combine data and process to some extent and exhibit behavior independent of other elements. These are defining qualities of objects, as described in *Chapter 2: The Object Model*. Thus, it makes perfect sense to implement them as objects. The very purpose of OpenStep, as a platform, is to make this easy. The three business-oriented OpenStep systems apply specifically to business components, business entities, and interaction with users.

Component Objects

Business components, being shared resources, must have a means of communicating with each other and with the other elements of the business application. The natural model suggested by objects is one in which the elements make requests and transmit information by sending messages to one another. Because components are often separate programs distributed across a network, though, basic Objective-C messaging isn't enough.

OpenStep's Distributed Objects facility addresses this issue by extending the Objective-C messaging metaphor to the network. This allows objects on disparate machines to send messages to one another exactly as if they were running in the same program. The object model remains the same, allowing application developers to focus on implementing business process and policy rather than on basic communication. Distributed Objects is also available apart from OpenStep on several UNIX platforms, making these systems available for deploying business components as well.

Business Objects

Because business objects must have lasting identities, their state has to be managed by a robust data repository such as a relational database. Relational databases, however, organize data quite differently from how objects organize it. To enable real business objects, an application must be able to translate between the rows of a database and the objects that add behavior to the raw data.

Bridging the gap between raw data and the OpenStep object model, NeXT's Enterprise Objects Framework embodies business entities as true objects while preserving their state in the database. The Enterprise Objects Framework maps the relational data model into the business application's object model, transforming rows into unique instances within a program, rendering relationships between rows as pointer references between objects, and tracking all changes to the state of the live objects for propagation back to the database. This leaves the business objects to carry on their processes without concern for the external storage that gives them their identity.

Presentation Objects

To be of any real use, business objects must have some means for letting users view and modify their data. OpenStep would seem to have a ready answer for this in the graphical objects of the Application Kit. These objects are simply a mechanism, however—it's up to the data-bearing objects to know how to make them display and edit values. Not only does this place an unnecessary burden on business objects, it ties them down to that mechanism.

To free business objects from having to drive display objects, an additional element is needed to move data to and from the display objects. This element can monitor business objects for changes, request data on their terms, and display it according to whatever presentation mechanism is available. Similarly, when the user changes values, the presentation element accepts the new data from the display object and passes it back to the business objects.

OpenStep currently supports two such presentation elements. The first is part of the Enterprise Objects Framework, a mechanism that binds business objects to the display mechanism of the Application Kit. The second is NeXT's WebObjects framework, which turns business data from objects into HTML for display in any standard World Wide Web browser and accepts requests on behalf of the objects. These two presentation elements both display data to users and accept data from them, passing it back to the business's objects. In this way, they connect the business's data, process, and policy to the world at large.

A Unified Approach to Business Applications

OpenStep offers tremendous benefit to business applications, and to business application developers, by providing a single object model for all of their elements. The encapsulation of all three elements as objects, and their integration into a single object model, enables them to be developed rapidly—and further, to evolve as business processes and policies evolve. When a process or policy changes, only the objects involved in that process or policy need change. Since these same objects can be reused throughout the business's application suite, changes are both easily made and easily deployed.

OpenStep's Distributed Objects facility and business frameworks make all this possible. Business components can be implemented as objects both within programs and across the network. Business entities can be given life from static data and operate entirely as objects. Data from all elements can be viewed and edited by users, through the Application Kit or more widely through the World Wide Web. The following chapters present OpenStep's business frameworks, showing what they do, presenting simple examples, and explaining how they work.

9 *Distributed Applications*

Distribution, though it works largely behind the scenes, is one of the defining characteristics of many business applications. Large systems with centralized, expensive, or simply rare resources—whether data or services—must share those resources, and distribution is the way it's done. Any framework for creating business applications must include a distribution mechanism; OpenStep's is called Distributed Objects (DO). Distributed Objects is an integral part of the OpenStep Foundation Framework, and is also available as a standalone product called Portable Distributed Objects™ (PDO®) on several UNIX-based operating systems.

In this chapter we show Distributed Objects in action, turning the sample application developed in Part One into a distributed application. Next, we explain how DO works, in great detail. Our reasons for doing this are to show you how much DO gives you and to allow you to determine how appropriate this model is for your needs. The final sections cover other distribution models and present some design issues that distribution forces on application development.

What Distributed Objects Does

Distributed object systems in general make objects in a remote process look like they exist in the local process. OpenStep's Distributed Objects facility allows the client of a remote object to use that object exactly as it does a local one, with the same expressions and methods used for any object. Using a local or remote object is identical, apart from the code needed to create the **id** for the object. Beyond this small difference, clients of a remote object need never know that the object exists in another process. Of course, robust applications *want* to know in some circumstances when an object isn't local; Distributed Objects allows those that care to find out.

That's all there is to it. But behind this simplicity lies a host of complex issues. The latter parts of this chapter describe many of them.

PayPerView with Distributed Objects

See *Appendix B: PayPerView with Distributed Objects* for the complete source code.

Before exploring the inner workings of DO, let's show how you use it in a client/server application, by putting PayPerView's program list on a server. To do this, you change only two methods in ProgramController, **init** and **updateList:**, to contact a server object and retrieve the program list from it. You also add a new instance variable of type **id** called **programServer** and implement **init** like this:

```
- (id)init
{
    NSConnection *serverConn;

    self = [super init];

    serverConn = [NSConnection
        connectionWithRegisteredName:@"ProgramServer"
        host:@"*"];
    programServer = [[serverConn rootProxy] retain];

    if (!programServer) {
        NSRunAlertPanel(@"No server",
            @"Can't connect to the program server.",
            @"Quit", nil, nil);
        [NSApp terminate:nil];
    }
```

```
    [(NSDistantObject *)programServer
        setProtocolForProxy:@protocol(ProgramServer)];

    programList = [[programServer programs] retain];
    return self;
}
```

Instead of creating the Programs here, the ProgramController relies on a central server to provide them. The messages to the NSConnection create a proxy to a remote object and assign its **id** to **programServer**. The server object runs in a different process, but its proxy looks just like any other Objective-C object here in the client. After checking for an error, **init** invokes **setProtocolForProxy:** to define the methods that the server is known to respond to and gets the list of programs using a method in the ProgramServer protocol:

```
@protocol ProgramServer

- (bycopy NSArray *)programs;

@end
```

This protocol has only one method, **programs**, that returns a copy of the server object's program list (without the **bycopy** specifier, it would return a proxy to the program list). The reasons for defining and using a protocol are explained later, under "The Role of Protocols."

updateList: can now be implemented to actually get new information, by releasing the old program list and getting a new, possibly altered one, from the server:

```
- (void)updateList:(id)sender
{
    [programList release];
    programList = [[programServer programs] retain];
    [table reloadData];
    return;
}
```

Note that although this is an extremely trivial example, we've made a design decision—using **bycopy** for the program list—that reflects the distributed nature of this application. The **programs** method returns a copy of the server's program list instead of a proxy. The reason for this is obvious. If you're going to be interacting a lot with a basically static object, you don't want every message going across the network. Far better to get a local copy of it, which you can replace, than to congest the network unnecessarily.

The server class defines an **init** method that creates the list of Programs using the same code that ProgramController did in the original PayPerView—it's just moved to this class. The protocol method, **programs**, simply returns an immutable copy of the list:

```
- (NSArray *)programs
{
    // Guarantee bycopy transmission by making immutable.
    return [[programList copy] autorelease];
}
```

Now, because the server is a separate program that doesn't use the Application Kit, it has to have a **main()** routine that creates the server object and makes it available to clients:

```
#import <Foundation/Foundation.h>
#import "ProgramServer.h"

int main (int argc, const char *argv[])
{
    NSAutoreleasePool * pool = [[NSAutoreleasePool alloc]
        init];
    ProgramServer *server;
    NSConnection *defaultConn = [NSConnection
        defaultConnection];

    server = [[ProgramServer alloc] init];
    [defaultConn setRootObject:server];
    if ([defaultConn registerName:@"ProgramServer"] == NO) {
        NSLog(@"Failed to register server. Exiting.\n");
        exit(EXIT_FAILURE);
    }

    NSLog(@"Server successfully launched.\n");
    [[NSRunLoop currentRunLoop] run];

    [pool release];
    exit(0);
}
```

This function uses the standard autorelease pool class to handle autoreleased objects outside of the run loop and sets up a ProgramServer object within the pool's scope. To make the ProgramServer available, it gets an NSConnection object, makes the ProgramServer the root object with a **setRootObject:** message, and registers the NSConnection with a **registerName:** message.

This might seem like a fair amount of code, but in a large project this is small indeed. Converting a simple OpenStep application to a client/server architecture is this simple, as far as the code itself is concerned. More complex applications require substantially more work, of course.

How It Works

As simple as it is to use Distributed Objects, a lot goes on behind the scenes. Understanding this can help you to decide whether DO will work for your projects. If you decide it will, your understanding will help you take full advantage of DO and diagnose any problems you encounter in your applications.

This part of the chapter examines the setup of a client/server application in chronological order, starting with the server and proceeding to the client. The first sections, "Advertising an Object" and "Contacting the Server," explain just what happens when a server advertises an object and when a client connects to it. The following section, "Remote Message Processing," describes the steps involved in trapping a message to a proxy and forwarding the message across the connection. "Transferring Data and Objects" explains how DO handles argument and return values and shows how you can bypass the normal proxy creation mechanism to have an object duplicated across a connection. The last section, "Handling Failures," explains how to correct problems that can occur in distributed messaging.

Advertising an Object

As we've already shown, a Distributed Objects session involves NSConnection and proxy objects. The example made two NSConnections and one proxy visible in the code; in fact, each adver-

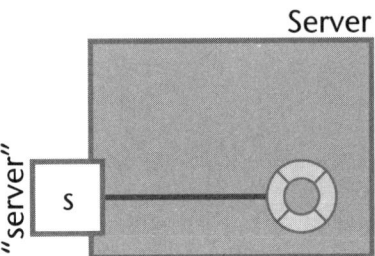

Figure 1. Server Process Advertising an Object

tised server object is managed by a *root connection*, and each process that contacts the advertised object creates another pair of NSConnections and proxies. The new PayPerView, then, actually creates three NSConnections. Here's how that all gets built up.

First, the server program creates the object that handles messages from clients. Then it creates an NSConnection, assigns the server object as the NSConnection's root object, and gives it a name. Recall the code from the previous section:

```
ProgramServer *server;
NSConnection *defaultConn = [NSConnection defaultConnection];

server = [[ProgramServer alloc] init];
[defaultConn setRootObject:server];

if ([defaultConn registerName:@"ProgramServer"] == NO) {
    /* Handle error. */
}
```

This code takes advantage of the fact that every thread has a default NSConnection object, which can be set up as a server. An NSConnection can advertise only one root object, however, so the default NSConnection might not be available. If you want to advertise several objects, you can create additional NSConnections with the usual **alloc** and **init** methods.

The result looks something like Figure 1, where a lone NSConnection (the square labeled **s**) advertises the name "server" to other processes. This NSConnection object acts as the matchmaker for other processes requesting the services of the object. It's worth noticing that the name is bound to the NSConnection, not to the server object. You can assign a

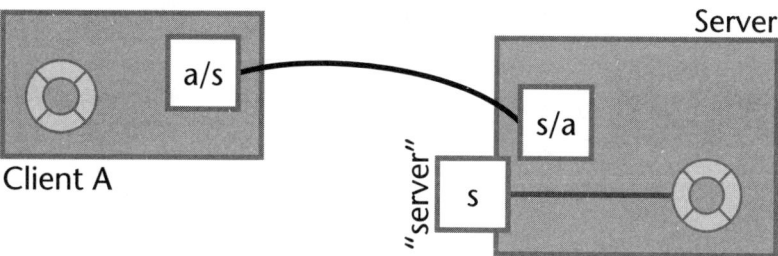

Figure 2. Client Process Connecting to the Advertised Object

new root object to an NSConnection at any time, changing the object that new clients connect to. You can change the name as well, perhaps to make one server unavailable when an upgraded one is brought on line.

While setting up the root connection, the server can also configure its behavior with regard to timeouts, concurrent message handling, and so on. Servers that use the Application Kit are finished setting up at this point. Most servers, however, don't present graphical user interfaces, using only the facilities of the Foundation Framework. Such servers must start the run loop explicitly in order to receive incoming messages:

```
[[NSRunLoop currentRunLoop] run];
```

The role of the run loop is explained in "Remote Message Processing."

Contacting the Server

When a client starts up, it seeks out the server's NSConnection using **connectionWithRegisteredName:host:**. The name used is whatever the server advertised. The host can be a specific machine's name, or "*" to connect to the first machine on the local network that responds to the request.

```
NSConnection *serverConn;

serverConn = [NSConnection
    connectionWithRegisteredName:@"ProgramServer"
    host:@"*"];
```

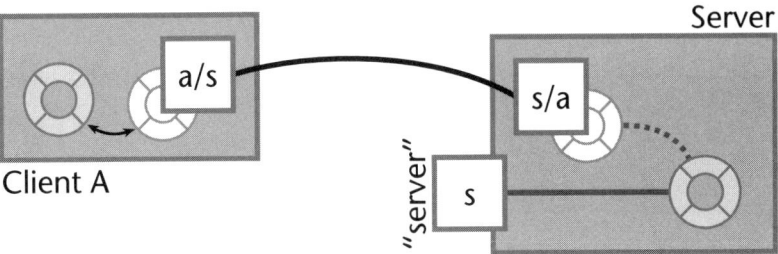

Figure 3. One Client Connected

This method causes the server's root NSConnection to create a child NSConnection associated with the client process and creates an NSConnection in the client that talks to it. The client can accept the new NSConnection as it is or set various configuration options before sending any remote messages. Figure 2 shows the state of things at this point. The letters in each box indicate each NSConnection's *receive* and *send ports*, which play reciprocal roles in the two processes and together identify the connection between them. Ports are an abstract notion with regard to the OpenStep specification, but NeXT's implementation realizes these as actual objects of the NSPort class. "Remote Message Processing" describes the role ports play in sending remote messages.

After setting up the connection, the client gets the proxy to the server object:

```
id <ProgramServer> programServer;

programServer = [[serverConn rootProxy] retain];

[(NSDistantObject *)programServer
    setProtocolForProxy:@protocol(ProgramServer)];
```

When a DO program returns a proxy to one of its objects, it's said to be *vending* that object. As a result of the **rootProxy** message, both the server connection **s/a** and the client connection **a/s** create proxy objects, as shown in Figure 3. The server creates a *local proxy* (the hollow object under the square **s/a**), so called because its real counterpart, sometimes called the target object, exists in the same process and thread. In its turn the client creates a *remote proxy*, which communicates with the target through the NSConnection objects. "Remote Message Processing"

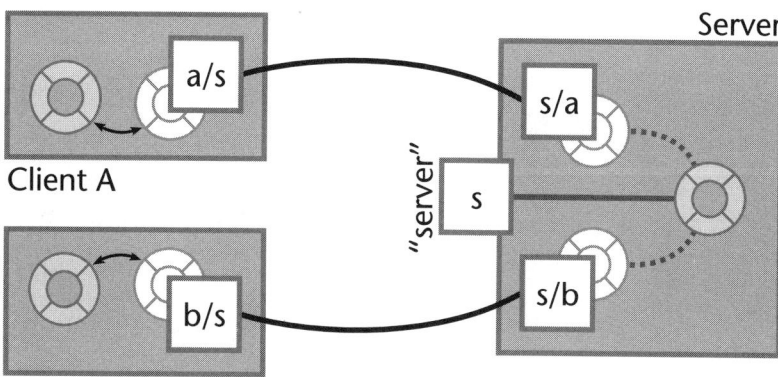
Figure 4. Two Clients Connected

describes the responsibilities of each of these objects, as well as the purpose of the **setProtocolForProxy:** message.

This is the basic scenario. By way of elaboration, Figure 4 shows what things look like when a second client connects to the server. It gets its own NSConnection pair, **s/b** and **b/s**, and another pair of proxy objects. Both Client A and Client B are communicating with the same object in the server, however. In similar fashion, if a client connects to two different servers, there will be two connections in the client and two proxies, representing the two different server objects.

In another common situation, suppose the server object returns a new object in response to a remote message. Here the client receives a new proxy, shown in Figure 5, which shares the child NSConnection **a/s**. Messages to or from either object in the server pass through this pair of NSConnection objects.

These are the most typical arrangements that develop among the components of a Distributed Objects application. Others are possible. A client might send one of its objects to the server, for example, which then ends up getting sent to a different client, resulting in a new connection between the two clients. Or, a program might be designed to run in multiple threads, using DO internally to preserve each thread's flow of control. In all cases, the NSConnections perform the necessary coordination and optimization of proxy relationships among vended objects.

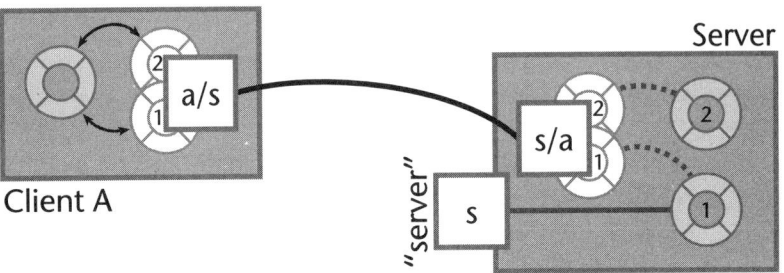

Figure 5. Two Objects Vended over One NSConnection

Remote Message Processing

On establishing the state in Figure 3, the client process is ready to send messages to the remote object and to receive replies. As mentioned before, the client can send any message to the remote object, passing and receiving just about any type of data except for unstructured or open-ended types such as unions, pointers to **void**, and pointers embedded in structures other than **char *** and objects. The Distributed Objects system itself allocates temporary buffers as needed for received data, allowing the recipient to use or cache the data without having to deallocate it. All received objects and data are temporary; you must retain or copy them if you intend to keep them.

You might want to refer back to Figure 3 as you read this process.

With that out of the way, let's consider what actually happens when a message is sent to a remote proxy. Because proxies implement very few methods of their own, the odds are that the remote proxy doesn't respond to the message. An unrecognized message causes the standard Objective-C method **forwardInvocation:** to be invoked, with an NSInvocation object representing the message and its arguments. In NSObject this method raises an exception to indicate a run-time error, but in the remote proxy class, NSDistantObject, it sends the invocation across its connection along with the **id** of its real counterpart.

The client's NSConnection takes the invocation, encodes it for network transmission, and sends it out on the local send port (which is connected to the server's receive port). The client port transmits the encoded message onto the network, where the server's receive port picks it up and the run loop is notified of pending input. The run loop sees that the message gets read and hands it to the server NSConnection, which decodes the invocation from the message, assigns its target to be the real object, and invokes it. (Local proxies are used only for bookkeeping purposes.)

The NSInvocation sends its message to the target object with the proper arguments, and if all goes well it squirrels away the return value, which the server NSConnection then packages up again and sends back to the client. There the client NSConnection passes the return value back to the remote proxy, where the Objective-C run-time system recovers it and hands it to the sender of the remote message.

The server might also crash or hang while executing a remote message. These cases are covered under "Handling Failures."

If all doesn't go well, meaning that the method invoked raises an exception, the NSConnection object traps the exception and sends it back to the client instead of a return value. The client NSConnection, on decoding an exception, immediately raises it in the client, duplicating what would happen if the remote message were in fact a local one.

The Role of Protocols

The sequence of events recounted above left out a small detail. It turns out that, in order to forward a message properly, the Objective-C run-time system needs information about the size and order of a method's arguments and return value. Within a single process, this can be handled by examining the run-time method tables, but in a distributed application, where the receiver of a message—and therefore its methods—aren't present, this information must be looked up before the remote invocation, resulting in an extra round-trip to the server.

Because network transmission is orders of magnitude slower than in-process lookup of messages, it makes a lot of sense to do away with this lookup if possible. To this end, the remote proxy class allows you to set a protocol of methods that the remote object is known to respond to. This is why the **setProtocolForProxy:** message is used in the code example above. It immediately records the method signatures for the methods in that protocol so that they don't have to be looked up when they're invoked later. You can still send any message to the remote proxy;

those not in the protocol simply cause remote lookup to occur. However, for most efficient use of the network, it makes sense to bundle the server object's remote methods in a protocol and advertise that to client programs via a header file. (If you're concerned about using multiple protocols with a proxy, remember that it's a simple matter to incorporate any number of protocols into another.)

Configuring an NSConnection

NSConnection defines reasonable default behavior for handling remote messages, but also allows you to adjust some of the parameters of this behavior. An NSConnection uses two different timeouts: one for messages waiting to be transmitted, called *requests*, and one for replies yet to be received. If either timeout is exceeded, the NSConnection raises an exception. You can set either to adjust the tolerance of an NSConnection for the vagaries of network performance.

When an NSConnection is awaiting a reply to a remote message, it puts its thread's run loop into a special mode, which preempts other run-loop modes and can block other sources of input from arriving. This mode is public, however, so you can base high-priority input sources on this mode, or add other modes to the one NSConnection uses, in order to have the input sources for those modes checked along with remote message replies.

Finally, you can set how an NSConnection handles multiple incoming remote messages. By default, an NSConnection handles them as they come in through the run loop. If your application returns to the run loop while handling a remote message—by invoking another remote message, for example—that remote message can be preempted by another one coming in. Normally, this is fine behavior; it allows for arbitrary levels of callbacks between the client and server to negotiate a transaction. However, for remote methods that must complete to assure consistent state, or that simply put application state into a temporarily inconsistent state, it can cause problems. The incoming messages then either return incorrect results to the sender or corrupt the server's state altogether. To address this issue, NSConnections can be configured to accept and handle only one incoming remote message at a time, through the **setIndependentConversationQueuing:** method. This limits the available server resources, of course, and can cause deadlock if the server attempts to send a message back to the client, so it must be used with care. Used appropriately, however, it solves several classes of problems, such as a secure login session that requires a single challenge-response cycle.

NSConnection's Delegate

An NSConnection can be assigned a delegate, which is given the opportunity to intercede in two operations: the creation of a root connection's child when a client makes contact, and the authentication of remote messages. This allows it to refuse new connections and to perform security checks on existing connections.

When a connection request arrives at a root connection, it checks with its delegate before actually creating a child connection, using the **connection:shouldMakeNewConnection:** method. The delegate can return YES to approve or NO to reject the new connection. This technique is useful for limiting the load on a server, for example.

The delegate's other responsibility, message authentication, isn't officially part of the OpenStep specification, but both NeXT's and SunSoft's implementations include it. When an NSConnection is preparing a remote message, it checks the delegate for data that the peer NSConnection can use to authenticate the message by sending it an **authenticationDataForComponents:** message. The delegate typically hashes the array of message components into a value that the peer can verify. When the message arrives at its destination, the NSConnection there checks for authentication data; if it's present, the destination NSConnection asks its own delegate to confirm the data with an **authenticateComponents:withData:** message. The delegate in the receiving process can hash the components and compare the result to the data provided by the sending process, returning YES or NO as appropriate. This feature allows you to capture illegal messages.

Transferring Data and Objects

The kinds of data that can be sent as arguments and received as return values and filled-in arguments have been hinted at so far. Here's the scoop on what exactly works and what doesn't. Naturally, all scalar C types and Objective-C objects can be passed back and forth in a remote message. Complex structures are allowed as long as they contain no pointers other than **char** * and objects. The Distributed Objects system assumes that any item declared as **char** * is a null-terminated C string, so plan your method parameter types appropriately. Pointers to other data types are allowed outside of structures and are assumed to point to a single element of the pointer type. Pointers must have valid values or be NULL at the time they're passed to a remote message, because the Distributed Objects system must access and send those values to recreate valid pointers in the receiving process.

Explicitly disallowed are unions, which are highly architecture-dependent, pointers to **void**, and structures as return values. You can pass structures or pointers to structures as arguments, but structures must always be returned by pointer reference, since returning structures by value requires significant manipulation of the stack. To avoid potential problems with this, the Distributed Objects system allocates memory for a returned structure on the heap, and you accept a pointer to this returned structure. This memory is reserved only temporarily though, so the receiver must copy it to hold on to it.

Passing or returning an object normally results in a new proxy being created if necessary. In this way programs can naturally share references to multiple objects, which makes their code look quite transparent to distribution, but can of course cause all sorts of performance and debugging problems. These problems are explored later under "Design with Distributed Objects." You can also set up particular object classes to support actual transfer over a connection, whether upon request or—overriding the normal behavior—by default. This is explained below.

"The Role of Protocols" mentioned an optimization that can be made at run time by specifying which methods a remote object is known to handle, thus saving two extra network trips per message. In declaring this protocol, you can also specify which method arguments and return types are actually transmitted over the network, saving on packet size and round-trip time. This is done with several special Objective-C keywords, used only in protocol declarations and only in forwarding remote messages:

Keyword	Effect
inout	Method parameter is sent to the receiver and returned (if a pointer value). Default behavior for all parameters except those declared **const**.
in	Method parameter is sent to receiver but not returned. Default behavior for parameters declared **const**.
out	Method parameter isn't sent to receiver but is returned to sender. Valid only for pointer values.
oneway	Causes a message with a **void** return value to return as soon as it's queued, and not block waiting for a reply.
bycopy	Causes objects to be replicated across the connection instead of having proxies created. Requires support from the class (see below).
byref	Explictly causes proxies to be created, overriding any objects that might normally copy themselves across the connection.

These keywords should be fairly straightforward, except for **bycopy** and **byref**. The effect of **bycopy** is simple in nature but requires the cooperation of the object being passed to actually work. In transmitting an object value, the Distributed Objects system invokes a special method, **replacementObjectForPortCoder:**, which normally causes a proxy to be created.

Classes that support **bycopy** transmission must override this method to return **self** when a copy should be provided instead of a proxy (which NSObject's implementation does by default). The receiver can check for this by sending **isBycopy** to the NSCoder provided in the message. The class must also adopt the NSCoding protocol, which allows it to be encoded into the remote message and reconstructed as a new, independent instance by the receiving process.

Some object classes, typically those representing simple, constant values, might override **replacementObjectForPortCoder:** to *always* return **self**, thus causing a copy to be transmitted any time an instance is passed in a remote message. NSString and NSData do just this, for example. It makes little sense to require the overhead of network traffic in order to repeatedly access the same value, so this is perfectly appropriate behavior. NSMutableString and NSMutableData, of course, are transmitted as proxies, just like most other objects with variable state. A similar mechanism allows objects to change their class when transmitted, which is useful for hiding a private subclass implementation by transmitting the object as an instance of the public superclass.

To make sure you get a proxy instead of a copy, you can use the **byref** keyword, which causes even objects that copy themselves by default to be sent across connections as proxies instead. Unlike with **bycopy**, though, the object itself need do no special work to be sent as a proxy. NSConnections already know how to create proxies for any object class.

Handling Failures

Distributed applications make use of network resources that can become unavailable at any time. Server processes can crash, machines can lose power or network connections, the network can become bogged down with traffic, and so on. The result is that a connection can vanish at any time, and remote messages can occasionally fail, unlike local messages, which are always delivered (unless the process itself crashes, of course).

NSConnections handle the death of a peer process by posting an NSNotification and invalidating themselves. This allows programs to notice when resources have become unavailable and shut down gracefully or look for new resources. Clients, for example, can try to restart the server or contact another; can tell the user to contact the system administrator; or perhaps they can quit and try later. Servers can clean up state associated with the failed client process and continue handling other requests.

When a remote message times out, an NSConnection raises an exception that the program can catch. Because a single message failure may result from temporary conditions, the program can try sending the message again a few times, check in some other way that the server is indeed still available, or take whatever action is needed.

Other Distribution Models

The Distributed Objects facility is the one distribution mechanism guaranteed to an OpenStep application and is of course the one best integrated with OpenStep. Still, applications are free to use whatever means necessary to share data and resources. DO doesn't prohibit these other mechanisms; OpenStep applications can still use database client libraries, TCP/IP routines, or whatever else is available on the host system. DO running on Windows NT also interoperates with Microsoft's OLE Automation facility, allowing OpenStep and Windows-native applications to invoke each other's functionality. As an added bonus, DO's network capability allows OLE to work across machines, something it can't do by itself (as we write this book, at least).

Microsoft OLE Automation

DO support for OLE is limited to OLE Automation. It doesn't support linking, embedding, and in-place editing.

With OpenStep DO or the standalone PDO for Windows (sold as D'OLE™ or Distributed OLE), Objective-C objects and OLE Automation objects can communicate with each other in their native languages and object models. The Objective-C objects can reside on the same machine as the OLE Automation objects, on a different Windows NT computer, or on any computer with a DO or PDO system installed. This cross-communication allows non-OpenStep Windows applications such as Microsoft Excel to retrieve data and invoke operations from an OpenStep server or application; allows OpenStep applications to access the OLE services of Windows applications; and permits Windows applications on different machines to communicate through OLE.

This is made possible through an object request broker (ORB), a server that understands both OLE and Objective-C and translates requests between the two object models. The current DO-OLE ORB works only with these two object models; it isn't a generic ORB—more specifically, it isn't CORBA-compliant. Still, it's a highly useful addition to Distributed Objects and OLE.

Contacting DO Objects with OLE

The DO-OLE ORB is available to Windows applications as the OLE Automation server NEXTORB.OLE. Through it, you can access advertised DO objects as well as OLE Automation objects on other computers. For example, if there's a DO server object named "server", a Windows Visual Basic® application can contact it in these two steps:

```
Set orb = CreateObject("NEXTORB.OLE")
Set server = orb.connectTo("server", "NSDO", "*")
```

The call to **CreateObject()** returns the ORB as an OLE Automation object, whose **connectTo()** method retrieves the server object from another host. The first argument is the advertised name of the server object. The middle argument, "NSDO", specifies that the object being contacted is in fact a DO object. (It's also possible to connect to OLE objects on other hosts by specifying "OLE", as we'll show later.) The last argument is the host where the server object resides; passing "*" indicates that the first host to respond to the request will be used.

Instead of using this two-step connection process, you can use the **orbreg** tool provided with DO on Windows to register the server:

```
C:\>orbreg add -olename do_server -doname server -protocol NSDO
```

This command registers the name "do_server" in the OLE namespace for the DO object named "server". When the server is registered like this, programs can contact it in one step, which automatically launches the ORB if necessary, contacts it, and gets the registered object:

```
Set server = CreateObject("do_server")
```

You can register objects that must exist in running servers to be contacted, or you can register dynamic link libraries (DLLs) that are automatically loaded when you contact the object. Once you have the server in hand, you can issue messages to it just like any other OLE Automation object. The ORB translates message names in a straightforward manner, handling all possible names where the OLE system supports named arguments. Here are some examples:

Objective-C Expression	OLE Expression
[obj name]	obj.name()
[obj setTitle:"Memo"]	obj.setTitle("Memo")
[obj setString:@"notes"]	obj.setString("notes")
[obj multiply:3 :4]	obj.multiply(3, 4)
[obj multiply:3 by:4]	obj.multiply(3, by:=4)
[obj multiply:3 by:4]	obj.sendMsg("multiply:by:", 3, 4)

Note that Objective-C string objects are automatically converted to and from C strings. Also, the last example shows how Objective-C method names with extra keywords can be accessed on OLE systems that don't support named arguments. The ORB defines a **sendMsg()** method that takes the method name as the first argument, followed by the message arguments. In this way, OLE clients can invoke any Objective-C method.

In addition to translating message names, the ORB converts references to OLE properties into a pair of special Objective-C accessor methods **setOLEPropertyNamed:to:** and **getOLEPropertyNamed:**. The Visual Basic statement

```
obj.title
```

for example, is rendered into a message equivalent to this:

```
[obj getOLEPropertyNamed:@"title"];
```

Objective-C classes must implement these two methods to access the appropriate instance variables.

Contacting OLE Objects with Objective-C

Going in the other direction, Objective-C code can contact an OLE Automation server, such as Microsoft Excel, through DO messages. In this case, the ORB's name is NEXTORB.NSDO. This code fragment connects to Excel and has it run the "countEmployees" macro:

```
#import <nxorb.h>

id <NEXTORB> theOrb;
id excelApp;
int employeeCount;

theOrb = [NSConnection
    rootProxyForConnectionWithRegisteredName:@"NEXTORB.NSDO"
    host:@"*"];
[theOrb setProtocolForProxy:@protocol(NEXTORB)];

excelApp = [theOrb
    objectWithRegisteredName:@"Excel.Application"
    protocol:@"OLE" host:@"farHost"];
[excelApp retain];
[[excelApp workbooks] open:@"C:\\EMPS.XLS"];
employeeCount = [excelApp run:@"countEmployees"];
```

Note, in comparing this example to the next one, that the ORB takes care of translating the case of method names.

Connecting OLE Objects on Different Hosts

The same thing can be done between OLE Automation objects on different hosts, using Distributed Objects as a bridge. This Visual Basic example does the same thing as the Objective-C example:

```
Set orb = CreateObject("NEXTORB.OLE")
Set excelApp = orb.connectTo("Excel.Application", "OLE",
    "farHost")
excelApp.Workbooks.Open("C:\EMPS.XLS")
employeeCount = excelApp.Run("countEmployees")
```

OMG's CORBA

In many businesses, particularly those with UNIX-based workstations rather than PCs, an alternative to OLE is CORBA. CORBA, now in its second release, is an industry-standard, language-independent, operating-system–independent, distributed object specification developed by the Object Management Group and endorsed by over 300 companies, including Sun, HP, IBM, SGI, NeXT, DEC, AT&T, and others. CORBA-2 includes both an API specification, an inter-ORB protocol specification, and a specification for APIs for various services that vendors can implement if they so choose. CORBA compatibility is planned for a future release of DO.

Because CORBA is language-independent, object interfaces are specified using a declarative language named Interface Definition Language (IDL). IDL interfaces look very much like C++ header files and serve much the same purpose that Objective-C protocols do for DO. When writing code, the IDL interface files are processed by a compiler to generate language-specific bindings.

It's possible to access CORBA services before DO provides direct support for CORBA, by using a bridge server—a server that maps requests in one environment to requests in another. On Windows, several ORB vendors (such as Iona) provide ORBs with an OLE interface; these can provide the same bridge functionality by using OLE to communicate between DO and the ORB. Using SunSoft's NEO system in conjunction with OpenStep Solaris, it's easy to write a DO to CORBA bridge server, which maps DO messages to CORBA messages, and vice versa. This entails writing some custom code but should provide higher performance than using OLE as an interoperability protocol.

Where Distributed Objects Falls Short

Now that we've spent 20 pages explaining how nifty DO is, let's look at its limitations and flaws. Some relate to the distribution mechanism itself, some to services that make using the mechanism easier, and others to the tools needed to develop distributed applications.

Limitations in the Distribution Mechanism

DO's communication model is one of point-to-point, nonverifiable message delivery. You can't send a true broadcast message via DO: An individual message has exactly one destination. Also, if no timeout occurs, you can be confident the message was delivered; but if a timeout does happen, there's no inherent way to be sure the message actually wasn't received. This can cause coordination problems between distributed components of an application. More reliable messaging can be implemented on top of the basic model by adding services that check for sequencing of messages. Nonetheless, it's important to note that DO today doesn't provide this capability.

Distributed Objects is solidly rooted in the Objective-C object model and language and currently interoperates only with OLE Automation objects. Other distributed object standards, notably CORBA, simply aren't supported yet. DO neither conforms to nor interoperates with these standards. NeXT is pursuing CORBA support for a future version of DO or OpenStep, but that support is lacking today.

One thing that isn't so serious is performance. DO used to be pretty slow, but NeXT has recently sped it up to the point that it's on a par with RPC.

Absent and Incomplete Services

About the only service that DO itself provides is simple naming and lookup of server NSConnections. There's no generic name registry, hierarchical or otherwise. Also, you must either know which host the server resides on or be limited to the local network when looking up the server. Nothing about Distributed Objects prevents a more elaborate naming service from being developed; there just isn't one right now.

The same can be said for the various services defined by CORBA, such as Life Cycle, Persistence, Events, Transactions, and Properties. DO and

Objective-C have informal support for large parts of these services, such as the reference-counting life cycle management, notification objects for broadcasting events, and so on. An add-on product, the Enterprise Objects Framework, offers persistence, transaction management, and uniform access to properties. However, these various informal services aren't codified the way CORBA's are. When CORBA support comes to DO, these informal services may be used to implement the formal ones, but for now DO does its own thing.

DO's security features are limited to a few delegate hooks on NSConnection for authentication of incoming messages. There are no standard services for encryption, authorization, auditing of remote messages, or licensing.

Finally, in the areas of replication, scalability, and load balancing, DO offers very little above its raw remote messaging facility. You can build on this to create a support structure for these features, however. One way is to create a server of servers, which vends objects from different machines and performs no other tasks. Another way is to create a multi-threaded server than can handle multiple requests at once.

Missing Tools

Project Builder is useful for managing the source code of both the client and the server in a distributed application. However, no tools are available for quickly repartitioning the components of a distributed application, for monitoring the performance of the application's components as a whole system, or for monitoring individual objects within a process. Repartitioning must be done manually, by shuffling code around from project to project. Administration and performance monitoring are supported only at the process level.

Also completely lacking in DO is any kind of backup/restore system for cleanly bringing down a distributed application and restarting it. As with the services discussed above, you have to develop your own tools and solutions until NeXT, SunSoft, or another company starts selling them.

Design with Distributed Objects

The key strength of OpenStep's Distributed Objects facility is its transparency. Remote objects look just like local objects, and it's very easy to get remote objects and to pass references around the network. This ease of use, however, leads directly to DO's greatest flaw: It's also very easy to create a distributed application that scatters objects across the network, saturates the network with remote messages, and bogs down the whole system. The default mode of handling messages, whereby a remote message can be received while another is being processed, can also cause problems of concurrent access. And of course, the transparency of Distributed Objects breaks down to varying degrees when other distribution models must be included. In designing a distributed application, then, it's vitally important to address these issues before committing to a particular architecture.

The key to good distributed design is to know when you have to disbelieve the illusion of locality and take explicit care to handle problems caused by the vagaries of interprocess communication. If your application's design allows for any number of dropped messages or connections with no data loss or other serious consequences, you can happily code away as if every object is local. Another application might require the server, as the more authoritative component, to take a more defensive stance with regard to network errors, while allowing the client to ignore errors or simply repeat its requests until it gets a response. The most delicate systems, where errors in either the server or the client can cause problems, must take the most care and necessarily be more complex.

The complexity of a distributed design is driven by many characteristics, enough to fill an entire book. The following sections briefly introduce four such characteristics, examining the sorts of measures that must be taken to ensure a robust application.

Performance

The performance of any distributed application, outside the efficiency of the network and the distribution mechanism itself, is perhaps most significantly affected by these factors:

- the ratio of client components to server components;
- the number and size of individual messages between components;
- the time it takes the server to process each message;
- the number of distributed components (both objects and processes).

The most obvious performance factor is likely the ratio of clients to servers. If there are too many clients, the server becomes overburdened. At first blush it's an easily solved problem: Just add more servers (or perhaps get a faster server). The application's design, however, must allow for this, explicitly considering resource contentions among multiple servers providing the same services, probably with the same data. Three-tier systems, in which clients deal with a single central server through a number of intermediate or "buffer" servers, introduce coordination problems of their own. Clients can remain simple with regard to this factor, but servers must be designed with these issues in mind.

Beyond the ratio of clients to servers, the balance of message number and size can have a great effect on network performance. Millions of tiny messages clog the network just as much as hundreds of huge ones, causing either incredible traffic noise on the network as each message vies for its transmission time, or long delays as interminable streams of data make their way across the net. Some room must be left for messages to be transmitted, without undue collisions or delays.

This problem is a bit more difficult to solve than that of the client-to-server ratio. It requires analysis of the interfaces between distributed components and of the sizes of messages sent, both in the design itself and in the running system. Once you have measurements, you can tune the system to achieve acceptable performance. In any case, both the client and the server are affected by this factor.

Closely related to number of messages is how fast the server can process each one. If it takes a long time to respond to each message, the server is more easily overwhelmed by many clients with many requests. Like the first factor, however, it's a problem that only the server need address, by working to make every remote method as fast as possible.

The last factor, number of components, is easily exemplified by an application in which a large database of items is represented as objects in the server, which vends each and every one of those objects as needed to clients. With potentially thousands of proxies in each client, the bookkeeping burden on the server becomes prohibitive, the network becomes saturated with messages between these varied components, and the potential for conflict becomes a certainty.

This is the most serious problem for the object-oriented approach, in which each data item is supposed to carry its own behavior. In order to achieve reasonable performance, the objects in the server must be duplicated *en masse* to each client rather than rendered as proxies; a mapping scheme must be used to relate each client's copies to its originals in the server; and a transaction or conflict resolution scheme must be used to prevent corruption of the server's state. As with message number and size, this factor affects both the client and the server, though in a more dramatic way, since whole systems must be added to both.

Reliability

Though performance is crucial if a system is to be of any benefit, it must also produce correct results without failure. An application's reliability is therefore the other face of its robustness. Applications that can be affected by failures in remote messaging must take care to check for those failures and handle them. In this area Distributed Objects offers concrete help. Objective-C programs can anticipate problems at run time by asking any object if it's a proxy, using the **isProxy** method. NSObject's implementation, naturally enough, returns NO, while NSProxy's returns YES. Application code can use this method to base certain decisions on the nature of an object.

With regard to actual errors, programs can discover both broken connections and individual messaging errors. In the more drastic case when a process terminates prematurely, any NSConnection that was communicating with it notices this occurrence and posts an NSConnectionDidDieNotification. Both clients and servers can put an observer in place for this notification and take whatever corrective measures are necessary upon receiving it.

For failures in delivering individual messages, the Distributed Objects system raises various exceptions. Some of these, such as NSInvalidSendPortException and NSObjectNotAvailableException, clearly indicate that a message wasn't delivered. Others, like NSPortTimeoutException, mean only that a timeout has occurred, leaving you in the dark about whether the message failed to arrive or whether the confirmation that the message was received failed to arrive. Still, you can define handlers to catch these various exceptions to take action when they occur.

Concurrency

Concurrent access to shared state has the potential to create infinite snarls of twisted logic. Like distributed design in general, the topic of concurrent access can fill an entire book. Clients can often remain ignorant of the steps necessary to ensure proper concurrent access, but servers must take care here, whether they handle their state in a single, well-managed flow of control, through multiple threads running concurrently in a single task, or through multiple servers running against a single store of data.

OpenStep provides some help here with NSConnection's independent conversation queuing and with the various locking classes, each of which defines a slightly different style of mutex. The basic NSLock class blocks the current thread when another holds it and you send it a **lock** message, continuing only when the first thread sends an **unlock** message. You can also use the **tryLock** method, which returns NO instead of blocking when the lock is held by another thread.

A variation on this class is the NSRecursiveLock class. NSLock causes a deadlock if the same thread tries to lock it twice in a row. NSRecursiveLock, on the other hand, makes a note of which thread holds it and allows the same thread to lock it any number of times in a row. That thread then has to unlock it an equal number of times before the lock can be acquired by another.

The third lock class is NSConditionLock, which allows its users to acquire it only when it enters a specific integer state. You can send it an unconditional **lock** message; a **lockWhenCondition:** message, which blocks until the lock both enters the condition specified and is acquired; or **tryLockWhenCondition:**, which immediately returns NO if the lock can't be acquired. When finished, you send it either an **unlockWithCondition:** message to establish a new condition, or an **unlock** message to leave the condition as it is. You can also ask for the current condition with a **condition** message.

Interoperability

The last aspect of distributed design we survey is interoperability between distribution mechanisms. This falls more in the realm of implementation than design, but in fact, the availability of commercial products, which do vary in the distribution mechanisms they use, has a direct effect on the amount of work you must put into developing your own system.

The obvious goal of distribution standards like CORBA is to make it easy for clients to access distributed objects in their different native languages and object models whenever possible. CORBA, of course, requires both client and server developers to work with other tools or to program to a different interface than the native application's language or libraries.

Barring its present feeble level of interoperability, the nice thing about DO is that you can still use the Objective-C language to access distributed objects of varying types, as exemplified by the OLE ORB. Some incompatibilities between object models may need to be considered, but in general DO allows for quite natural use of distributed components.

Interoperability requires consideration of many tradeoffs in a system's design. DO tends to weigh programmer productivity heavily when making these tradeoffs. Systems like CORBA, on the other hand, are highly flexible in terms of environment—objects can be anywhere, written in nearly any language or object model, and addressed by any of several protocols. Such generic qualities require several levels of abstraction and add substantial burden to developers trying to address a specific problem. DO's roots are firmly planted in Objective-C, which has an object model and run-time system that lend themselves well to distribution. There's one language for the client and the server, and a developer who's familiar with that language will have a good idea of how to use the system. DO isn't as flexible or generic as raw CORBA, but development happens much faster in DO. Preserving the speed of development will be a guiding factor as NeXT and SunSoft add more support for CORBA, OLE, and other distribution mechanisms.

Perspective

Distributed Objects is the interprocess communication mechanism of OpenStep. Its transparent extension of the Objective-C messaging model across process boundaries makes it incredibly simple to use and also makes breaking up and redistributing application components a breeze. By changing a few lines of code here and there, you can have your business application take advantage of a new compute server or can split its burden among several replicated components.

Because DO is so easy to use, though, many forget that it's fundamentally an inter*process* (or interthread) communication mechanism, and only by happenstance is it an interobject communication system. Distribution adds a number of issues to application design that you can't ignore, even with a largely transparent mechanism. Nonetheless, using a familiar model for remote messaging does make the programmer's job a lot easier in the long run.

10 *Database Applications*

The most important function of any business application is to support the practices and data of the business. In order to do this, the application must provide ready access to business data, enforce business policies regarding that data, and keep the data up-to-date and internally consistent. Vast amounts of business data are currently stored in relational databases, which have proven themselves as robust, powerful engines for storing data. Modifying the data in relational databases, however, has been a rather sticky problem in some ways: Though the database excels at storing and retrieving data, the logic for altering that data, enforcing policies, and ensuring consistency has never found a sure place.

Database servers offer a home for business logic in the form of stored procedures. These have the advantage of centralizing policies, but they must be implemented in nonportable SQL that varies between database vendors. Further, the scalability of such a system is limited, since all business logic must be executed on the database server and can't be distributed across the network.

Client development systems such as 4GLs try to address these problems by putting business logic in the client application's user interface. This solves the basic scalability problem but has its own shortcomings. Tying business logic to the user interface limits both its reusability and maintainability. Business logic depends explicitly on the user interface and can't easily be reused for other interfaces. This leads to client applications being developed independently, which can produce inconsistencies in policy and makes revisions to policy difficult to deploy. Even scalability returns as a problem, since client machines don't have the processing power to handle complex calculations on large data sets.

A few software companies have decided to address these issues with object-oriented tools, mapping relational models to object models and placing the business policies in the hands of the objects. NeXT's offering in this area, the Enterprise Objects Framework, does this in terms of the OpenStep object model. With it, developers focus on modeling the business in Objective-C classes, and the Enterprise Objects Framework does all the work of translating between the database and the objects and of managing the display of data in the user interface. This frees business logic from dependence on either the database server or the user interface.

What the Enterprise Objects Framework Does

The goal of the Enterprise Objects Framework is to enable your business objects to execute business logic purely in terms of the object model. Business objects that need to know how their data is stored in a database are limited to use with that database. Similarly, business objects that must interact directly with the user interface can be used only with that particular interface. Both are often needless restrictions, and the Enterprise Objects Framework aims to remove them altogether.

It does this by making business objects dependent on the Framework rather than on external components, though in a minimal way. This allows the business objects to focus on their own behavior. The Enterprise Objects Framework then does all the work of translating between the database and the business objects, monitoring changes, and updating the user interface.

What's an Enterprise Object?

Objects can be categorized in many ways; for example, by whether they represent values or complex entities, by whether they draw themselves, or by how much they interact with other objects. A business object is characterized by its role as part of a business or other process model and by having transient local state in its running application that maps to more persistent state in a shared data repository. This repository can be a relational database, a flat-file database, or a real-time data feed. An *enterprise object* is a business object that plays along with the Enterprise Objects Framework to enable that mapping.

The Enterprise Objects Framework defines just one method that enterprise objects must use and a few optional methods that they can use or implement for specific functionality. These methods are quite general in nature, and introduce no unmanageable dependencies on components external to the enterprise objects.

The principal requirement of an enterprise object, for which you must explicitly write code, is that it notify the Framework when its state is about to change. This allows the Framework to examine the object's state before and after the change and to update the database accordingly. The Framework defines the means for doing this by adding a method called **willChange** to NSObject, which every other object therefore inherits. All the enterprise object need do is invoke it before changing any instance variable:

```
- (void)setTitle:(NSString *)aString
{
    [self willChange];
    [title autorelease];
    title = [aString copy];
    return;
}
```

Everything else is optional, and just about as generic. The Enterprise Objects Framework provides a number of other methods, some of which it implements for enterprise objects to use and some of which it uses if enterprise objects implement them. For example, there are special "awake" methods that enterprise objects can implement to be told they've just been fetched from the database or created anew in the application. Enterprise objects can also implement methods for validating state, which the Framework invokes automatically to check for constraints. Later parts of this chapter highlight the individual methods in context.

Model–View–Controller Revisited

The Enterprise Objects Framework bridges databases, enterprise objects, and the client application's user interface by acting as a big controller, in two different ways (Figure 1). The bottom part of the Framework treats the database as the model and the enterprise objects as an abstract view, handling the logic required to synchronize the two. You provide a mapping between the database schema and your object model, and the Framework translates between database rows and objects.

The top part of the Framework treats the enterprise objects as the model and the user interface as the view, defining a generic mechanism to move values between enterprise objects and interface objects. All you have to do is define the associations between interface objects and the properties of enterprise objects that they display.

Between these two is the part that manages the enterprise objects themselves, monitoring them for changes and propagating those changes up or down as needed. This part allows you to group enterprise objects into

> **Models, Models, Everywhere**
>
> The term *model* is potentially confusing, since it's often used to refer to different things. We've talked about object models so far, meaning both the Objective-C way of defining what an object is and your design of custom classes to represent your business. In the database world, schemas are sometimes called models. And now there's the Enterprise Objects Framework, which says that a model is a mapping between your custom object model and a database model. We've tried to make clear what kind of model we're talking about as we go along, but this is something you'll just have to live with.

Chapter 10: Database Applications 167

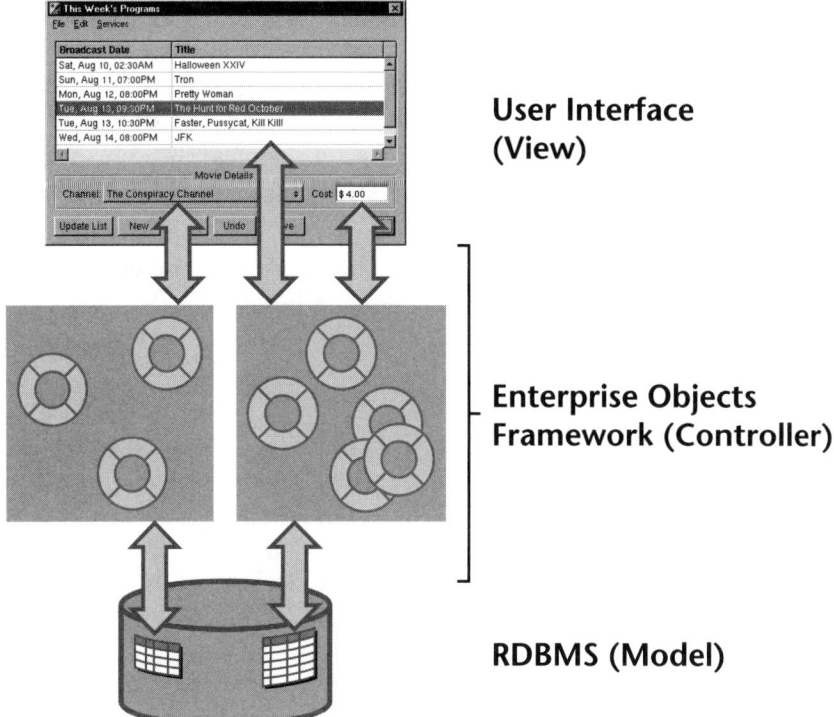

Figure 1. Model–View–Controller in the Enterprise Objects Framework

separate editing contexts, each of which tracks changes separate from the others and allows you to save and undo changes as they're made.

Specific Features

So far we've described what the Enterprise Objects Framework does in extremely general terms. Here's a list of the major features that the Enterprise Objects Framework offers your business application. The last part of this chapter explores the details behind many of these features.

Flexible object-to-relational mapping. You can map object classes to tables in the database; map object properties to columns in multiple tables; and define relationships across databases. You can even map an inheritance hierarchy to the database in several different ways.

Complete in-memory manipulation of objects. All of your business objects' actions are defined in terms of the in-memory object model. The Framework automatically tracks primary keys, resolves relationships between objects to foreign key references in the database, performs uniquing on fetched objects to avoid duplication, and creates fault objects that fetch their data on being accessed.

Flexible editing. The Framework tracks changes to enterprise objects based on a small hook method; allows enterprise objects to validate changes; provides in-memory transactions, qualifiers, and sorting; and can undo any change.

Automatic synchronization with user interface. Whenever enterprise objects change, the Framework automatically updates all user interface objects displaying properties of the changed objects.

Efficient use of the database. The Framework avoids fetching data it doesn't have to by creating fault objects that fetch when accessed. You can tune this mechanism to prefetch these objects when you know you'll need them, or to have them automatically fetched in groups, reducing the number of discrete fetch operations performed.

PayPerView with Enterprise Objects

Before we examine how the Enterprise Objects Framework realizes all these features, let's have a brief look at application development by converting the PayPerView application to use it. This process will reveal several aspects of the Framework's power. The ProgramController class bows out entirely, being replaced by standard Framework classes that deal with the database and user interface for you, allowing you to hook everything up in Interface Builder. These classes also support undo and editing of values with no code, so we'll show how to add these features too.

Defining the Relational-to-Object Mapping

Before you create an application, you must define the mapping between objects and the database. You do this with the Enterprise Objects Framework's database-mapping tool, EOModeler. This application creates *model files* that define entities for the tables in the database, each of which contains attributes and relationships based on columns in the various tables of the database (or even of different databases). Each entity is assigned to a particular object class, whose instances represent individual rows from the database tables in the client application.

EOModeler can read in an existing database schema, which you then tune to match your object model, or it can create a model file from scratch and use that to build a schema in the database. This example assumes the schema has already been defined, with one table for programs, one for channels, and a many-to-one relationship between programs and channels:

PROGRAM Table Columns	**CHANNEL Table Columns**
PROGRAM_ID (primary key)	CHANNEL_ID (primary key)
TITLE	NAME
BROADCAST_DATE	DIAL_NUMBER
COST	
CHANNEL_ID (foreign key)	

We've broken channels out from programs because this is how it would likely be done in a real database, as well as to demonstrate how the Framework handles relationships.

When you launch EOModeler and create a new model file, you're prompted to choose a type of database server (Oracle®, Sybase®, and so

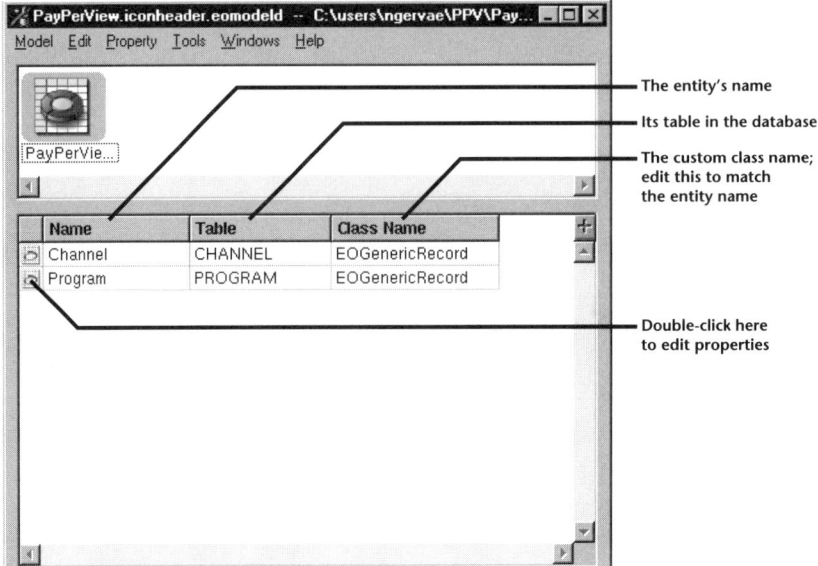

Figure 2. The New Model

on), asked for login information for the server, and then presented with the model editor in Figure 2.

Editing Entities

EOModeler automatically reads the database tables and constructs entities for them. In this case, the CHANNEL and PROGRAM tables in the database have been rendered as Channel and Program entities. The first thing to do is define how they map to Channel and Program objects in the application. To specify the classes themselves, edit the Class Name column for each entity, changing it from the default EOGenericRecord to the appropriate value.

> **Generic Enterprise Objects**
>
> EOGenericRecord is a simple class that can store any kind of property by key, much like an NSDictionary. You can use it when you have enterprise objects with no custom behavior. In fact, the Program and Channel classes don't have any custom behavior yet, but since the whole point of this example is to show enterprise objects....

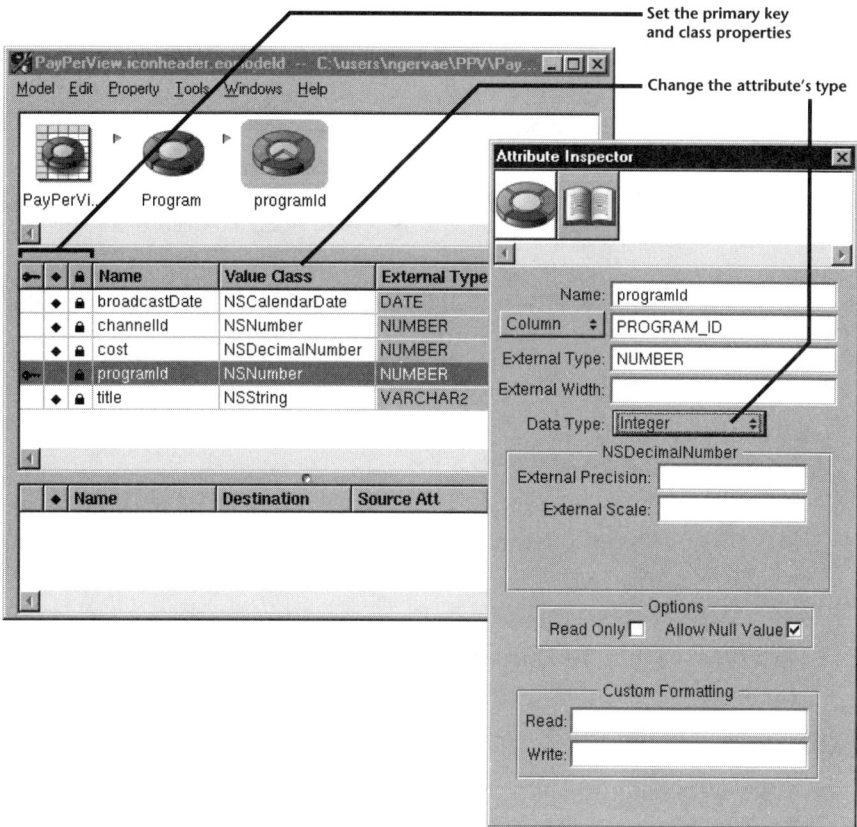

Figure 3. Tuning Attributes

Appendix C: PayPerView with Enterprise Objects contains a summary of the model file definitions.

For other changes, double-click the edit icon at the left of each row, which brings up a table of attributes and a table of relationships (as shown for the Program entity in Figure 3). EOModeler reads these from the database schema, making a best guess at the names and value classes to use in the client application. You need to specify which attributes are primary keys, which should be fetched into the application, and which should be used for locking during updates. You also need to change the value classes where EOModeler's guesses don't fit the object model.

The three columns on the left represent which attributes:

- define the entity's primary key (⊶);
- are class properties fetched into objects from the database (♦);
- are used for locking when making an update (🔒).

The "programID" attribute is the PROGRAM table's primary key, so set that by clicking the cell below the ⚷ icon. Also, since EOF manages primary keys automatically, it doesn't need to be fetched into the Program objects; turn off the ◆ so that the primary key isn't stored in the objects.

The only other change you need to make to the Program entity is to correct the value class for "programID" and "channelID" (a foreign key you'll use to set up a relationship to the Channel). EOModeler assigned NSDecimalNumber, which is normally used for fractional values such as dollar amounts, but these columns actually store integer values. To reflect this, use the Attribute Inspector panel to change the data type to Integer.

That wraps up the Program entity. After making these same adjustments to the Channel entity, you're ready to define the relationships between the two. To create a relationship from Program to Channel, select the Program entity and choose Add Relationship from the Property menu. This adds a row to the relationships table at the bottom of the model editor. You establish the nature of this relationship with the Relationship Inspector (Figure 4), typing "channel" as the name, choosing the destination entity, and selecting the source and destination attributes (which correspond to the foreign and primary keys in the database schema). For the relationship from Program to Channel, specify the relationship as To One. Next, select the Channel entity and create a relationship from Channel to Program as well, specifying this relationship as To Many.

Generating Classes

See Appendix C for the source code of the Program and Channel classes.

With the model finished, save it and add it to the project. Now you can use the Create Template command to generate code for the two classes. The generated code includes instance variable declarations for the class properties in the model and actually defines accessor methods for all these properties, as well as a **dealloc** method. It doesn't define an initialization method, of course, because the enterprise objects' state will be set automatically by the Framework. Though you already have code

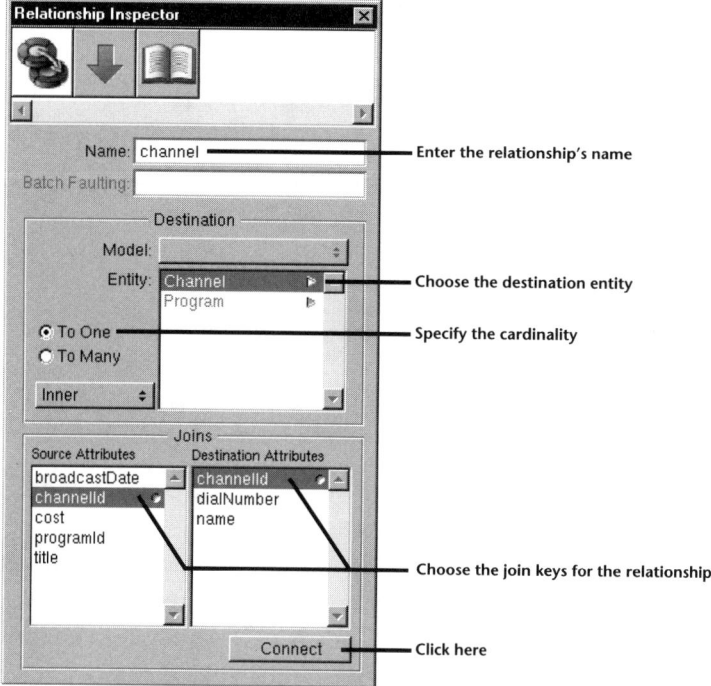

Figure 4. Defining a Relationship

for the original Program class, it's all related to accessor methods, so it's safe to just replace it here (you can compare the code in the appendices to see the minor differences).

Note: Because the accessor methods are bracketed by an **#ifdef** preprocessor directive, they're not used by default. You typically implement accessor methods only when they have to do more than return or set a value, since the Framework can read and write instance variables directly. See "Translation Between Value Dictionaries and Enterprise Objects" on page 186 on for more information on direct variable access.

That's all there is to defining the database-to-object mapping. Now you can move on to redefine the user interface. After that, we'll review the changes that must be made to the code.

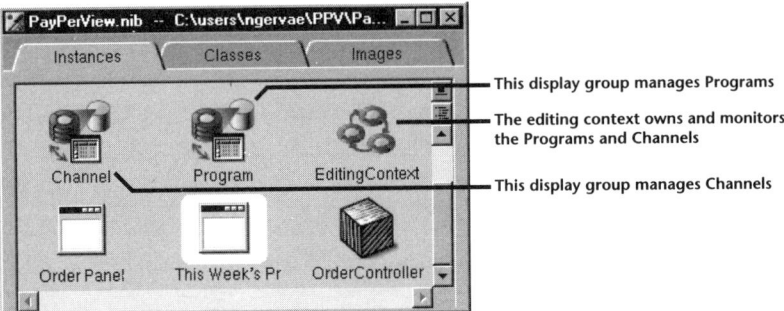

Figure 5. Display Groups in the Nib File Window

Revising the User Interface and Code

Opening the PayPerView nib file in Interface Builder, the first thing you do is delete the ProgramController object. The Enterprise Objects Framework provides its own interface controller, so the entire ProgramController class, as well as some code in the OrderController class, can be removed. To this end, you can delete ProgramController's source files from the project entirely and remove from OrderController its instance variables and message expressions related to displaying Program information, as shown in Appendix C.

Now, to set up the new interface controller, return to EOModeler, select the Program entity, and drag its icon into the nib file window. This creates a *display group* for that entity (Figure 5), an object that contains all Program objects fetched from the database and coordinates their display in the user interface. Do the same for the Channel entity. These display groups take the place of the old ProgramController object. You'll be connecting the user interface objects to them.

Binding the Interface to the Display Group

To establish the display group as the controller of the Program window, you create *associations* between each user interface object and the display group. An association watches both its interface object and the display group for changes. When the user edits the interface object, the association tells the display group to change the appropriate property of the selected enterprise object. When an enterprise object's property changes

Chapter 10: Database Applications   175

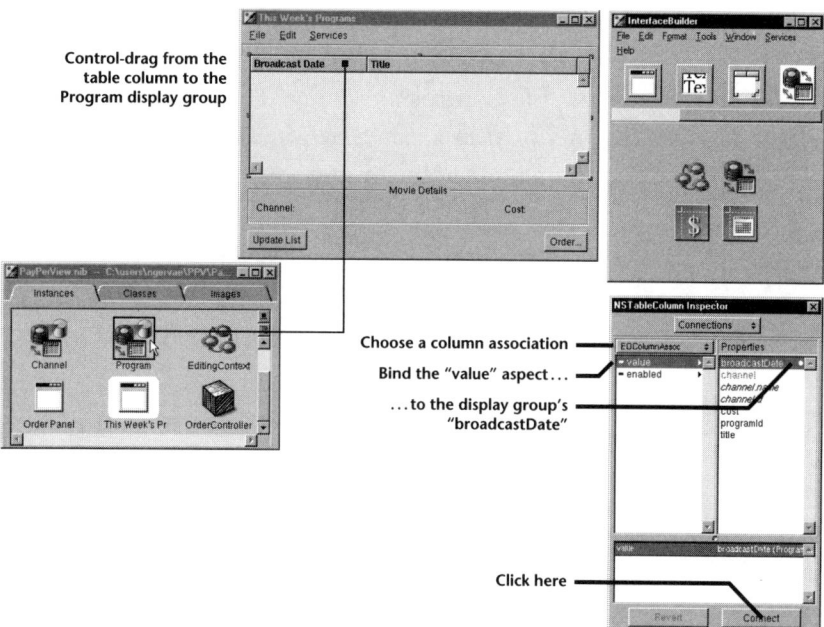

Figure 6. Making an Association to the User Interface

in the display group, the association updates the display of the interface object. Thus, associations replace much of the code that was in ProgramController. They also make it trivial to allow the user to edit values, so you can add this feature without writing any code.

See page 272 in Appendix C for a complete diagram of the associations in the nib file.

To create the first association, select the Broadcast Date column in the table view, then Control-drag to the Program display group, just as though you were making an outlet connection (Figure 6). When the Connections Inspector appears, click on the Outlets pop-up list and choose the item labeled EOColumnAssociation. Associations come in several varieties, tuned for different types of interface objects and behaviors. For a table view's column, only this one is available.

When you select the association, the browser changes to display *aspects* on the left, with property keys on the right that they can be bound to. Aspects govern different properties of a user interface object, such as the value it displays, whether it's enabled, and so on. In this case, you simply want to bind the **value** aspect to the broadcast date, so select that aspect and key, and click the Connect button.

> Note the use of the attribute key "channel.name" in Appendix C. The Framework uses this notation to traverse relationships automatically.

You do the same thing for the other interface objects—the Program Title column and the text field that displays the cost—except that you use an EOControlAssociation for the text field. You'll be altering the channel field in a different way soon, so leave that alone. After making these changes to the Program window, repeat this procedure for the text labels in the order panel. Leave the customer name and credit card fields alone, though; the OrderController still has to manage those itself.

Formatting Values

> Formatters are actually in the Foundation Framework, but Interface Builder doesn't support them by default.

The original version of PayPerView had to explicitly define the format for dates in code, and used strings for the cost of each show to avoid the problem of formatting money amounts. The Enterprise Objects Framework adds special formatter objects to Interface Builder, allowing you to dispense with a bit more code and to use a robust decimal number object for money values. The Framework provides access to date and money formatters; you can define others by creating custom subclasses of NSFormatter.

To add the formatters, drag them from the palette onto the Broadcast Date table column and onto the text fields in the main window and the order panel. Once you've done that, the Inspector panel's pop-up list includes a Formatter inspector (Figure 7), which you can use to specify any number of display formats.

The date formatter inspector provides a number of standard date formats, along with a text field where you can type a custom format, using a number of special codes for the various parts of a date expression. There's also a check box for natural language parsing, which makes the formatter try to interpret expressions that don't fit its format.

The number formatter inspector allows you to specify the precision and decimal places for a number, whether to display negative values with a minus sign or in red, whether to use a thousands separator, and whether to switch the comma and period for the decimal point. You can also include arbitrary currency or other symbols around the digits.

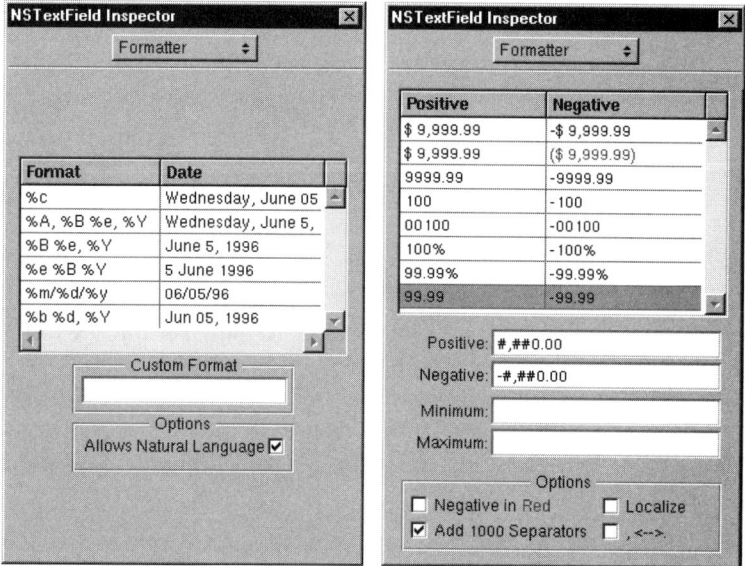

Figure 7. The Date and Number Formatter Inspectors

Making Things Editable

Display groups and associations give you a lot of functionality for free, the most significant examples of which are editing values, a general undo mechanism, and saving changes to the database—all with no need to write code. You can make entities, attributes, and relationships read-only in EOModeler, but by default they're automatically editable. In PayPerView, then, the table view is now editable by virtue of the Framework, and making the Cost text field editable also allows the user to change the cost of a Program.

For setting a Program's Channel, however, a text field isn't a good choice, since there's a limited set of channels that programs are broadcast on. A pop-up list is a good replacement, so delete the field and drag one to its place in the box. To get the Channel names, you need the Channel entity from the model, so Control-drag from the pop-up list to the Channel display group to form the association. Choosing EOPopUpAssociation in the Connections Inspector, you'll see these aspects: **titles**, **selectedTitle**, **selectedTag**, **selectedObject**, and **enabled**. Bind the **titles** aspect to the "name" key in the Channel display group, so that the pop-up list will contain all of the Channel names in the database.

To show the selected Program's Channel in the pop-up list, Control-drag from the pop-up list to the Program display group. Because Channels are objects, bind the **selectedObject** aspect to the "channel" key. Now, when the user selects a Program in the table view, the pop-up list will automatically change to show that Program's Channel, and when the user changes the Channel by manipulating the pop-up list, the corresponding Channel object will be set in the selected Program.

For creating new Programs and deleting the ones that are there, you can add buttons to the window and label them New and Delete. By connecting these buttons to the Program display group's **insert:** and **delete:** action methods, you get these two functions for free, without having to write any code. Supporting the creation of new objects does, however, require the database to provide primary key generation, something that normally requires no code, but that must be recorded in EOModeler. (The means for generating primary keys, and recording this in EOModeler, vary with the database used.)

While you're doing all this, you might as well add Undo and Save commands to the application. These features are controlled by the display group's *editing context*, which is where all enterprise objects, both Programs and Channels, live. The editing context is in charge of recording all changes to its enterprise objects so that they can be reversed or saved. To add the Undo and Save commands, drag some buttons onto the window, and make target-action connections from the Undo button to the editing context's **undo:** method and from the Save button to the editing context's **saveChanges:** method.

Testing the Interface

Now that you've made these changes, you can test the model and interface to see if the basic stuff works. Since all of the Framework objects exist right in Interface Builder, you can run them directly to see that the display groups do indeed fetch data from the database and synchronize

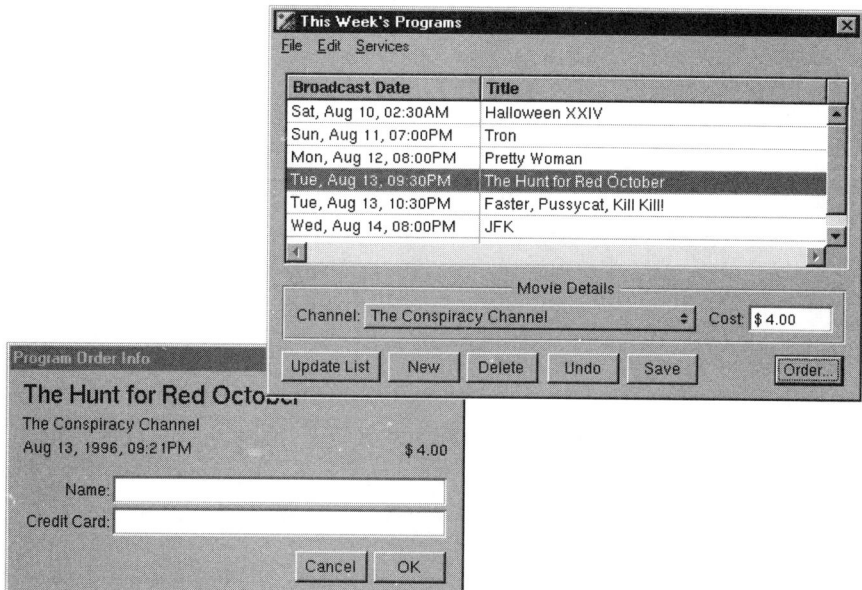

Figure 8. Testing the Interface in Interface Builder

the display of values in the table view and fields. To do this, choose Test Interface from the Document menu. Suddenly, PayPerView appears to be running, without even compiling the application (Figure 8). This is a skeletal but live application, which you can use to demonstrate how the user interface works. Doing so allows you to prototype the interface with end users, even changing it on the fly to see what might work better.

In this simulation, the OrderController hasn't been compiled and linked, so you can't place an order. Similarly, in the absence of the Program and Channel classes, Interface Builder substitutes instances of EOGenericRecord. Because these classes don't yet define any custom functionality, though, everything besides placing an order actually works, right inside Interface Builder. You can select different programs, and the pop-up list and text fields all change to reflect the selection. You can choose a different channel using the pop-up list (Figure 8) and edit the table view and cost text field. The New button creates a new program (provided the model file includes primary key generation), and

Delete removes the selected program. Undo undoes each change made; Save writes changes to the database; and Update List fetches the data again.

Now you can build the application and actually run it, gaining the functionality defined by the custom classes. Note, however, that a huge amount of functionality is available immediately from the Framework. PayPerView fetches data, displays and formats it properly, and allows the user to edit it—all with no code.

Changes to Existing Code

Let's examine the changes made to the Objective-C code:

- The ProgramController class is completely gone.
- The code in OrderController that set values in the order panel is gone.
- EOModeler automatically generated the definitions and code for the Channel and Program classes.

In all, the amount of code related to managing the data and coordinating the user interface fell dramatically. This allows you to focus on the custom code: that for placing an order and, of course, that for the business objects themselves.

If you compare the source code for the Program class between the original version of PayPerView and the Enterprise Objects version in Appendix C, you'll notice that apart from the new data types, only one kind of change was really made. Each method that sets a property begins by invoking the **willChange** method:

```
- (void)setTitle:(NSDecimalNumber *)value
{
    [self willChange];
    [title autorelease];
    title = [value retain];
    return;
}
```

> "Change Tracking" on page 190 explains this process in a bit more detail.

The Enterprise Objects Framework implements **willChange** for you. This method posts an NSNotification that the object's editing context listens for, so that when enterprise objects change, the Framework automatically updates all of the relevant state affected by that change: the user interface, the undo stack, and any snapshots or other records needed for synchronizing changes to the database. (Recall that even these accessor methods aren't needed unless they do something more than just set an instance variable.)

How It Works

Just like Distributed Objects, the Enterprise Objects Framework makes your job easy by doing the hard work behind the scenes. Distributed Objects, however, provides a single, straightforward service, while the Enterprise Objects Framework performs many complex functions to support your business objects. Despite all the automatic functionality, you may well need to alter how these functions work in some ways or extend them to work with new databases and interface objects. The Framework defines several specific customization points where you can do this.

Architecturally, the Enterprise Objects Framework comprises three layers, each with its own responsibility (Figure 9). The core is the Control layer, which manages enterprise objects in memory, tracks changes, and forwards them down to the Access layer. The Access layer defines an object-oriented interface to relational databases and maps enterprise object state to database state. Above the Control layer is the Interface layer, which maps individual properties of enterprise objects to OpenStep user interface objects and coordinates display and editing of those values. The following sections explore each of these layers, from the bottom up.

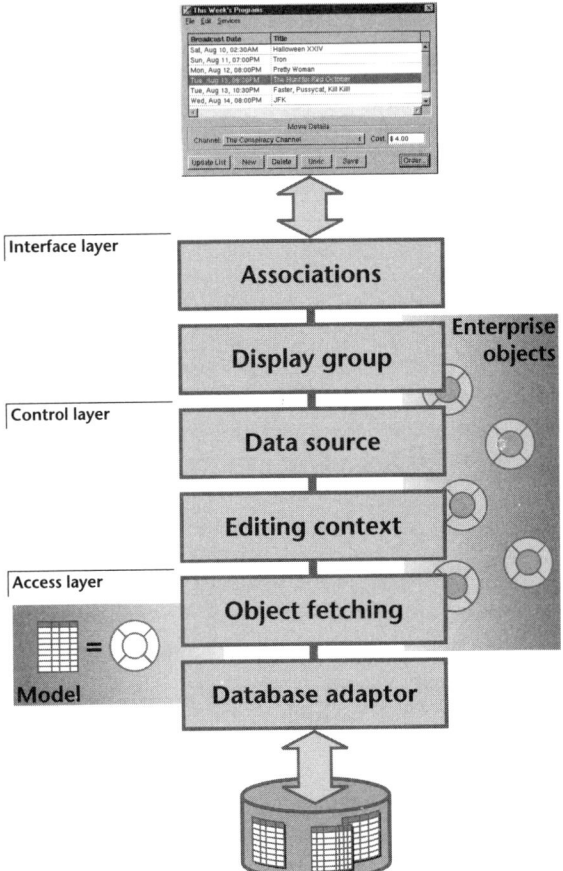

Figure 9. The Enterprise Objects Framework Architecture

The Access Layer

The job of the Access layer is to transfer data between a relational database and your enterprise objects. It retrieves raw data from the database, recasts it in a form usable by enterprise objects, and creates the enterprise objects from that data. Then, on the return trip, it transforms the enterprise objects' data into database-specific form and writes it back to the database. The Access layer does this with two distinct layers of objects and with a database-to-object mapping defined by EOModeler. The lower layer defines a portable adaptor API for interacting with relational databases in terms of basic Foundation types such as NSDictionary, NSString, and NSCalendarDate. Above this, database objects handle the conversion of this generic data to and from enterprise objects.

Model Files and the EOModeler Application

Model files map database-specific tables to generic entities and custom classes, relating table columns to attributes and rendering relationships as concrete pointer references between objects. The revision of PayPerView introduced a number of specific features of model files and of EOModeler, the model editor. Details aside, the significant features of these two components of the Enterprise Objects Framework are that:

- Models provide an abstraction between application code and a specific database's schema, eliminating the need for code to perform this kind of translation. You can even retarget an application to a new database by simply changing the model. (In fact, an application can switch servers at run time by switching models.)

- Entities can be arranged in an inheritance hierarchy with three kinds of table reuse (see the sidebar).

- Models can span several databases, bridging the various entities through relationships defined between them. Entities are stored in separate files and loaded incrementally at run time as needed.

- EOModeler can both read an existing database schema into a model and generate a schema from a model built by hand.

- EOModeler can generate basic code for enterprise object classes, which includes the interface declarations and definitions of optional accessor methods.

Database Adaptors

A model defines how database-specific types are converted to object types. The objects that perform that conversion are called *adaptors*. There are three cooperating adaptor classes: EOAdaptor, which manages the others; EOAdaptorContext, which manages transactions; and EOAdaptorChannel, which performs individual operations. The Access layer's adaptor classes define a single general interface to any relational database. Database-specific adaptor subclasses translate this general interface into that of the database's client library.

The adaptor interface is defined in terms of NSDictionary objects, each of which represents a single row of values in the database. The keys of the dictionary name the model attributes corresponding to columns in the table. Dictionaries read from the database are used to create enterprise objects, and those extracted from enterprise objects are used to

> ### Entity Inheritance
>
> You can map class hierarchies to database tables in three different ways. The first, called *horizontal inheritance mapping*, specifies no table for the superclass and duplicates the superclass's attributes in tables mapped to the subclasses. Suppose you have a Person superclass with Employee and Customer subclasses. In this case the Person class contains generic instance variables such as **name** and **age**, but there is no Person table. Instead, the Employee and Customer tables each contain identical columns for the generic attributes.
>
>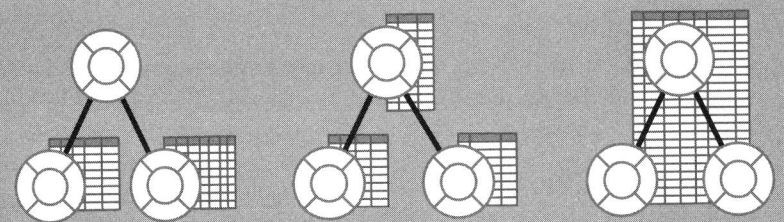
>
> In the second mapping technique, *vertical inheritance mapping*, you define a table for the superclass (Person) that includes the generic information, along with subclass tables that provide more specific information (Employee and Customer). When the Access layer fetches a row from the Employee or Customer table, it also fetches the row with the same primary key value from the Person table and combines all the values to create the instance.
>
> Finally, in *one-table inheritance mapping*, you lump all columns for the related classes into one table, using a special attribute and restricting qualifier to map individual rows to their appropriate object classes.

perform inserts and updates. These processes are described later, under "Object Fetching and Updating."

The adaptor interface is the Access layer's main customization point. Adaptors can be assigned delegates, which are asked to approve or alter the parameters of many types of operations—such as beginning, committing, and rolling back transactions, selecting and fetching rows, and executing stored procedures—and are informed when they've been executed. You can also create a custom adaptor to work with a new data repository, whether a relational database or some other kind of storage system. The Enterprise Objects Framework includes adaptors for Oracle, Sybase, Informix®, and ODBC databases.

Value Conversion

Adaptor methods that perform database operations, such as inserts, selects, updates, and deletes, all take an argument that identifies an entity from the application's model. The adaptor uses the entity's attribute mapping to convert values between the database's external types and internal types, which can be Foundation value classes or custom classes that you define. As you might expect, string types map to NSString, dates to NSDate, numbers to NSDecimalNumber (a high-precision variant of NSNumber), and large binary types to NSData. The Enterprise Objects Framework also defines a special EONull class to represent NULL values in the database.

Stored Procedures and Evaluation of Raw SQL

The adaptor classes provide "trap-door" methods for invoking database-specific functionality when you want it, while still generalizing the interface enough to reduce the amount of nonportable code you have to write. EOModeler allows you to record the names and arguments for stored procedures in the database server. You can then run those stored procedcures by using a special adaptor method, **executeStoredProcedure:withValues:**, which takes the procedure's name and an NSDictionary containing its arguments. Another method, **returnValuesForLastStoredProcedureInvocation**, provides the return value and output parameters of the last stored procedure invoked. All of the parameter values are converted between the database types and value classes just like attribute values.

There's also a method, **evaluateExpression:**, for sending a raw SQL expression to the database server. Since this bypasses many checks that the adaptor objects perform, you have to take special care to handle the effects of the expression. After evaluating an expression, you can ask the adaptor if it resulted in a select operation and begin fetching, but in general you have to know what the result might be.

Object Fetching and Updating

Adaptors manipulate a database in a generic, low-level way, but in most applications adaptors are handled automatically by higher-level "database" objects, which define a true object-oriented interface to a relational database (or other repository), using your custom enterprise objects where the adaptor uses dictionaries. Database objects take value dictionaries from the adaptor and produce enterprise objects, as well as extract values from enterprise objects and use the adaptor to write them back to the database. The three database classes—EODatabase, EODatabaseContext, and EODatabaseChannel—correspond to the adaptor classes.

Translation Between Value Dictionaries and Enterprise Objects

The database objects, and other parts of the Enterprise Objects Framework, translate between value dictionaries and enterprise objects using a mechanism added to the NSObject class, called *key-value coding*. This mechanism allows any object's instance variables to be accessed directly through the methods **takeValue:forKey:** and **valueForKey:**. These methods use dynamically determined information for the enterprise object classes, invoking accessor methods for the key provided if they exist, otherwise directly accessing the instance variable named by the key.

As an example using the PayPerView application, suppose the adaptor reads attributes for the Program entity, among them "title" and "cost".

When setting values in the Program object, **takeValue:forKey:** invokes a method of the form **setTitle:** or **setCost:** if it exists. If the Program class doesn't have such a method, it sets the instance variable directly (releasing the old value and retaining the new). Similarly, **valueForKey:** invokes methods named **title** and **cost** if they exist, otherwise directly retrieving the instance variables.

The key-value coding mechanism frees you from having to write basic accessor methods for your enterprise objects but still allows you to implement them and have them invoked automatically. When your enterprise objects need to change property values themselves, you can be assured that the Framework will honor it.

Updates to the Database

When writing changes back to the database, the database objects essentially reverse the process described so far, extracting values from enterprise objects and passing the resulting dictionaries to the adaptor objects. Because databases typically have many users concurrently accessing them, however, it's possible for an update to fail due to a conflict. The Access layer's database objects offer several means of managing updates.

The first is the strategy that the database objects use for updates. You can configure them to be pessimistic, locking every row fetched during a particular transaction so that nobody else can access their values. This increases the chances of an update succeeding, though at the cost of blocking other users' attempts to read the values being changed. You can configure them to not lock anything and blindly overwrite whatever values are there, regardless of what other users may have done. This is useful for read- and insert-only systems. Or, you can leave them with the default strategy, which compares the last-known state of the enterprise object being updated with the values in the database to see if a conflict has occurred. This more optimistic strategy balances the granularity of locking against the odds of a conflict.

The last-known state of an enterprise object is called its *snapshot*. Whenever an enterprise object changes, the database objects record a snapshot for comparison with the state in the database. Snapshots are always taken, but only for changed objects, and they're cleared when the update is written back to the database. This constant presence of snapshots allows pessimistic updates outside a transaction to fall back to the optimistic locking strategy.

The Control Layer

The Control layer is the core of the Enterprise Objects Framework, defining the context within which enterprise objects exist and managing changes to them. Its two primary classes, EOObjectStore and EOEditingContext, define the abstract interfaces to external and internal repositories of objects, respectively. Other classes enable such features as object uniquing, undo management, multidatabase support, and in-memory filtering and sorting of objects.

Object Stores and Editing Contexts

An object store serves as liaison to an external repository of objects for an editing context, which does most of the work of managing enterprise objects. An object store fetches objects from its external repository and saves changes to those objects back to the repository. It also creates temporary stand-ins for unfetched objects, called *faults*, which are used to make the relationships of fetched objects appear valid without actually fetching the destination objects for those relationships. The EODatabaseContext class of the Access layer is a concrete object store that interacts with a relational database.

The Control layer's other customization point is the EODataSource interface.

The object store interface is one of the Control layer's two customization points. You can create a subclass of EOObjectStore to manage any kind of external repository of data, such as an object database, a real-time stock feed, or even a file system.

An editing context defines a space that enterprise objects live in, independent of any other editing context in the same application. An editing context maintains a single instance of each of its enterprise objects and records a global identifier for each one, which it uses with its object store when accessing the external repository. Editing contexts also monitor their enterprise objects for changes, recording those changes in an undo stack and collecting them for saving to the object store.

Uniquing and Relationship Construction

When an object store first fetches an enterprise object for a particular editing context, it creates a global identifier and records the new object in that editing context. This establishes a unique instance within that editing context. All subsequent fetches or requests for that object in the editing context then return the unique instance.

Global identifiers aid in the construction of relationships based on external information, such as foreign keys in a database table, since they prevent duplicate objects from being created for every relationship. They also enable prebuilding of a relationship when the destination object or objects haven't been fetched yet, since a fault object can be created and assigned the global identifier based on the entity and primary key of the destination object. When the real enterprise object is fetched (see "Fetch Optimization" immediately ahead), its fault can be

Initializing Enterprise Objects

Although enterprise objects are created with an **init** message by default, the Framework uses more specific methods if they're available. An enterprise object can implement a more detailed method called **initWithEditingContext:classDescription:globalID:**, which gives it more information about where it's being created. This method provides the editing context the object will live in, a class description object that relates it to the database, and a global ID that distinguishes the object from those in other editing contexts that were created from the same database row.

Two extra initialization methods, **awakeFromFetchInEditingContext:** and **awakeFromInsertionInEditingContext:**, inform a new enterprise object that it's just been fetched from the database or other repository or created in the application.

located based on the global identifier and overwritten with the object's fetched data, keeping all in-memory references to it intact.

Fetch Optimization

As mentioned, when an enterprise object is fetched, objects for its relationships aren't immediately fetched; instead, faults are created to hold places for those objects when they're eventually fetched. The reasons for this are obvious: Fetching through relationships would quickly result in the entire object graph being pulled in on the first access, which is completely unnecessary and would take up far too much time and memory.

Faults are an excellent protection against too much fetching, but the limits they impose can be too strict, resulting in many small fetches when fewer, larger fetches could be made. Suppose you fetch a group of Program objects, which creates faults for their Channels, and run through them accessing the Channels. Each time you do this, a single-object fetch is performed even though you'll be running through the whole group of Programs. EOModeler lets you specify a batch fetch amount for relationships, so that when you access a fault created for a relationship, a group of faults is resolved all at once, instead of just one fault at a time.

Batching makes fetches happen in clusters after faults have already been made. Another kind of fetch optimization involves forcing specific relationships to be fetched immediately, descending a short way into the object graph. This is called *prefetching*, and it allows you to reduce the number of fetches necessary when you know you'll be traversing a number of relationships in the process of performing an operation.

Change Tracking

After creating the object graph from fetched objects, an editing context's most important job is to track changes to enterprise objects in memory and relate those changes to operations in its object store. This is where the **willChange** method introduced earlier comes in. The Control layer defines this method to send out a notification to any interested observers that the receiver is about to change in some way.

When an editing context first records a new enterprise object, it registers itself as an observer of that object. Then, whenever that object receives a **willChange** message, the editing context hears about it and can examine the object's state before and after the change to determine what happened. The editing context also keeps track of insert and delete messages sent directly to it.

The editing context caches all of these various changes, typically through a single pass of the run loop. At the end of the loop, it cleans up any relationships that may have been affected by deletions, records the old and new states for undo, and records the changes for saving to the object store. It also posts a notification that causes the user interface to be updated based on the changes.

In addition to fixing relationships, an editing context applies delete propagation rules defined in the model whenever an enterprise object is deleted. You can specify that deletion be denied if the relationship has any destination objects; that deletion cascade through the relationship, deleting all the destination objects; or that deletion simply remove the object and any references to it through relationships.

Undo Management

As an editing context records changes to its enterprise objects, it also records the nature of these changes in an undo stack, represented by the EOUndoManager class. Editing contexts record all operations on enterprise objects—such as inserts, changes to attributes and relationships, and deletes—as single, undoable actions. An **undo** message reverses the last change in the undo manager's editing context, and a **redo** message reverses the last undo. EOEditingContext defines action methods that you can hook up to menu items or controls in Interface Builder, relieving you of the need to write any code related to basic undo management.

Multiple Object Stores

Support for multiple databases or other repositories is made possible by the EOObjectStoreCoordinator class, which pools together the objects created from its member object stores (such as EODatabaseContexts). A coordinator acts as the representative of its members, forwarding messages to the appropriate object stores based on which enterprise objects they provide.

Suppose the PayPerView application stored Programs in an Oracle database and Channels in a Sybase database. In this case, a fetch message sent to the object store coordinator results in a fetch message to the Oracle object store for the Programs and another fetch message to the Sybase object store for the Channel objects. The coordinator then constructs the relationships between the two. If you have two different legacy databases and must integrate them, this is a useful feature indeed.

When saving changes to its various data repositories, an object store coordinator guides its members through the operation in several passes, in which each member store saves its own changes and then forwards remaining changes to the other stores that need to perform them. For example, if the Channel object store deletes a Channel, it might inform the object store containing Programs to delete all the Programs belonging to that Channel.

Multiple and Nested Editing Contexts

As object stores can branch below a coordinator, different editing contexts can use a single object store and can be nested one within the other, creating in-memory transaction scopes that buffer changes from peers and parents until they're saved. This allows you to create independent document windows in an application or detail views that allow a number of changes to be grouped together as a single procedure in the user interface. A later version of PayPerView, for example, might allow customer account management, which involves many complex tasks. Using nested editing contexts, you can easily create a drill-down interface in which the user performs a complex task by opening a new window to enter information. If the user enters incomplete or incorrect information, it doesn't affect the parent editing context; if the user aborts the operation, the application need only release the nested editing context.

Validation

Enterprise objects can validate changes made to them independent of the database or the user interface by simply implementing methods that the Framework invokes on performing particular operations. This allows enterprise objects to enforce business policies in the form of value limits, interdependencies between objects, and other constraints.

The most general method is **validateValue:forKey:**, which is used before the Framework sets a property. This method, like the key-value coding methods, has a default implementation that checks for a property-specific validation method. For example, the Program class can implement a **validateCost** method that's invoked whenever the Framework sets the Program's "cost" attribute.

Other validation methods are invoked before the enterprise object's changes are communicated to the database. **validateForInsert** and **validateForUpdate** allow the object to approve values about to be written to the database. A more general **validateForSave** method can be implemented to cover both cases. **validateForDelete** verifies that the object can be deleted from the database.

In-Memory Filtering and Sorting

In addition to all the heavy-duty graph management classes, the Control layer defines classes to filter and sort arrays of enterprise objects. EOQualifier and its subclasses form a general-purpose filtering mechanism, which can match enterprise object properties to specific values, relate one property of an enterprise object to that of another, and combine basic qualifiers using the AND, OR, and NOT logical relations. EOSortOrdering records a property key to sort by and an object method to use for sorting.

The Access layer uses qualifier and sort ordering objects to limit and sort the results of a fetch, but these objects can also be applied in memory to arrays of enterprise objects. This filters and sorts enterprise objects directly, without generating a new SQL query and fetching from the database. The Control layer adds methods to NSArray that apply qualifiers and sort orderings to produce a new filtered or sorted array.

Data Sources

EOEditingContext is a sophisticated class, with a lot of methods for performing very specific and sometimes esoteric operations. To present a simpler interface for higher-level objects, the Control layer defines the EODataSource class. EODataSource is an abstract class that defines a very simple interface for managing enterprise objects, consisting primarily of the methods **createObject**, **insertObject:**, **deleteObject:**, and **fetchObjects**. Concrete subclasses must implement these methods appropriately. An EODatabaseDataSource, for example, uses an editing context that gets objects from a relational database through the Access layer.

The Control layer's other customization point is the EOObjectStore interface.

The data source interface is one of the Control layer's customization points. Just as you can create custom adaptors to handle new kinds of relational databases, you can create custom data sources to handle completely different data repositories, such as flat-file databases, structured file systems, and real-time stock feeds.

The Interface Layer

The third system within the Enterprise Objects Framework is in charge of synchronizing the values in enterprise objects with the application's user interface. The Interface layer is actually quite simple in design, comprising two focal classes, EODisplayGroup and EOAssociation. Display groups collect enterprise objects from an EODataSource and watch for changes to the objects in the EODataSource. Associations tie user interface objects to the display group, with different subclasses handling different kinds of interface objects.

Display Groups

A display group manages the display and updating of values for enterprise objects in a single EODataSource. In this capacity, it filters the EODataSource's objects using a qualifier, sorts them as needed, and manages the display of values for those enterprise objects. The display group maintains a selection of zero, one, or many enterprise objects, which is reflected in the user interface through association objects.

The primary job of a display group, however, is to wait for changes to its enterprise objects and to its associations' interface objects, and to propagate those changes up or down accordingly. A display group registers itself as an observer of its EODataSource's editing context, so that when the editing context posts a notification that its objects have changed, the display group updates all associations tied to it. It also gets notified by its associations when their interface objects change, updating the selected enterprise object with the interface object's new value.

Associations

Associations play the same role with the user interface that adaptors do with database servers. The generic association class, EOAssociation, defines an abstract and automatic mechanism for synchronizing the user interface with the state of a display group's enterprise objects. Subclasses of EOAssociation handle the different kinds of interface objects, such as table views, text fields, and pop-up lists. EOAssociation is the Interface layer's customization point: You create custom subclasses of EOAssociation for new kinds of interface objects.

Each kind of association defines a number of *aspects* that relate to some characteristic of the interface object it manages, such as the value displayed, whether the interface object is enabled, the set of possible values, and so on. Interface Builder displays these aspects in its Connections Inspector, through which you bind them to keys in the display group that identify properties of enterprise objects. As a simple example, in the PayPerView application a table column's **value** aspect was bound to the "broadcastDate" property of the Program display group. A more complicated association was that from the pop-up list, which had a **titles** aspect bound to the "name" property of the Channel display group and a **selectedObject** aspect bound to the "channel" property of the Program display group. This caused the pop-up list to create items for every Channel and to show the name of the Channel for the Program selected in the table view.

Associations aren't restricted to actual interface objects. They can be used to link a display group to any other object that presents values—even another display group. The Interface layer defines several such associations, which provide for different kinds of master-detail views. For example, to create a table view that shows departments with a detail table showing all the employees in that department, you just link the two tables' display groups with a master-detail association.

Perspective

That covers what the Enterprise Objects Framework does and how it does it. The biggest take-home point is probably this: Putting business logic in objects gives you a centralized, reusable, and highly manageable structure for developing business applications. You can put your business objects into a library or framework of your own, providing a consistent view of the business model to all of your engineers and users.

You can also put your business objects on high-end machines for compute-intensive operations, adding a third tier between the traditional server and client. Combined with Distributed Objects, this makes for a flexible system that can be repartitioned across your network as requirements and hardware change. As noted in Chapter 9, however, you don't want to distribute the enterprise objects themselves, as this will only flood the network with distributed messages.

Finally, using interface controllers, you can present your business objects to the user with very little coding. You can even put them on the World Wide Web, as the next chapter shows.

11 *World Wide Web Applications*

Unless you've been living under a rock since the mid-1990s, you've heard of the explosive growth of both the Internet and the World Wide Web. These technologies represent a revolution in communication, making information immediately available to millions of people, direct and on demand. The business advantages of the World Wide Web over traditional print and broadcast media are obvious: Printing and broadcast costs are eliminated, since information doesn't have to be sent to a wide potential audience to reach the appropriate targets; content can be tailored to specific audiences, who can retrieve the information they're most interested in; and information can be updated and made available immediately.

The World Wide Web started out as a simple hypertext system, with static pages that presented information and contained links that led to other static pages. As the Web grew, people made it more interactive by generating pages on the fly, tailoring their content to requests made by the user. The typical way to do this has been using HTML forms to send data to the Web server, which is then processed by various programs and scripts to generate a page based on that data.

Unfortunately, without a coherent architecture for Web scripting, these solutions are extremely difficult to implement and maintain. Raw scripting mixes HTML generation with data retrieval and business logic, offering no encapsulation and hampering reusability. (Sound familiar?) The end result of all this is a large, brittle set of pages and scripts with limited functionality and no flexibility.

Handmade scripts also fall prey to the basic mode of the Web, which is based on discrete transactions. Each interaction between the client browser and the Web server involves a separate request–response pair. There's no standard system for maintaining state across transactions, so each company developing Web sites has to roll its own session management scheme from scratch.

Enter Java, from Sun, and WebObjects, from NeXT. These two systems enhance Web development from either end, namely the client Web browser and the server. Each separates the presentation of information from the logic and data behind it, though in somewhat different ways.

> See the JavaSoft Web site at **www.javasoft.com** for more on Java.

Java is a programming language that looks like C++ but has a lot in common with more dynamic languages like Smalltalk and Objective-C. Web browsers such as Netscape Navigator™ download Java programs, called *applets*, and run them on the user's computer. This sidesteps the issue of HTML generation on the server, instead having the client machine do the work in Java. With Java, you can write programs that work on any computer or operating system that includes a Java interpreter (or virtual machine). There are literally dozens of books available on Java, so we won't be exploring it much here.

> See NeXT's Web site at **www.next.com** for the latest news on WebObjects.

WebObjects is an object-oriented framework for developing Web applications on the server. With WebObjects an application can be divided into discrete, reusable components, whether whole pages or individual design elements such as navigation bars and corporate identification information. This framework includes a number of classes that encapsulate various aspects of HTML generation and defines a coherent session management system that accumulates each user's state separately. It works with the Enterprise Objects Framework to connect Web applications to corporate databases. In addition, to support application development without requiring compiled code, it provides a simple object-oriented scripting language. The rest of this chapter is devoted to describing WebObjects.

Working on opposite sides of the browser–server connection, Java and WebObjects form a complementary pair of tools that you can use to build powerful, dynamic Web sites. As of this writing, NeXT is working to integrate WebObjects even more with Java, as well as with other popular Web technologies.

Note: Web and Internet technology is moving fast. As we write this book, WebObjects is shipping in version 2.0. However, NeXT has announced plans to include a graphical editor much like Interface Builder, to support additional scripting languages, and in general to add many new features that will make using WebObjects easier and easier. For these reasons, we haven't shown how to revise PayPerView in this chapter—by the time you get this book, the process we would have described would already be obsolete! Instead, we recommend that you visit NeXT's Web site at **www.next.com** for the latest information.

What WebObjects Does

WebObjects applies object-oriented principles to Web page design, treating pages as components that you build from basic elements. When a Web application receives a request, it looks for a page definition that matches the request and constructs an instance of that page using data in the request. It then sends a message to the page, asking it to generate an HTML response, and sends the HTML to the Web server for transmission to the browser.

The Parts of a Page

A WebObjects page definition is composed of three parts. The first is an HTML template that lays out the static structure of the page. The template includes the basic elements of a page, such as text, lists, images, links, and forms, as well as special WEBOBJECT tags, which tie the template to objects that generate dynamic content. You can think of the template as a window in a nib file that contains text fields, buttons, and other items—or as the view in the model–view–controller paradigm.

The second part of a page definition is a script file or compiled class for the page, which contains variable declarations and methods that can be invoked. This part determines the dynamic content of the page, as well as how it responds to input. You can think of this part as a custom object or controller that manages the items in the page, just as PayPerView's ProgramController in Chapter 7 manages the table and text fields.

The third part is a list of declarations that link the template to the script or compiled class. Declarations are like the connections or associations you create using Interface Builder. All three parts are stored together in a directory on the Web server under a common name, with the extension **.wo**. For example, a page definition named **Main.wo** contains the files **Main.html**, **Main.wos** (the script), and **Main.wod** (the declarations).

NeXT's upcoming page editor neatly hides this file structure.

That accounts for the view and the controller, which leaves the Web page's model. Just as PayPerView put the model in three different places in its three incarnations, a WebObjects application can embed the model in the script, use Distributed Objects to share them among multiple Web servers, or use objects derived from a database using the Enterprise Objects Framework. Because WebObjects applications share the OpenStep object model, they have access to all of these mechanisms. More significantly, through WebObjects these mechanisms have access to the Web, so that you don't have to limit your application to deployment on an OpenStep system.

Reusable Components

Page definitions represent the unique components of an application. Each page, however, may well include standard elements such as a navigation bar with links to the Web site's home page, a search tool, and other useful facilities. You might duplicate the HTML and script for such elements in each page, but this quickly becomes unwieldy as the number of pages increases. Not only does this consume disk space unnecessarily, but it makes changes to such elements an onerous task.

With WebObjects, you can define such elements as standard components, with template, script, and declarations files appropriate to the element. A component can be made reusable simply by omitting top-level HTML tags such as HTML, HEAD, and BODY, and putting the files in a globally accessible location. Page definitions can then include this reusable component with a WEBOBJECT tag, just like any other. This makes a single definition available to all the pages in your application, or even your entire Web site, collapsing the storage and maintenance burden to a single set of files.

Session State Management

Although a WebObjects application can run as a continuous process for as long as users interact with it, this interaction is still limited to unconnected request–response cycles. The Web's transfer protocol defines no inherent management of state across them, so WebObjects does this for you by allowing you to declare the scope of script variables. In the simplest cases, variables declared inside a script method last for the duration of the method's execution, while those declared outside methods in a component script last for the duration of a request–response transaction. Global variables that exist as long as the WebObjects application runs can be declared in a special script for the application itself.

Most useful for tracking the state of multiple users' interactions with the application, however, are *persistent* and *session* variables. Such variables retain their values across transactions, for as long as the user interacts with the application. Persistent variables are declared in a component's script using the **persistent** specifier and are accessible only by that component. Session variables are declared in the application's script using the **session** specifier and are available to every component in the application.

WebObjects allows applications to keep persistent state on the server or to place it in the pages sent to the client as special hidden fields in forms. Each approach has its advantages and disadvantages. State kept in the server keeps the application simple and is more secure than putting it within the user's reach, but it also increases the application's memory usage and can be lost if the server crashes. State kept in pages reduces the storage burden of the application and remains valid even if the application terminates and restarts. However, large amounts of state add to the transfer time of both requests and responses; also, since the data exists in the browser, the user can tamper with it, or the wrong state can be sent to the application if the user backtracks to an earlier page. The good news is that wherever it's stored, WebObjects transparently handles the actual management of the state.

A Sample Page Definition

By way of example, let's take a look at the WebObjects equivalent of the classic Hello World program, available as part of NeXT's WebObjects documentation. This application displays a form with a message asking the user for his or her name, a text field to type the name in, and a submit button to send the information to the server. When the user types his or her name and clicks the submit button, the Web application returns a page that greets the user by name. Here's the template for the main page, **Main.html**:

```
<HTML>

<HEAD>
    <TITLE>Hello World!</TITLE>
</HEAD>

<BODY>
  <FORM>
  What's your name?
  <P>
  <WEBOBJECT NAME = "NAME_FIELD">
    <INPUT TYPE = "TEXT">
  </WEBOBJECT>

  <WEBOBJECT NAME = "SUBMIT_BUTTON">
    <INPUT TYPE = "SUBMIT">
  </WEBOBJECT>

  </P>
  </FORM>
</BODY>

</HTML>
```

Note the use of the WEBOBJECT tags around the INPUT fields. These tags identify the text field and the submit button, which are represented in the application by instances of the built-in WOTextField and WOSubmitButton classes. The declarations file, **Main.wod**, makes the association between the tags and the classes:

```
NAME_FIELD: WOTextField {value = nameString};
SUBMIT_BUTTON: WOSubmitButton {action = sayHello};
```

The classes that represent standard HTML tags are called *dynamic elements*, as they're primitive classes built into WebObjects. You can also associate WEBOBJECT tags with scripted components, simply by referring to the **.wo** directory name.

The last part of each declaration lists the bindings between aspects of the dynamic elements and variables and methods in the script. Just like an association in Interface Builder, each kind of dynamic element or component manages its own set of attributes or aspects. A WOTextField, for example, stores a string value in its **value** attribute, while a WOSubmitButton triggers a message stored in its **action** attribute. In **Main.wos** below, the script contains a variable called **nameString** and a method called **sayHello**:

The scripting language used here is based on Objective-C and is called WebScript™. NeXT is also planning support for scripting languages such as Visual Basic and JavaScript™.

```
id nameString;

- sayHello
{
  id nextPage;
  nextPage = [WOApp pageWithName:@"Hello"];
  [nextPage setNameString:nameString];
  return nextPage;
}
```

When the user types his or her name in the text field and clicks the submit button, the value of the text field is stored in **nameString** and the **sayHello** method is invoked. This method has the global application object look up and create a page from a definition named "Hello". This definition can come either from a **Hello.wo** directory or from a compiled class in the application named Hello. Once it has this page, **sayHello** hands it the string the user typed in the form and returns the page as the result to send to the Web browser. The **Hello.html** template says "Hello" followed by whatever the user typed:

```
<HTML>
<HEAD>
  <TITLE>Hello World!</TITLE>
</HEAD>

<BODY>
  Hello <WEBOBJECT NAME = "NAME_STRING"></WEBOBJECT>!
</BODY>
</HTML>
```

The declarations file, **Hello.wod**, associates the NAME_STRING tag with a WOString, which simply holds a string value. The value is bound to the **nameString** variable:

```
NAME_STRING: WOString {value = nameString};
```

The script file, **Hello.wos**, contains only the definition of the **nameString** variable:

```
id nameString;
```

Note the absence of a **setNameString:** method. Like the Enterprise Objects Framework, WebObjects can dynamically set and get attributes based on their names.

That's about all there is to defining WebObjects pages. The next section dives inside WebObjects to show how it performs its dynamic magic.

How It Works

All Web applications currently interact with users on a page-by-page basis. The browser displays an entire page, with links and forms. When the user clicks one of these, the browser sends a request to the Web server, which returns a new page that the browser then displays. With static pages, the request must indicate an existing file on the server machine. With dynamic pages, the server invokes a program that generates the page. This program can be a command-line program, a **perl** script, or a WebObjects application.

A WebObjects application communicates with a standard Web server through an adaptor that converts incoming requests into Distributed

Objects messages to the application's WOApplication object. Just like the Application Kit's NSApplication, this object takes incoming events (requests) and distributes them to the appropriate destination. In this case, it does so by looking up component and page definitions, creating objects for them, and sending them messages. The application's executable can be a custom program with compiled business objects, or it can be the **DefaultApp** program, which knows how to handle scripted components but does nothing else.

> WebObjects also supports the Netscape Server API (NSAPI).

An individual WebObjects application stores its page and other component definitions in a subdirectory of the Web server's documents directory. Users start the application with a URL that names the WebObjects **cgi-bin** application with the application directory; for example:

```
http://wwwsite/cgi-bin/WebObjects/HelloWorld/
```

When the Web server gets this request, it starts up the WebObjects application and passes it the URL. The WebObjects application then enters the *request–response loop*.

The Request–Response Loop

For a WebObjects application, an incoming request is always associated with a page, called naturally enough the *request page*. (Initial requests are assigned to the page named "Main.") The request page is given the task of handling the incoming request and producing a *response page*, which is rendered as HTML to be sent back to the browser. This process takes place in three steps:

> These steps apply to any component, not just pages.

1. The WOApplication object prepares for the request by looking up the request page and restoring its persistent and session state. If the request page already exists, the WOApplication uses that; otherwise it finds the page definition and creates an object with it. It then restores the persistent and session state and adds any input that came with the request (such as the user's name in Hello World).

2. The WOApplication has the request page produce a response by invoking whatever action was specified in the request (such as **sayHello** in Hello World). If no action is specified, the request page itself is used as the response.

3. The response page is told to generate HTML based on its state, which is then returned to the browser.

At each stage, the WebObjects system checks the request and response pages for standard methods, invoking them if the pages define them. When first created from its definition, any page or component can receive an **awake** message that allows it to initialize transaction and persistent variables. The request page or component can define methods such as **willPrepareForRequest:inContext:** and the corresponding **didPrepareForRequest:inContext:**, substituting a different page in its own place if needed. Similarly, the response page or component can define the optional methods **willPrepareResponse:inContext:** and **didPrepareResponse:inContext:**. These methods in particular are useful for implementing login pages and for cleaning up state after a request–response transaction completes.

Following Hello World

Needless to say, this example glosses over a lot of detail. See NeXT's Web site for the particulars.

To clarify the request–response loop, let's examine what happens when a user runs Hello World from a Web browser. When the user accesses the URL **http://*wwwsite*/cgi-bin/WebObjects/HelloWorld/**, the Web server launches the WebObjects **cgi-bin** program, which starts the default application executable. This starts the first pass through the request–response loop:

1. The application looks in the HTML directory for **HelloWorld** to find a request page. Since this is an initial request, it creates a page from the **Main.wo** definition.

2. This initial request doesn't contain an action, so the Main page is used as the response page.

3. Finally, the Main page is made to generate HTML for the form with the text field and submit button. This HTML is then sent back to the user.

So far, so good. Now, when the user types a name and clicks the submit button, the Hello World application receives a request for the Main page that indicates that the submit button was clicked. This begins the second pass through the loop:

1. The application looks up the Main page and puts the contents of the text field into its **nameString** variable, in accordance with the binding in the declarations file.

2. Then, since the request came from the submit button, the application gets the action bound to the submit button, **sayHello**, and invokes it. **sayHello** creates the response page from the **Hello.wo** directory, assigns the **nameString** variable to the new page, and returns that page.

3. The Hello page, with the user's name, is made to generate HTML, which is sent back to the user.

And that's all there is to it.

Perspective

WebObjects provides for easy creation of dynamic Web pages, which you can use to present your business's object model to the world. With support for the Foundation and Enterprise Objects Frameworks built in, it provides your business objects with a wide channel for presenting your message and interacting with your customers. Not only can your business objects be used in custom client applications using the Application Kit, they can be made available to the world on the World Wide Web using WebObjects.

Part Three: Development Topics

12 *Development Topics*

To conclude this review of OpenStep, we've added a few chapters that examine specific issues related to developing applications. The goal is to show how OpenStep fares in such areas as project management, debugging, and performance. This should give you some idea of its particular strengths and weaknesses in day-to-day development.

Project management is by far the largest topic, since it's a general subject open to much discussion. *Chapter 13: Project Management and the Development Life Cycle* covers the major aspects of a development project, from small- to large-scale management of resources to the development of a business model. It also reviews specific development styles particularly well suited to OpenStep—rapid prototyping and iterative development—and addresses their impact on scheduling.

The other topics, being more particular, merit only short surveys of specific problem areas and general remedies to those problems. Chapter 14 covers the first topic, portability, which everyone wants to know about before committing to a particular technology. The short answer, of course, is that OpenStep applications are as portable as OpenStep. The long answer depends on whether those applications use resources outside of OpenStep, some of which will be portable, some of which won't.

Just after portability is everyone's favorite activity, debugging. Since OpenStep defines such a variety of mechanisms and interacting components, things can and will go wrong in your application. Chapter 15 highlights the problems most commonly seen in code and suggests some remedies and preventative measures.

The last development topic is performance, an eternal bugbear of software and hardware developers alike. OpenStep, being an advanced application system, certainly makes its demands on hardware. The elegance of its object model can also seduce developers into writing beautiful—but slow—code. Objects have their place, and aren't appropriate for every programming task. Chapter 16 points out both general techniques for managing and improving performance that apply more than usual to OpenStep, as well as some techniques unique to OpenStep.

13 *Project Management and the Development Life Cycle*

In a business environment, the requirements that a software system must fulfill are always changing, usually right through the development process and beyond. Software systems must evolve throughout their useful life to keep up with changing business conditions. Software that doesn't keep up quickly becomes a liability and can make the difference between success and failure for the whole business. Building a software process that assists in coping with this fact of life helps a lot, but it doesn't happen by accident.

There are two scales of project management—management in the small and management in the large. *Management in the small* refers to version control, configuration and change management, and other file-oriented aspects of working in groups. There are few changes that OpenStep development brings to this aspect of project management; it's still somewhat tedious, detail-oriented, and absolutely necessary.

Various tools available on UNIX and Windows platforms assist with these issues. You need a system that, at a minimum, lets you track who has edited what and what has changed, keeps team members from stepping on each other's toes when editing files, remembers which versions of files make up a version of the whole system, and provides a repository or workspace for sharing all the on-line artifacts of the development effort—code, design documents, review comments, perhaps even electronic mail messages. As of this writing, for NeXT's Mach operating system, RCS/CVS is a good, freely available tool that manages all this data. On Solaris, SPARCWORKS™/TeamWare, based on SCCS, is a good one and is well integrated with the rest of the Solaris Workshop development environment. Decide on one or another of these tools,

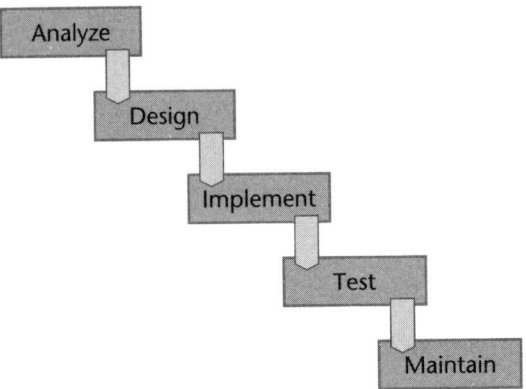

Figure 1. The Waterfall Model

train your team to use them effectively, and then use the tools religiously.

Management in the large deals with understanding the problems that the system must address and with building a team and a process that allow for changing requirements and that enable reuse. Many of the potential benefits offered by object-oriented development techniques in general—and OpenStep development specifically—don't come for free. They need organizational support to be realized; there's more to building applications that help your business than just picking the right tools. If your organization isn't already familiar with OO tools and development processes, then you won't be able to take full advantage of the benefits OpenStep development offers without changing the way you deal with the software life cycle and development process in your organization.

Much has been written about the software life cycle, ever since people first figured out that developing software isn't trivial. Several models of software development processes have been put forth, starting with the "waterfall" model (Figure 1). The waterfall model was based on five consecutive stages of development: analysis, design, implementation, testing, and then maintenance. The engineering team completed each stage before moving onto the next. In some cases, each stage was performed by different groups. This process presumed that it was possible to learn—and communicate—everything there was to know about the analysis before proceeding to the design stage, learn and

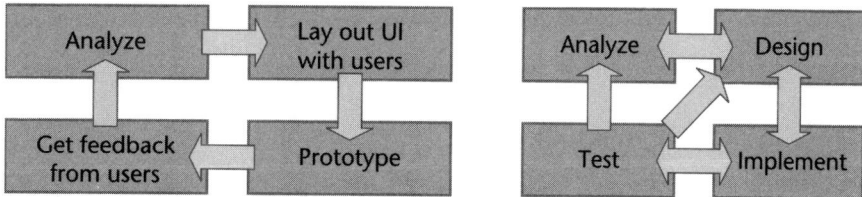
Figure 2. Rapid Prototyping and Iterative Development

communicate everything there was to know about the design before proceeding to implementation, and so on. Developers working in the waterfall model typically spent most of their time documenting each stage in exhaustive detail, leaving a bulletproof paper trail, rather than actually creating code. This had to be done, because the model said you couldn't easily go back to a prior stage, and because often you'd be handing your material to another group to do the next stage while your group started up a new project.

As might be expected, the waterfall process is a pretty inefficient way to develop most forms of software. Each stage in the development process teaches you something about the other stages, and it's at best counter-productive—at worst, impossible—to set any one part in stone before moving on to the next stage in the cycle. However, those five stages in a program's life are very clear, and most life-cycle models incorporate them, in roughly the same order. The differences are in what happens when, in the point at which a given phase can be considered complete, and in how often each stage is entered over the course of development.

Two interesting development models created over the past 15 years work particularly well for OpenStep development. During the initial development efforts, which includes learning the users' requirements and designing the program's interface, the *rapid prototyping* model (Figure 2) assists in developing a requirements document and a user interface layout. Rapid prototyping works well at the beginning of a project, where the development team is discerning the users' requirements and the users themselves are figuring out what those requirements are. Once the requirements have been uncovered in some detail and the rate of change slows down, the *iterative development* model allows for more manageable progress and scales better to more developers, while retaining the ability to react quickly to changing requirements.

Building Business Models

While building applications is the primary focus of this book, it's important to be able to build the *right* applications—the applications that solve the problems you're facing. Object-oriented languages were originally developed to build models and simulations; a good software system is in many ways a simulation of your business. It should be based on the same basic things that drive your business's operation. You need a model that represents the entities that make up your business—what they know, how they behave, and how they interact; in short, the data and the processes of the business. Much of the actual work of a business reengineering effort should consist of building and verifying this model.

Constructing the Model

Developing a business model primarily involves defining and categorizing the objects that make up the business process. This model is different for every business, but many aspects are similar for all businesses. For instance, most models have representations of people, and the representations of people are often specialized into employees and customers. Each person probably has an address, perhaps more than one. Employees typically have payroll information and job descriptions, while customers have order histories and pending invoices. The distinctions come in determining the details—is a job description a characteristic of an employee, or is it a separate object that the employee object refers to? The answers to questions like these depend on the history and practices of the business and on which groups in the company will be accessing the data.

The process of building the model will probably reveal some redundancy in the business practice. For instance, many businesses have multiple definitions of the word "customer." The marketing department may want to track buying patterns and future demand; the sales department may want to track individual pending sales and credit limits; the customer service department is worried about customer satisfaction; while the product development department wants feedback and demand projections on new products. All of these things come from "customers," but each is a different kind of data that must be tracked. When building the model and defining a Customer entity, the development team must merge these multiple definitions as much as is practical. Different departments will still see distinctions and want to track different data, but the common ground between the definitions should be abstracted out and kept in one place.

It's also important to consider the life cycle of entities in the model. What happens when a new Customer entity is entered into the system? What happens when a Customer is removed? When an Order is fulfilled, does it create an Invoice object? How long does the Order remain in the system? Is it recorded forever, is it deleted automatically, or does a human being need to sweep it out? The Warehouse and Fulfillment divisions may be finished with an Order entity as soon it's been shipped and invoiced, but the Customer Service and Legal departments may need it to remain for some length of time. If the Order is deleted, does that cause the Invoice to be deleted as well? How are other entities in the model, and other groups and departments in your company, affected by these events?

Much of the model's construction can be facilitated by developing scenarios or *use cases*—writing down a script of the flow of a business process and then making sure that the model does in fact model it. These scenarios provide lots of information about what the objects in the model should be, what they should do, and what other objects they need to interact with. The scenarios should script out the execution of various business processes as they occur now (before a reengineering effort is implemented), such as taking, fulfilling, and invoicing an order; responding to a customer complaint; and generating a marketing report. Different scenarios from different departments in the business will highlight overlaps between departments and indicate areas where there are conflicting definitions.

Verifying the Model

As the model is developed, it can also be verified by running various trial scenarios through it. If the model doesn't support the process, then the model probably needs to be modified to do so. It's also possible that the scenario is inefficient or even incorrect, and the model might suggest an improved way of carrying out the process. It's important to include some negative cases to check for scenarios that should be prohibited. For example, with regard to an Employee entity, only certain employees should have access to payroll information; a good scenario might be to check that employees who shouldn't have access to payroll data are prevented from seeing it.

Another technique for verifying the model is to expand and evolve it. This is good for identifying things that share common traits. For example, consider the ways in which an order can be paid. It can be paid with cash, a purchase order, a credit card, a check, a money order, or by other means. They're all valid means of payment. They share common traits, such as how much they're worth and the date they were received, but they also have distinctive individual traits, such as how they're processed, whether they're prepaid or not, and the cost of processing the payment. The commonality can be abstracted out into a supertype, perhaps called Payment. The model needs to support both abstraction of shared elements into a supertype, such as treating purchase orders, cash, and credit cards as kinds of Payments, and addition of more subtypes, such as adding a new type of Payment, say some form of electronic cash or electronic funds transfer. If the model doesn't support this type of extension, then you've identified a potentially major weakness in the model. Models usually need to evolve in some unanticipated ways, but you can catch many of the problem areas with some forethought about what your customers will want.

A final area for verification is that of concepts that don't have explicit representation in the model. Occasionally some "real-world" objects are best represented in the model in abstract ways, especially when the model is being evolved. Given the existing model, some real-world concepts may turn out to look like relationships between objects rather than brand-new objects. This is usually wrong—make a new object to represent the connection. For instance, an Order contains a set of Products. Special data about the Products being ordered is specific to an individual Order—quantity, price charged, date shipped, and others. These are usually represented as something like an Order Line Item. Order Line Items can be independent objects, or they can be a kind of relationship between an Order and a Product. Use the implementation that makes the most sense, but model the object explicitly. In the example above, include real Order Line Item entities in the model, not just Orders and Products. It's crucial that all the real-world entities used in the application be modeled as first-class entities.

Building and verifying a business model is an iterative process that can take months for a complex business. Involvement from all aspects of the business is required to develop canonical meanings for the elements of the model and to ensure that the elements in the model actually represent the things they're meant to represent. It's also important to schedule enough time for several iterations and changes. The basic framework needs to be in place before development starts. Once the framework is in place and most of the key entities and their interrelationships are known, then development can begin. The software development efforts will uncover areas where the model is inaccurate or incomplete, and this information should be used to improve the model.

Choosing a Methodology

Equally important as developing the business model is choosing the methodology you'll use to develop it. Some methodologies specifically support modeling objects, while some are more geared to modeling relational data. It's important to choose one that allows you to model the whole system—the back-end data store, the middle-tier business logic, and the front-end representation. Otherwise, you run the risk of miscommunication and imprecise mappings between different models. A major reason for building a model in the first place is to have consistent definitions and meanings between users, developers, and analysts—lack of consistency slows things down and makes the development process more error-prone.

Once you have the model, you can quickly build applications that manipulate these objects, and changes to the underlying objects in the model can be reflected across all the applications. Building the applications then becomes a relatively low-effort task—the applications inspect, connect, and modify the objects in the model; this is where much of the reuse benefit of object technology occurs.

One simple modeling development technique worthy of consideration, especially for development efforts that involve people outside the information systems department, is the Class–Responsibility–Collaborator (CRC) system from Wirfs-Brock and Beck. This system makes it easy for people unfamiliar with information systems technology and object-oriented concepts to take an active role in developing the model by representing each basic entity on a 3×5 index card. Each card lists an individual entity's data and responsibilities. The relationships between entities are described by how the cards are arranged. This simple technique allows modeling teams to experiment with different organizations of the model by moving the cards around on a whiteboard or table. It doesn't provide enough information to lay out the user interface and fully implement the system, but it can help you settle down very quickly into a base architecture that describes user-domain objects, like Orders, Customers, and Invoices, rather than the buttons, windows, and controllers that your system will need to implement.

As of this writing, object modeling methods continue to be a focus of much effort and refinement. The CRC system is a good place to start. More-complex and richer systems from Grady Booch and James Rumbaugh, Ivar Jacobsen, Peter Coad, and others, are all worthy of consideration. Don't forget, however, that the modeling methods are tools, not religions. Try a few, and see which techniques work best for your organization.

Rapid Prototyping

One of the most important components of OpenStep is the Interface Builder application, which allows the rapid construction of user interfaces and even some behavior, without writing code. Interface Builder introduces a distinction between what things are on the screen, where they are, and what they do. This lets the developer add, remove, connect, modify, and rearrange the objects that make up the user interface without needing to modify the code behind the user interface and recompile it. This is perhaps the most significant advance that an OpenStep development environment offers. Most other user interface builders and screen painters either tie you to a specific tool with few hooks to the rest of the system or generate code that you then compile and link into your system. Interface Builder doesn't need to generate any code at all—the objects are read in and unarchived at run time by the Application Kit, so the entire user interface can be updated without needing to recompile the program, merge code, or even have access to the source in many cases. Interface Builder also supports the use of custom-crafted palettes of objects, allowing the partial assembly of applications from prebuilt components.

Often during the initial stages of analysis, the customers and users of the software being developed have only a rudimentary idea of what they want. They have a clear understanding of the problems they want to solve, but not necessarily a good understanding of how those problems should best be addressed. In the rapid prototyping model, the developer lays out a prototype interface, preferably with a user assisting, and then proceeds to evolve the interface of the application with the user's input. It's easy to try out ideas and throw away the ones that don't work. The user interface layout usually proceeds very quickly and should be concerned only with the user interface itself—object design and implementation issues should be postponed for now. In general, this process of successive approximation should take less than a team-week (a person-week for every member of the team) per major component in the system.

Developers and users should also concern themselves with determining what output the system needs to provide. The reporting requirements, and mockups of the reports themselves, are important as a check for the user interface and as input for the developers implementing a database schema. If a field appears in the report, it needs to be entered or calculated somewhere, and if a field appears in the user interface, it should probably appear on a report somewhere as well. If a piece of data appears in one domain and not the other, there's probably an inconsistency somewhere. From a consistency standpoint, the actual layout of the report isn't as important as the contents, but it's useful for designing the user interface—the layouts of the reports are often a good starting point for a layout of the user interface itself.

As this process moves forward, the developer gains an understanding of the requirements the application needs to fulfill. Many requirements have nothing to do with the user interface, but the users can describe how they'd like the application to behave even though there's no code there to implement the behavior. You may want to implement prototype objects, often called "smoke-and-mirrors" objects, that make the user interface react to user actions using precomputed data and canned results so that the users can get a feel for different ways of working with the application. Capturing this information is the primary purpose of the rapid prototyping model in this stage of the development cycle, and some added incremental effort spent building smoke-and-mirrors objects can help you avoid throwing away fully implemented modules that don't meet the application's requirements.

At some point, the rate of change in the user interface and reports falls off. The developers have a pretty good idea of what to build, and the users have a pretty good idea of what to expect. When this happens, it's time to start taking other factors into account. This is when a shift to the iterative development model makes sense.

Iterative Development

As the rapid prototyping stage in the development process winds down, the user interface layouts need to have some behavior put behind them—the business rules and processes that the application supports need to be implemented.

In the software classic *The Mythical Man-Month*, Fred Brooks wrote: "Plan to throw one away; you will anyway." Given the luxury of time, it's a great way to build really good software—you learn a tremendous amount by doing a full-blown dry run, and these lessons feed into the second pass. However, Brooks later decided that it was bad advice. There are ways to speed up the process that allow you to get the most useful information without most of the trouble.

The iterative development model takes the waterfall model and applies it to smaller pieces of the problem and then repeats itself. The development process passes through each stage as often as needed—as Grady Booch said, "Analyze a little, design a little, code a little, test a little." Then go back and do it again.

As the team progresses through each step, the team members will find that they learn useful information about the other steps. Sometimes this knowledge is painful; you may discover that you've decomposed a problem into a design that you might not be able to build efficiently. The sooner a problem like this is found, the better! When things like this happen, the reasonable approach is to stop and try to solve the problem, perhaps by prototyping a few proposed solutions. If the problem can't be resolved, go back and reevaluate the analysis and the design with this new information in mind.

This process plays into one of the fundamental concepts of object-oriented development—the split between interface and implementation. The interface of an object defines what it does, but should say very little about how it does what it does. Once an interface is defined, the internals of the object can be filled in as needed. This allows the developers to write interfaces based on what the model says the objects should do, and then implement a first cut at the behavior. They can then assemble the objects into a prototype of the application, employing the user interface prototypes developed earlier, and actually run and play with the prototype application. The developers can find out what users like and dislike about the prototype and feed that input into the next iteration of the process.

Occasionally the users will ask for a feature change and then decide that they liked it better the old way. The tools for management in the small, discussed in the beginning of the chapter, help a lot here. It should be possible to roll back to a previous version of the code without much effort.

It's possible for the iterative development model to degenerate into a state in which everyone is fighting fires and working in different stages, and there's no apparent control. Some small amount of this is occasionally unavoidable, but it needs to be very carefully monitored. This is best managed in the same way as any other project; have a schedule that both management and developers believe in, and carefully track how the developers are progressing against the schedule. The next section presents some useful scheduling techniques.

Scheduling and Milestones

Software development is notoriously hard to schedule. Predictability was one of the few benefits of the waterfall model discussed previously. It took forever, but you could usually guess fairly accurately how long that would be. The iterative model is somewhat less predictable, so it needs to be more actively managed. The iterative development process needs to be grounded in reality in terms of both schedule and expectations. A good rule of thumb, often forgotten in software project management, is that any schedule event should have as much chance of being early as of being late, but engineers almost always give best-case dates and then end up late because they were too optimistic. Scheduling can be a delicate balancing act, but there are some techniques that help.

Users usually ask for systems in terms of features—lists of things they'd like the system to do. When you're planning how to build the system, however, having more structure is helpful. Build things in terms of both modules and features, not just features. After all, you're designing the system in terms of modules—collections of related objects that work together—so you should schedule your development effort in these terms as well. Identify the modules that form the foundation of the system, and implement them first. Then, implement the modules that add more features to the whole system, module by module rather than feature by feature, in the order that the users need them. You'll need to strike a balance between postponing modules whose requirements are most in flux and building the most important parts of the system first; often they're the same chunks.

Thinking in terms of both modules and features makes it easier to schedule and to decide what to cut if time gets short (or what, if anything, to add if you're early). If delivery dates change, it's better to have several things that work well and some things that don't work at all, rather than a bunch of things that partially work. Building modules also helps with motivation—it's very satisfying to have a whole, consistent module ready and working.

Schedule regular milestone builds; take the whole system and make sure that everything that's ready fits in and works. This provides several major benefits: It makes sure that everyone is coordinated on one set of code, class interfaces, and database schemas on a regular basis; it makes sure that everyone knows where they stand with regard to the schedule—features and modules that are scheduled to be ready for a given milestone are either ready or they aren't; and it provides a fixed base of code for testing and demonstrating to users. Milestone builds do incur some cost. They bring added overhead to the engineers coordinating the build, and it's a distraction from pressing ahead for everybody. Nevertheless, this is one of the most powerful ways to make sure everyone is pointed in the same direction, and it can provide insight on which parts of the project need help.

Defining Milestones

Ask developers to commit to a prioritized listing of modules and features and then to develop a mapping of features to milestone builds. This ensures that developers think in terms of bite-size chunks; it's much easier for engineers to predict what they can do in three or four weeks rather than in three or four months. Having a deadline in the near future helps to keep motivation and enthusiasm levels high. This plays into the *iteration* of the iterative development process—schedule both getting a part of the system working and then improving it.

An important question to consider is whether the milestone builds are date-driven or feature-driven. In the early stages of the iterative development process, it makes more sense to have these builds be feature- and module-driven. The most basic parts of the system are under construction, and having a stable milestone release is more important than making schedules in the early stages of the game. The milestone process provides information on how realistic the first cuts at schedules are and on which parts of the system are proving to be hard to implement. Don't be afraid to move the dates if things aren't ready. "Declaring success" by changing the definition of an early milestone can come back to haunt you for three reasons. First, you lose information about how long it took to implement that milestone's features. Second, you cause problems for any part of the system that depends on the pieces you're implementing. Third, you also silently change the definitions and timetables of all subsequent milestones, since you have to apply effort both to the items that caused the slip and to the things that were originally slated for the next milestone. Later in the process, as less-fundamental parts of the system are being added, be more and more fussy about dates. If features aren't ready, postpone them to a later milestone, or consider dropping them altogether. Features and modules should be added in order of decreasing importance.

Another important question to consider is how often to do milestone builds. They should be relatively far apart in the beginning of the process, perhaps every four to six weeks for a fairly complex project. This spacing accommodates broad changes such as class redesign, class interface changes, and user interface changes. As the project progresses, speed them up to one every week or two. The added overhead of doing the build should decrease because there should be no drastic changes late in the game, and having more precise information about the schedule's agreement with reality becomes more important as the completion date approaches. At any rate, you should schedule builds often enough to keep a sense of urgency in the project; there should be a deadline just around the corner, but not so soon that there's not enough time to do a quality job. This often proves to be a delicate balancing act.

Most milestones are specific to the project, but some milestones occur in nearly every project, and they should be especially significant. These are the builds that mark such events as the user interface being complete, the class interfaces being frozen, whole modules being implemented and tested, the system reaching feature completion, and builds being released outside your group. These builds should be treated somewhat differently. The full state of the system—source code, nib files, design documents, database dumps, and schema files, the whole thing—should be backed up to tape or some other off-line medium if you're not backing up all of the builds. These milestones might impose some conditions on further development which are important to respect—if the user interface is considered frozen, then changing it should be a big deal and not done lightly, even though it's easy to make a small change quickly with Interface Builder. Lastly, these milestones should be cause for some celebration. Buy your team dinner or throw a party when the build is finished and working.

Revising the Schedule

External constraints often impose nonnegotiable finish dates on the development process. The milestone build process allows you to track with some precision how development is going with regard to hard-and-fast dates and to direct the development process when circumstances change. You can add or drop features and whole modules in response to changing requirements, and slating these changes for a specific milestone allows changes to fit in without destroying the schedule's validity. On the other hand, external events can cause the finish dates to move without concern for your convenience. The milestone build process gives some leverage to deal with this; there's usually a mostly working system ready to go. You can redeploy resources to polish up a milestone build for release if need be, and there should be little confusion about which parts work and which ones don't. For these reasons, it's useful to keep fairly detailed notes that record the state of the system as of the build date.

Always remember that schedules should have something to do with reality. If your developers are working 80-hour weeks to make a 40-hour-week schedule, then your group isn't late—the problem is that the schedule is wrong and needs to be revised. Some 80-hour crunches are tolerable, and they can even be fun, but there are dire consequences if it's a matter of policy. In the short run, your developers will check in quick-and-dirty, untested hacks to make the dates, and in the long run, they'll burn out and be frustrated that they're not allowed to do good work. Revisit the schedule, update your estimates and dates, and decide where you can push out dates and what things to cut to bring the date back in. Your developers will be much happier because they'll be able to believe the schedule; your customers will be happier because you'll be delivering a higher-quality piece of code; and you'll be richer because you'll be better than the competition in your ability to guess right at how long things will take and how much they'll cost.

The Benefits of Reuse

As you develop more systems with OpenStep, you'll find that certain modules are needed over and over again. These modules may map directly onto database entities, such as a Person object, or may be more generic visual components, such as a specialized table view or check box. Take some time to flesh these objects out into reusable components so that they can be more easily used over and over again. It's been reported that you need to build the component three times before you know how to make it reusable and that you then need to use it three times before you start seeing payback. The combination of Objective-C and Interface Builder's target–action paradigm can make reuse somewhat cheaper and faster than that, but getting reusable code is still hard, and it still isn't free. Most developers enjoy taking the time to make reusable code (given the opportunity), but if you don't allow some time for this in the schedule, it can't happen.

As you build or buy a library of objects, you'll find that many simple applications that manipulate the data model can be constructed out of components that are already built, from the OpenStep Application Kit or the WebObjects framework, from your own custom visual components, and from the objects that make up your data model. These component-built applications are usually quite small, many consisting of well under a thousand lines of code to hook the components together, and can often be built by one or two engineers in under two weeks. For these small applications, the full milestone build process is too heavyweight and doesn't make much sense. Depending on the complexity of the application, the process can be simplified to something as simple as a code review by someone knowledgeable about the system and the data model.

Even with a library of reusable components, don't skimp on the front-end part of the process—developing a prototype with the users. Given a rich enough component set and a simple enough application, the prototype may end up being almost the whole system, but if you don't build the prototype, you run the risk of building the wrong application. It's seldom feasible to skip the prototyping stage—it's a powerful validation of the specification.

All of this is applicable to any iterative development process, not just OpenStep systems, but it's especially important for OpenStep applications because the development tools make it so easy to change things. Most of the time, this is a great advantage of the OpenStep environment, but there are times when making it a little harder to change things provides the advantage of knowing where you stand and how much farther you have to go.

14 *Portability*

The basic intent of the OpenStep specification is to guarantee source portability across platforms by defining a standard programming interface. The reality of application development, however, means that you need to use libraries and other resources outside of OpenStep. These can be parts of the system underneath the OpenStep frameworks or products added alongside or on top, such as a third-party library of C or C++ routines and classes, or even NeXT's Enterprise Objects Framework.

As with many aspects of development, you rarely decide to write completely portable or completely nonportable code. Rather, you work toward making your code easier to port by encapsulating the parts of it that aren't inherently portable. This makes it easier to locate when needed and to modify without affecting other parts of the system.

Encapsulation, of course, is one of the basic principles of object-oriented programming. The most natural way of integrating components into an OpenStep application is to create an Objective-C class that presents a stable interface to whatever external service you're using. This is precisely what the database adaptors do in the Enterprise Objects Framework, for example. When you need to port your application to a host system that provides that service in a different way, you can create a new subclass that implements the interface in terms of the new service.

Using a bridge or adaptor class is a well-known OOP technique, so we won't bother exploring it here. This chapter simply reviews the portability level of the various resources you use with OpenStep. First, we summarize what you can rely on to be transparently portable, followed by what definitely has to be encapsulated. The final section covers things that may or may not be portable, which you may or may not want to take the time to encapsulate.

Guaranteed Portable

By definition, all of the OpenStep specification's interfaces are transparently portable across host systems. This includes all of the classes, protocols, functions, and other elements in the Foundation and Application frameworks, but it also includes the Display Postscript System and additions. And of course, since the whole package is based on ANSI C, you can use any of the standard C library functions and definitions. You may not need to use them, since OpenStep provides higher-level interfaces to things such as string manipulation and time calculation, but for integrating legacy code it's a nice incidental benefit.

You may need to take a bit of care even here, though, if the specification recommends not using a particular method or function, whatever the level. There may be unforeseen interactions between high- and low-level API, and even some high-level API provides access to explicitly nonportable things, such as hardware codes that generate keyboard events. Fortunately, this subset of the specification is small indeed.

Guaranteed Nonportable

Using API outside of the OpenStep specification is sure to be nonportable if it would be nonportable anyway. Specifically nonportable are interfaces that are particular to an operating system or that depend on hardware information. These include interfaces defined by the operating system, vendor additions to OpenStep that use or provide access to system types, and OpenStep methods that provide information about hardware. For example, on Microsoft Windows, the NSWindow class has a method that returns the window handle used by the operating system, and NSEvent has a method that returns the keyboard code that generated the event.

One of the Foundation Framework's design goals is to provide system-level services, but there are times when you do have to call upon the operating system for an unusual feature. If you need to use such features, it's a good idea to encapsulate them as a portable class, using neutral data types and other OpenStep classes. The important thing is to always isolate code that's known to be nonportable.

Gray Areas

Some kinds of code lie between the poles of portability and nonportability. These are typically based on interfaces that are portable but whose implementations aren't necessarily available on other systems. Other items of uncertain portability include additions to OpenStep that happen to be available in all implementations and noncode resources whose formats might differ across platforms. In this gray area, you have to decide between the cost of encapsulating a partially portable interface yourself and the risk that it might not be available in every environment you develop in.

> ### Checking for Specification Conformance
> The OpenStep specification requires any additions to frameworks to be marked for conditional inclusion, using the STRICT_OPENSTEP compiler macro:
>
> ```
> #if !defined(STRICT_OPENSTEP)
> /* ... */
> #endif
> ```
>
> You can check that your application uses only OpenStep API by defining this macro when building it. If it is defined, classes and methods that are conditionally included aren't seen, resulting in compiler warnings wherever they're referenced.

System-Neutral Libraries and Tools

OpenStep's frameworks and applications can be viewed simply as libraries and tools that you use to build applications. Many other such libraries and tools exist, of course, and many of them provide valuable functionality that OpenStep doesn't, such as file indexing, numerical routines, and low-level database access. Libraries are clearly not portable if their interfaces are defined in terms of a specific operating system, but many of them use neutral interfaces defined in C, C++, or other standard programming languages. The portability of these kinds of libraries, and of development tools, depends simply on their availability.

The portability of a system-neutral library or tool is affected most by two factors:

- Source code availability. If you can rebuild it yourself on the new system, it's about as portable as it can get.

- Without source code, a product's availability on the market determines its portability. If you can be assured that the library or tools exist on your target platforms, you can take the chance of using it as is, without encapsulating it.

A special class of products that falls under the second point is that of frameworks built on top of OpenStep, such as NeXT's own Enterprise Objects Framework. These products are as portable as the number of OpenStep implementations they're available for. Of course, they have the added bonus of tight integration with OpenStep.

Additions to OpenStep

NeXT's and SunSoft's implementations of OpenStep share several components that aren't formally part of the specification. Among these are formatters and the table view classes. Using these is relatively safe, as they're quite likely to be included in a future version of the specification. The only real problem is that this makes the STRICT_OPENSTEP macro described in the sidebar less helpful in checking for compliance to the specification.

More problematic are additions not shared—or that differ—between the implementations. NeXT has its dozen or so additions to the Foundation Framework, along with the Application Kit's new text system. NeXT and SunSoft each has its own file-handling classes, with different interfaces. The future membership of these classes in the specification is less likely than that for those common to both systems. In any case, their presence on only one system or the other makes them nonportable right now. You might want to implement them yourself if you have the resources, or wait to see what becomes of them in the next version of the specification.

Noncode Resources

Portability considerations also arise outside the area of coding. Today's applications use resources of many types, from lists of strings to images, sounds, and video. OpenStep explicitly embraces some resource formats, such as RTF, PostScript, and TIFF, but remains mute with regard to many others you might use. In addition to the basic resource formats, though, system-specific transformations must be considered. A notable example is file compression, for which UNIX and Windows systems use quite different standards.

Text can also present a problem. OpenStep defines Unicode as its standard text encoding, but this is still an emerging standard. The encodings presently used by different systems and by different applications make this a potential problem. OpenStep's most significant problem in this area, however, is that only NeXT's implementations include text-editing classes that can handle Unicode characters. OpenStep's NSText and NSCStringText really work only with 8-bit encodings based on ASCII.

Some noncode resources are used not by the application but to build the application. Project Builder, for example, adds a pair of special files to each project, where you can define build macros and other options. How you make these definitions differs slightly between NeXT's and

SunSoft's implementations. You may need to keep separate versions of these auxiliary makefiles for each platform if they're very complex.

15 *Testing and Debugging*

Hunting errors in computer programs is both science and art. It requires a thorough understanding of how the code is structured, along with the intuition to glean the true cause of a problem from often cryptic clues. Knowing what's likely to cause an error is a big step toward both avoiding it in the first place and correcting it when it happens anyway.

Likely causes of errors vary with the programming language, the application architecture, and specific systems used in developing an application. OpenStep, with its Objective-C programming language, Foundation and Application frameworks, and related add-ons, certainly offers its own unique brands of errors. The goals of this chapter are to present the most frequently encountered kinds of errors and to explore how difficult they are to ferret out.

Although this chapter is devoted to fixing errors in the program code itself, it's important to remember that you can debug your application long before writing a single line of code. Examining your business object model and application architecture before proceeding to implement them can save hours of time with the debugger. Similarly, incorporating checkpoints and tests in your application architecture can speed pinpointing the causes of errors once you've begun testing.

That said, let's examine the testing and debugging aids that OpenStep offers and review the kinds of problems that can occur with OpenStep code.

Debugging in OpenStep

Despite its complexity, OpenStep offers a lot of help in debugging, from the integrated source debuggers, to the object model, to the pretested frameworks, to the graphical development tools. NeXT's and SunSoft's development environments both include a semigraphical Objective-C debugger, which offers push-button control of basic operations such as running and stopping the program, single-stepping, and examining objects. NeXT's debugger runs right within Project Builder, allowing you to set and manipulate breakpoints directly in the code editor. SunSoft's debugger runs from a terminal window and communicates with the Edit application, which displays the code being debugged and presents a panel with controls for stepping and examining data.

Objective-C's run-time dynamism is a great advantage, as it allows you to ask many questions about the state of the application and its objects that would be difficult or impossible to ask with a static language. If a message generates an exception because the receiving object doesn't respond to it, you can verify that it's of the proper type by asking what

> **Object Debugging**
>
> NeXT's Foundation Framework includes an extra header file, called **NSDebug.h**, that declares a number of unofficial, unsupported, but very useful environment variables, functions, and methods. Most of these items control debugging and recordkeeping behavior for memory allocation and object lifetime, such as logging multiple deallocations of objects and setting high-water marks on NSAutoreleasePools. You can set the values of the environment variables to turn on debugging and logging, then use the functions and methods to control other kinds of debugging behavior and to test various conditions at run time. These utilities are also quite useful for performance tuning (the topic of the next chapter).
>
> Solaris also adds debugging methods to its Foundation Framework, though not in a central location. The nice thing on Solaris, however, is that a lot of specific debugging tools have been integrated right into the debugger, including a speedy message-tracing feature that comes in handy for tracking prematurely deallocated objects and other reference-counting errors.

its class is or whether it conforms to a specific protocol. You can also set breakpoints on standard run-time error-handling methods, such as NSObject's **doesNotRecognizeSelector:**, NSException's **raise**, and NSAssertionHandler's various **handle...** methods.

The OpenStep frameworks and graphical development tools represent a huge base of code that you don't have to write. The easiest code to debug is the code that someone else has already debugged. By masking complexity with simpler interfaces, these frameworks reduce the amount of code you do have to write. Interface Builder and EOModeler even allow you to test parts of your application before writing that code.

Common Problem Areas

You've probably guessed that most errors particular to OpenStep are related to its dynamic mechanisms: Objective-C messages, asynchronous notifications, and the like. Far from certain indictment of dynamism, however, this simply reflects the fact that with any feature come problems specific to that feature. Run-time errors are the companions of dynamism, but they're by no means unmanageable, as the following survey of error classes shows.

Reference Counts

Though the Foundation Kit's reference-counting mechanism addresses many problems in sharing objects, it isn't automatic. You have to know when to retain objects and when to release or autorelease them, and you must make sure that you release an object exactly as many times as you retain it (explicitly or implicitly). If you release an object too many times, it will be deallocated early and your program will crash when it tries to use that object. If you retain it too many times, it will never be deallocated, resulting in a memory leak.

Debugging reference-counting errors can be difficult indeed, since the disposal of an object is often located nowhere near where it was first created or retained. NeXT has developed some tools for tracking and analyzing object lifetimes, including one that provides summary information for a running program and one that generates extremely detailed statistics of object allocation, **retain** and **release** messages, and deallocation for every class in the program. These tools help you both to find where objects are leaked and prematurely deallocated and to determine what caused that to happen. Solaris integrates some of this functionality right into the debugger.

Run-Loop Asynchrony

The Foundation Framework's NSNotification and NSTimer classes allow for messages to be sent to multiple recipients after a delay. Also, any object can register as an observer of a notification, supplying a method of its own to be invoked when that notification is posted. This is a useful and powerful feature, but when an error pops up it can be quite difficult to pinpoint the origin: Both notifications and timers, after all, remove the invocation of a method from the context that originated the message.

Tracking asynchrony errors can be time-consuming. It involves breaking at the offending method and examining the notification or timer included as an argument, then examining the code for the likely originators of the improper asynchronous message. After this, you can set breakpoints where these notifications and timers originate and examine the context.

Noncode Logic: Nib Files and Models

One of OpenStep's greatest strengths—reduction of code through tools such as Interface Builder and EOModeler—can lead to very frustrating errors if you forget that nib files and models represent program logic just as much as code does. Unlike code, though, you can't examine a nib file or model in the debugger; you must either intuit the source of an error or examine every connection manually to find the error's cause.

For nib files, an improperly made connection can cause any number of unexpected behaviors that appear impossible when you look only at code. The right message can be sent to the wrong object (or to no object, since a message to null is legal in Objective-C); the wrong message can be sent to the right object; or the wrong message can be sent to the wrong object. In the debugger, where the context of the interface isn't obvious, such errors can seem quite mysterious. A common cause of lost messages is changing a method name in a class's header file. You can forestall this error by reimporting the header into the nib file and checking the outlets whenever you edit it.

With the Enterprise Objects Framework, an entity missing a primary key, among many other possible model errors, can cause problems entirely unrelated to code and not obvious in the debugger. EOModeler is a bit friendlier than Interface Builder in some regards, since it offers a consistency check for detectable errors in a model file. Even so, there's a large number of problems it can't detect, which you have to intuit from the behavior of your application.

Exceptions

Exceptions are supposed to aid in debugging, but in fact they can be extremely unhelpful. The existence of exceptions is often justified in two ways. One view is that methods should always return meaningful values or none at all, rather than returning error codes. In this view, errors cause exceptions that you must catch and handle. The other view is that exceptions represent errors that should never happen in the first place, such as accessing an array past the last index, which therefore represent fundamental errors in program logic. Nonetheless, exceptions are often used for problems that have nothing to do with program correctness, such as Distributed Objects timeouts. In either case, you can end up with code that's cluttered with exception handlers, which is as bad as checking every return value for an error code and taking preemptive action.

To its credit, however, the Foundation Framework's exception model offers a wealth of information at run time that classic error codes and exceptions don't. Objective-C exceptions are objects with names that reflect the nature of the error. They can also be assigned a more elaborate description stating the likely reason for the exception, along with arbitrary information from the context in which the exception was raised. This information can be quite helpful in pinpointing and correcting the problem.

Weak Typing

Proponents of strong compile-time type checking may decry Objective-C's dynamism as dangerous, but the fact is that, like many things, it's a very useful feature when used properly. Typing every object as **id** is certain to cause errors eventually; like **void** *, this generic type is meant to be used sparingly, when the type is understood from context. The most common errors resulting from weak typing are sending a message that the receiver doesn't respond to, and sending a message that the receiver does respond to, but in an unexpected manner.

Unrecognized messages are easily avoided by statically typing your objects as much as possible, which produces warnings at compile time rather than errors at run time. Remember that in Objective-C, declaring an object with a particular class means the object is an instance of that class or of any subclass. You get the benefit of compile-time type checking, but polymorphism and run-time binding still apply.

An unexpected response to a message is typically caused by insufficient restriction in the definition of a method, most often through ambiguous naming and typing of arguments. Renaming ambiguous elements makes it clearer how they're supposed to be used, which reduces the chance of unexpected results. Statically typing arguments enables the compiler to warn of improper invocations. Consider a method named **insert:at:**, where the first argument is the thing being inserted, and the second tells where to insert it. Unfortunately, the name itself gives no clue as to the type of the thing being inserted or the location. A name like **insertObject:atIndex:** or **insertText:inRange:**, with properly typed object arguments, is much clearer.

Distributed Objects

Distributed Objects doesn't introduce too many problems that distributed programming in general doesn't already have. However, DO makes distributed programming so easy on the surface that you're more likely to do it and therefore to encounter these problems. If you plan on creating a distributed application, however complex, learn about the issues related to concurrent and distributed programming, resource contention, and deadlock first.

16 *Performance*

Performance is the rope in a tug-of-war between hardware and software. Just when new processors arrive that make software run acceptably fast, and disk storage doubles for the price, new software comes out that slows right down again and requires three times the storage. The major bottleneck, memory, has not shared the gains of mass storage in terms of megabytes per dollar, keeping the most straightforward way of improving performance the most expensive.

OpenStep, in any incarnation, is no exception to this trend. Its rich graphical nature, object model, and the amount of functionality it provides all require great processing power and memory for acceptable performance. Also, some of the convenience it provides the programmer makes it easy to write inefficient code. You have no direct control over OpenStep itself, but you can tune your application's use of it for maximal efficiency.

Measuring Performance

Finding and fixing performance bottlenecks takes time, and development speed is often far more costly than application speed. Hence, it makes sense to fix only the problems that users complain about—to ask users what they don't like about performance and to analyze the potential causes of those problems. Analysis itself can vary in sophistication from a quick eye review of code up through full profiling of every routine.

Code performance can be analyzed in two basic ways. The first is to measure the time it takes to perform a specific operation, called *timing* or *sampling*. This means following the user's perception into the code and measuring specific methods and functions for the time they take to execute. Time measurements give you the information to pinpoint problems with algorithms, memory usage, and other common causes of poor performance.

The second method, called *profiling*, involves measuring how often particular methods and functions are invoked, which offers additional insight into algorithm performance. It's also useful data for scatter loading or otherwise arranging compiled modules so that the code that executes together is grouped in memory. In virtual memory systems, where code must be paged in and out of memory, this is often a key part of performance tuning.

OpenStep doesn't define any standard tools for either sampling or profiling. These kinds of tools sometimes seem to be the poor cousins of compilers and debuggers. NeXT has some tools on Mach, such as the **gprof** profiler and its own **sampler** tool, but none yet on Windows, for example.

Improving Performance

Once you know where the problems lie, you can apply the appropriate techniques to correct them. The following sections summarize several techniques, some general, some specific to object-oriented programming and to OpenStep in particular. They appear in rough order of usefulness, with the more effective or commonly useful techniques first. (Also, see the sidebar "Object Debugging" on page 238 of *Chapter 15: Testing and Debugging*.)

In considering any performance technique, remember that maintenance can be far more costly than hardware or even users' time. If a performance enhancement renders code unintelligible or more prone to error, it's probably not worth implementing. That said, a great number of performance enhancements do no harm to clarity, modularity, or maintainability. Simply choosing the right level of abstraction, such as NSArrays versus C arrays, is a tremendous performance technique, and all it does is change the context of the problem.

If you decide to try a technique, be sure to measure performance both before and after applying it and to test the new code thoroughly. These techniques don't always produce benefits worth the impaired maintainability, and they may not even work at all in some situations. They may have no effect; they may make the code being optimized run more slowly; or they may produce an undesirable side effect elsewhere. Formal testing can save hours of developer and user time.

Tuning Algorithms

One of the first things to look at when you've isolated a slow routine is the kinds of algorithms it uses. To increase their own speed in developing an application, programmers do use slower algorithms that are easier to code. Often, they intend to replace them later with faster algorithms but forget once they've moved on to new features. They may also simply be unaware of faster algorithms.

For these reasons and more, it's a good idea to have people other than the original author review slow code. They may see or know something the author didn't. A fresh perspective can reveal potentials for dramatic improvement.

Reducing Memory and Disk Usage

Lack of memory was implicated at the beginning of this chapter as a major culprit in performance problems. Large systems with robust virtual memory have made it easy to program as though there's no limit to storage, but there's still a heavy price in performance. It pays richly to revise code so that it uses less memory, even at the cost of performing more calculations; loading a page of virtual memory from disk is orders of magnitude more expensive than performing even millions of calculations. This fact also suggests that resources stored on disk be compressed if possible, so that they can be read into memory more quickly and then expanded as needed.

Managing Autoreleased Objects

The Foundation Framework's autorelease feature reduces much of the burden of tracking object ownership, but it has a potentially huge impact on performance when many temporary objects are being processed. Blindly autoreleasing every object you create is not a wise tactic, as these objects accumulate in memory until the run loop finishes its current cycle. Always consider the scope of an object's use, autoreleasing only those passed outside a method and explicitly releasing all local objects at the end. Similarly, a class's **dealloc** method should autorelease only instance variables that may have been passed to other objects and should simply release private instance variables.

Another common cause of autorelease bloat is a loop that creates temporary objects in each iteration, whether explicitly or implicitly. To remedy this problem, you can create your own NSAutoreleasePool at the top of the loop and release it at the bottom, so that all objects autoreleased inside the loop are cleaned up on each iteration. This technique is tremendously useful for reducing the space occupied by autoreleased objects, though you must be careful to retain objects that you want to survive past the loop.

Loading Resources on Demand

OpenStep provides explicit support for loading compiled code, nib files, and other resources incrementally, as they're needed. This is managed by the Foundation Framework's NSBundle class, which defines methods for loading a group of related resources, for finding and dynamically loading compiled code, and for loading nib files and connecting their objects into the application. Loading resources only when they're needed greatly reduces the time it takes an application to launch, and results in only slight, one-time delays when the resources are first loaded.

Using C++ and Standard C

Objective-C is well suited to high-level application development, but it does have its limits when it comes to low-level efficiency. It would be ludicrous to use NSNumber objects for all calculations, for example. The purpose of that class is to allow numbers to be transported in collections, not to replace the native C types **int**, **float**, and so on. Similarly, although NSArray and other collection classes are quite useful, should performance needs dictate it, you can always bypass them for C arrays, hash tables, and so on. If your analysis reveals that an object easily replaced by a more basic data structure is taking too much time, by all means replace it.

Using Threads and Distribution

You can realize a significant gain in performance through concurrent programming, by taking advantage of multiprocessor support through threads, and through redesigning your application with a distributed architecture. The NSThread class, along with NSLock and its subclasses, provides a standard OpenStep interface to threads, and Distributed Objects provides remote method invocations. When using either technique, keep in mind that some parts of OpenStep aren't designed with concurrency in mind. An application's connection to the PostScript Window Server, for example, is a shared resource, whose use you must manage carefully in a multithreaded application (see the sidebar on page 60 for SunSoft's solution to this particular problem).

Overriding Reference-Count Methods

NSObject's **retain** and **release** methods work by keeping global hash tables of extra references to each object whose reference count is greater than one. This eliminates the need for every instance to store its own reference count, which saves a lot of memory, but isn't appropriate for objects that are frequently released and retained. For such objects, the delay in lookup outweighs the benefit of less storage for objects with no extra references.

To bypass the default mechanism, a class can override **retain** and **release** to increment and decrement a private instance variable. Doing so speeds up these methods at the cost of an extra instance variable for all instances, whether or not their reference counts go above one. You can determine whether this is appropriate by measuring performance with and without these overridden methods.

Overriding Objective-C Dynamism

If you need to squeeze the last bit of performance out of an Objective-C object, you can cache the implementation of a method and invoke it as a function, bypassing the Objective-C run-time system. This is a useful technique in tight loops where performance is essential but where you must still use objects. However, you must take great care to guarantee that every object treated this way is an instance of the class whose implementation you cache, and not an instance of an unrelated class or a subclass. If you don't, you could invoke a method that either doesn't apply to the object at hand or that applies to it improperly.

The NSObject class method **instanceMethodForSelector:** returns a pointer to the underlying C function that implements the specified method (a selector is a hashed method name). If you know the arguments it takes, you can invoke this directly with any instance of the class you got the implementation from. These kinds of invocations, being function calls, are as fast as C++ nonvirtual functions.

This particular trick shows the depth you can go to speed up an OpenStep application. In general, though, you should rarely need to do this. By using the appropriate technique for your performance requirements from the beginning, you can avoid having to use such hacks to nudge out performance gains.

Appendices

Appendix A: PayPerView Source

Here's the source code for the PayPerView application developed in *Chapter 7: Building an Application*. Code generated and maintained by Project Builder, such as the file defining the **main()** function, isn't included here.

PayPerView.nib

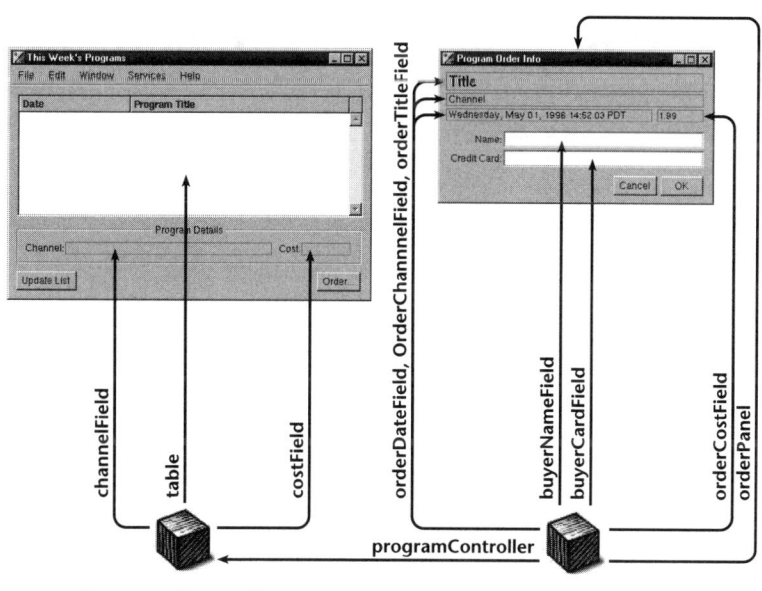

Figure 1. Connections from Custom Objects (Outlets)

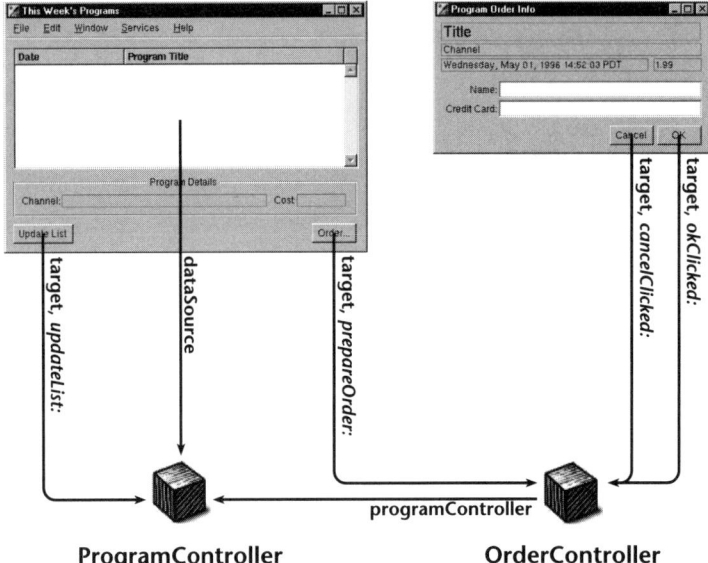

Figure 2. Connections to Custom Objects

ProgramController.h

```
#import <AppKit/AppKit.h>

@class Program;

@interface ProgramController : NSObject
{
    id   table;

    id   channelField;
    id   costField;

    NSMutableArray *programList;
}

- (id)init;
- (void)tableClicked:(id)sender;
- (void)updateList:(id)sender;
- (Program *)selectedProgram;

@end
```

ProgramController.m

```objc
#import "ProgramController.h"
#import "Program.h"

@implementation ProgramController

- (id)init
{
    NSCalendarDate *aDate;
    Program *aProgram;

    self = [super init];

    programList = [[NSMutableArray alloc] init];


    aDate = [NSCalendarDate dateWithString:@"8/13/1996 23:45"
        calendarFormat:@"%m/%d/%Y %H:%M"];
    aProgram = [[Program alloc]
        initWithTitle:@"Faster, Pussycat, Kill Kill!"
        channel:@"Cinerip" broadcastDate:aDate
        cost:@"$2.50"];
    [programList addObject:aProgram];
    [aProgram release];


    aDate = [NSCalendarDate dateWithString:@"8/14/1996 21:00"
        calendarFormat:@"%m/%d/%Y %H:%M"];
    aProgram = [[Program alloc] initWithTitle:@"JFK"
         channel:@"The Conspiracy Channel"
         broadcastDate:aDate
        cost:@"$1.50"];
    [programList addObject:aProgram];
    [aProgram release];


    aDate = [NSCalendarDate
        dateWithString:@"8/15/1996 19:00"
        calendarFormat:@"%m/%d/%Y %H:%M"];
    aProgram = [[Program alloc]
        initWithTitle:@"It's a Wonderful Life"
        channel:@"Movie Classics"
        broadcastDate:aDate
        cost:@"$1.99"];
    [programList addObject:aProgram];
    [aProgram release];

    return self;
}
```

```objc
- (void)updateList:(id)sender
{
    [table reloadData];
    return;
}

- (void)tableClicked:(id)sender
{
    Program *selectedProgram;

    selectedProgram = [self selectedProgram];
    [channelField setStringValue:[selectedProgram channel]];
    [costField setStringValue:[selectedProgram cost]];

    return;
}

- (Program *)selectedProgram
{
    int row;
    Program *theProgram;

    row = [table selectedRow];
    theProgram = [programList objectAtIndex:row];
    return theProgram;
}

- (int)numberOfRowsInTableView:(NSTableView *)tableView
{
    return [programList count];
}

- (id)tableView:(NSTableView *)tableView
    objectValueForTableColumn:(NSTableColumn *)tableColumn
    row:(int)row
{
    Program *theProgram = [programList objectAtIndex:row];
    id colID = [tableColumn identifier];

    if (!theProgram) return nil;
    if ([colID isEqual:@"title"]) return [theProgram title];
    else if ([colID isEqual:@"broadcastDate"]) {
        return [theProgram broadcastDate];
    }
    else return nil;
}

@end
```

Program.h

```objc
#import <Foundation/Foundation.h>

@interface Program : NSObject
{
    NSString *title;
    NSString *channel;
    NSCalendarDate *broadcastDate;
    NSString *cost;
}

- (id)initWithTitle:(NSString *)aTitle
    channel:(NSString *)aChannel
    broadcastDate:(NSCalendarDate *)aBroadcast
    cost:(NSString *)aCost;

- (void)setTitle:(NSString *)value;
- (NSString *)title;

- (void)setChannel:(NSString *)value;
- (NSString *)channel;

- (void)setBroadcastDate:(NSCalendarDate *)value;
- (NSCalendarDate *)broadcastDate;

- (void)setCost:(NSString *)value;
- (NSString *)cost;

@end
```

Program.m

```objc
#import "Program.h"

@implementation Program

- (id)initWithTitle:(NSString *)aTitle
    channel:(NSString *)aChannel
    broadcastDate:(NSCalendarDate *)aDate
    cost:(NSString *)aCost;
{
    self = [super init];
    if (!self) return nil;
    [self setTitle:aTitle];
    [self setChannel:aChannel];
    [self setBroadcastDate:aDate];
    [self setCost:aCost];
    return self;
}

- (void)setTitle:(NSString *)value
{
    [title autorelease];
    title = [value copy];
    return;
}

- (NSString *)title
{
    return title;
}

- (void)setChannel:(NSString *)value
{
    [channel autorelease];
    channel = [value copy];
    return;
}

- (NSString *)channel
{
    return channel;
}

- (void)setBroadcastDate:(NSCalendarDate *)value
{
    [broadcastDate autorelease];
    broadcastDate = [value copy];
    [broadcastDate setCalendarFormat:@"%B %d, %Y %I:%m %p"];
    return;
}
```

```objc
- (NSCalendarDate *)broadcastDate
{
    return broadcastDate;
}

- (void)setCost:(NSString *)value
{
    [cost autorelease];
    cost = [value copy];
    return;
}

- (NSString *)cost
{
    return cost;
}

- (void)dealloc
{
    [broadcastDate autorelease];
    [channel autorelease];
    [cost autorelease];
    [title autorelease];
    [super dealloc];
    return;
}

@end
```

OrderController.h

```objc
#import <AppKit/AppKit.h>

@class ProgramController;

@interface OrderController : NSObject
{
    id programController;
    id orderPanel;

    id  orderTitleField;
    id  orderChannelField;
    id  orderDateField;
    id  orderCostField;

    id buyerNameField;
    id creditCardField;
}
```

```
- (void)prepareOrder:(id)sender;
- (void)cancelClicked:(id)sender;
- (void)okClicked:(id)sender;

- (void)cancelOrder;
- (void)confirmOrder;
- (BOOL)verifyCreditCard;

@end
```

OrderController.m

```
#import "OrderController.h"
#import "ProgramController.h"
#import "Program.h"

@implementation OrderController

- (void)prepareOrder:(id)sender
{
    int result;
    Program *selectedProgram = [programController
        selectedProgram];

    [orderTitleField setStringValue:[selectedProgram title]];
    [orderChannelField setStringValue:[selectedProgram
        channel]];
    [orderCostField setStringValue:[selectedProgram cost]];
    [orderDateField setStringValue:[[selectedProgram
        broadcastDate] description]];

    [buyerNameField setStringValue:@""];
    [creditCardField setStringValue:@""];

    result = [NSApp runModalForWindow:orderPanel];
    switch (result) {
        case NSRunStoppedResponse:
            [self confirmOrder];
            break;
        case NSRunAbortedResponse:
            [self cancelOrder];
            break;
    }
    return;
}
```

```objc
- (void)cancelClicked:(id)sender
{
    [orderPanel orderOut:nil];
    [NSApp abortModal];
    return;
}

- (void)okClicked:(id)sender
{
    if (![self verifyCreditCard]) return;
    [orderPanel orderOut:nil];
    [NSApp stopModal];
    return;
}

- (void)cancelOrder
{
    NSString *status = [NSString
        stringWithFormat:@"Order for %@ was cancelled\n",
        [orderTitleField stringValue]];

    NSRunAlertPanel(@"Order Canceled", status, nil, nil, nil);
    return;
}

- (void)confirmOrder
{
    NSString *status = [NSString
        stringWithFormat:@"%@ ordered %@ using card #%@\n",
        [buyerNameField stringValue],
        [orderTitleField stringValue],
        [creditCardField stringValue]];

    NSRunAlertPanel(@"Order Placed", status, nil, nil, nil);
    return;
}

- (BOOL)verifyCreditCard
{
    if ([[buyerNameField stringValue] isEqual:@""]) {
        NSRunAlertPanel(@"No Customer Name",
            @"You must enter a customer's name.",
            nil, nil, nil);
        return NO;
    }
```

```
        if ([[creditCardField stringValue] isEqual:@""]) {
            NSRunAlertPanel(@"Invalid Card",
                @"Invalid credit card number for %@.",
                nil, nil, nil, [buyerNameField stringValue]);
            return NO;
        }
        return YES;
    }

@end
```

Appendix B: PayPerView with Distributed Objects

The Distributed Objects version of PayPerView has two projects, one a command-line server program, the other the graphical client application.

The Server Project

The server project, being a command-line program, has no nib file. Also note that it defines its own **main()** function, in **PPVServer_main.m**.

ProgramServer.h

This file declares the public protocol used by client applications as well as the interface to the class itself. Note the use of **bycopy** to indicate that the array of programs is returned by making a copy over the network, not by passing a proxy. In this example, the ProgramServer is distributed by reference. Client applications need only the protocol declaration, but this example doesn't bother to separate the two.

```
#import <Foundation/Foundation.h>

@protocol ProgramServer

- (bycopy NSArray *)programs;

@end
```

```objc
@interface ProgramServer : NSObject <ProgramServer>
{
    NSMutableArray *programList;
}

- (id)init;

@end
```

ProgramServer.m

```objc
#import "ProgramServer.h"
#import "Program.h"

@implementation ProgramServer

- (id)init
{
    NSCalendarDate *aDate;
    Program *aProgram;

    self = [super init];

    programList = [[NSMutableArray alloc] init];


    aDate = [NSCalendarDate dateWithString:@"8/13/1996 23:45"
        calendarFormat:@"%m/%d/%Y %H:%M"];
    aProgram = [[Program alloc]
        initWithTitle:@"Faster, Pussycat, Kill Kill!"
        channel:@"Cinerip" broadcastDate:aDate cost:@"$2.50"];
    [programList addObject:aProgram];
    [aProgram release];

    aDate = [NSCalendarDate dateWithString:@"8/14/1996 21:00"
        calendarFormat:@"%m/%d/%Y %H:%M"];
    aProgram = [[Program alloc] initWithTitle:@"JFK"
        channel:@"The Conspiracy Channel" broadcastDate:aDate
        cost:@"$1.50"];
    [programList addObject:aProgram];
    [aProgram release];
```

```
        aDate = [NSCalendarDate dateWithString:@"8/15/1996 19:00"
            calendarFormat:@"%m/%d/%Y %H:%M"];
        aProgram = [[Program alloc]
            initWithTitle:@"It's a Wonderful Life"
            channel:@"Movie Classics" broadcastDate:aDate
            cost:@"$1.99"];
        [programList addObject:aProgram];
        [aProgram release];


        return self;
}

- (void)dealloc
{
    [programList autorelease];
    [super dealloc];
    return;
}

- (NSArray *)programs
{
    // Guarantee bycopy transmission by making immutable.
    return [[programList copy] autorelease];
}

@end
```

Program.h/Program.m

The Distributed Objects version of the Program class adds one method to support copying instances across the network:

```
- (id)copyWithZone:(NSZone *)zone
{
    Program *newProgram;
    newProgram = [[[self class] allocWithZone:zone]
        initWithTitle:title channel:channel
        broadcastDate:broadcastDate cost:cost];
    return newProgram;
}
```

PPVServer_main.m

```objc
#import <Foundation/Foundation.h>
#import "ProgramServer.h"

int main (int argc, const char *argv[])
{
    NSAutoreleasePool * pool = [[NSAutoreleasePool alloc]
        init];
    ProgramServer *server;
    NSConnection *defaultConn = [NSConnection
        defaultConnection];

    server = [[ProgramServer alloc] init];
    [defaultConn setRootObject:server];
    if ([defaultConn registerName:@"ProgramServer"] == NO) {
        NSLog(@"Failed to register server as ProgramServer.
            Exiting.\n");
        exit(EXIT_FAILURE);
    }

    NSLog(@"Server successfully launched.\n");
    [[NSRunLoop currentRunLoop] run];

    [pool release];
    exit(0);
}
```

The Client Project

The nib files for the Distributed Objects client are identical to those in Appendix A.

ProgramController.h

The Distributed Objects version of the ProgramController class differs only by importing the interface for the ProgramServer class and changing the instance variables to reflect the use of the server. The array of programs is retrieved by copy, not as a proxy. In this example, the ProgramServer is the proxy.

```
ProgramContoller.h
import <AppKit/AppKit.h>
#import "ProgramServer.h"

@class Program;

@interface ProgramController:NSObject
{
    id table;
    id channelField;
    id costField;

    id <ProgramServer> programServer;
    NSArray *programList;
}

- (id)init;
- (void)tableClicked:(id)sender;
- (void)updateList:(id)sender;
- (Program *)selectedProgram;

@end
```

ProgramController.m

The Distributed Objects version of the ProgramController class differs in only two methods, **init** and **updateList:**. **init** establishes a connection to the server rather than building a list of Programs itself, while **updateList:** disposes of the current list of Programs and asks the server for another.

```
- (id)init
{
    NSConnection *serverConn;

    self = [super init];

    serverConn = [NSConnection
        connectionWithRegisteredName:@"ProgramServer"
        host:@"*"];
    programServer = [[serverConn rootProxy] retain];
```

```
        if (!programServer) {
            NSRunAlertPanel(@"No server",
                @"Can't connect to the program server.",
                @"Quit", nil, nil);
            [NSApp terminate:nil];
        }

        [(NSDistantObject *)programServer
            setProtocolForProxy:@protocol(ProgramServer)];

        programList = [[programServer programs] retain];
        return self;
    }

    - (void)updateList:(id)sender
    {
        [programList release];
        programList = [[programServer programs] retain];
        [table reloadData];
        return;
    }
```

Program.h/Program.m

See the listing under "The Server Project" earlier in this appendix.

OrderController.h/OrderController.m

The Distributed Objects version of the OrderController class is identical to that in Appendix A.

Appendix C: PayPerView with Enterprise Objects

In the Enterprise Objects version of PayPerView, note how much code is replaced by the more generalized model and nib files. The ProgramController class is gone, and changes have been shown here struck through or made bold.

PayPerView.eomodeld

This model uses an Oracle database for external types. Column names for attributes are made by capitalizing the name and adding underscores; for example, "broadcastDate" becomes BROADCAST_DATE.

Program Entity

Class: Program **Table:** PROGRAM
Attributes:

Name	Value Class	External Type
programID	NSNumber	NUMBER
title	NSString	VARCHAR2
broadcastDate	NSDate	DATE
cost	NSDecimalNumber	NUMBER
channelID	NSNumber	NUMBER

Relationships:

Name	Destination	Join Key	Join Semantic	Cardinality
channel	Channel	channelID	Inner	To One

271

Channel Entity

Class: Channel **Table:** CHANNEL
Attributes:

	Name	Value Class	External Type
🔑 🔒	channelID	NSNumber	NUMBER
♦ 🔒	name	NSString	VARCHAR2
♦ 🔒	dialNumber	NSNumber	NUMBER

Relationships:

Name	Destination	Join Key	Join Semantic	Cardinality
programs	Program	channelID	Inner	To Many

PayPerView.nib

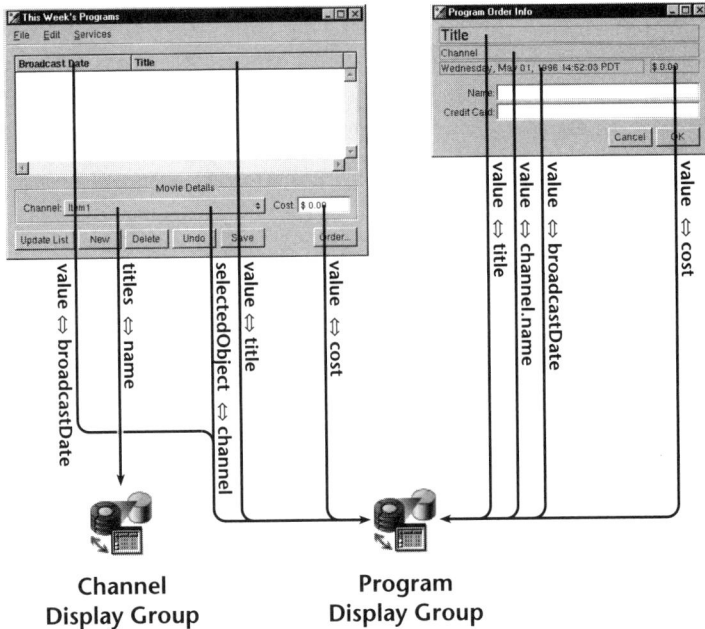

Figure 1. Associations with Aspects and Key Bindings

Appendix C: PayPerView with Enterprise Objects 273

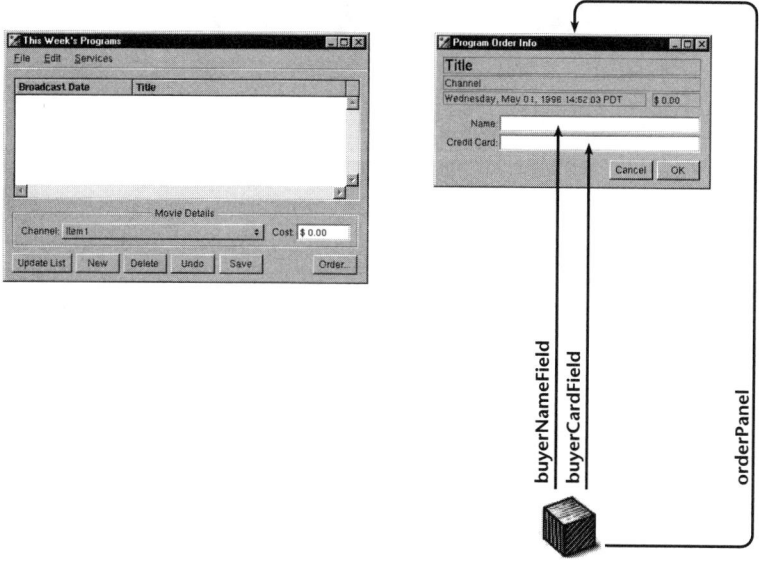

Figure 2. Connections from Custom Objects (Outlets)

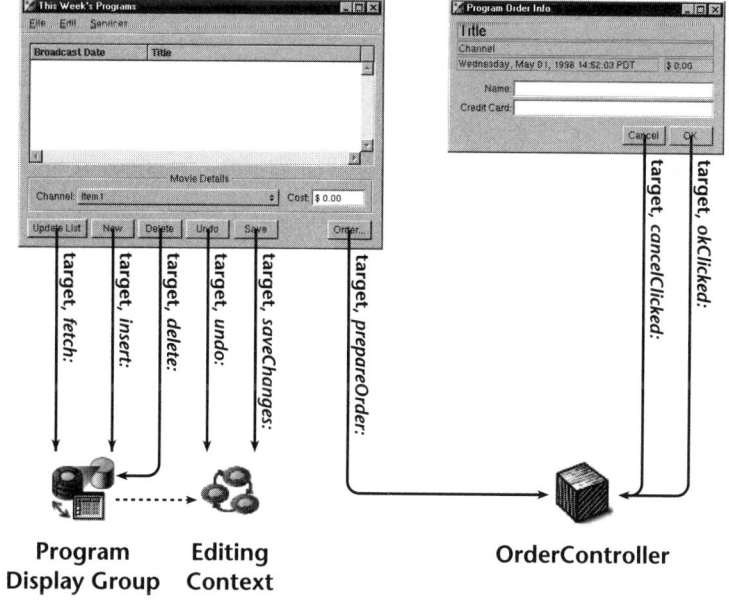

Figure 3. Connections to Custom Objects

OrderController.h

```
#import <AppKit/AppKit.h>

@class ProgramController;

@interface OrderController : NSObject
{
    id programController;
    id orderPanel;

    id  orderTitleField;
    id  orderChannelField;
    id  orderDateField;
    id  orderCostField;

    id buyerNameField;
    id creditCardField;
}

- (void)prepareOrder:(id)sender;
- (void)cancelClicked:(id)sender;
- (void)okClicked:(id)sender;

- (void)cancelOrder;
- (void)confirmOrder;
- (BOOL)verifyCreditCard;

@end
```

OrderController.m

```
#import "OrderController.h"
#import "ProgramController.h"
#import "Program.h"

@implementation OrderController

- (void)prepareOrder:(id)sender
{
    int result;
    Program *selectedProgram = [programController
        selectedProgram];
```

```
    [orderTitleField setStringValue:[selectedProgram title]];
    [orderChannelField setStringValue:[selectedProgram
        channel]];
    [orderCostField setStringValue:[selectedProgram cost]];
    [orderDateField setStringValue:[[selectedProgram
        broadcastDate] description]];

    [buyerNameField setStringValue:@""];
    [creditCardField setStringValue:@""];

    result = [NSApp runModalForWindow:orderPanel];
    switch (result) {
        case NSRunStoppedResponse:
            [self confirmOrder];
            break;
        case NSRunAbortedResponse:
            [self cancelOrder];
            break;
    }
    return;
}
```

Program.h

```
// Program.h
//
// Created on Fri Jun 07 19:11:35 PDT 1996 by NeXT EOModeler
// Version

#import <EOControl/EOControl.h>

@interface Program : NSObject
{
    int programId;
    NSString *title;
    NSCalendarDate *broadcastDate;
    NSDecimalNumber *cost;
    id channel;
}

#ifdef ACCESSOR_METHODS

- (void)setProgramId:(int)value;
- (int)programId;

- (void)setTitle:(NSString *)value;
- (NSString *)title;
```

```objc
- (void)setBroadcastDate:(NSCalendarDate *)value;
- (NSCalendarDate *)broadcastDate;

- (void)setCost:(NSDecimalNumber *)value;
- (NSDecimalNumber *)cost;

- (void)setChannel:value;
- channel;
```

#endif

```
@end
```

Program.m

```objc
// Program.m
//
// Created on Fri Jun 07 19:11:35 PDT 1996 by NeXT
// EOModeler.app Version

#import "Program.h"

@implementation Program
```

#ifdef ACCESSOR_METHODS

```objc
- (void)setProgramId:(int)value
{
    [self willChange];
    programId = value;
}

- (int)programId { return programId; }

- (void)setTitle:(NSString *)value
{
    [self willChange];
    [title autorelease];
    title = [value retain];
}

- (NSString *)title { return title; }
```

```objc
- (void)setBroadcastDate:(NSCalendarDate *)value
{
    [self willChange];
    [broadcastDate autorelease];
    broadcastDate = [value retain];
}

- (NSCalendarDate *)broadcastDate { return broadcastDate; }

- (void)setCost:(NSDecimalNumber *)value
{
    [self willChange];
    [cost autorelease];
    cost = [value retain];

}

- (NSDecimalNumber *)cost { return cost; }

- (void)setChannel:value
{
    // A TO-ONE relationship.
    [self willChange];
    [channel autorelease];
    channel = [value retain];
}

- channel { return channel; }

#endif

- (void)dealloc
{
    [title autorelease];
    [broadcastDate autorelease];
    [cost autorelease];
    [channel autorelease];
    [super dealloc];
}

@end
```

Channel.h

```objc
// Channel.h
//
// Created on Fri Jun 07 19:12:03 PDT 1996 by NeXT EOModeler
// Version

#import <EOControl/EOControl.h>

@interface Channel : NSObject
{
    int dialNumber;
    NSString *name;
    NSArray *programs;
}

#ifdef ACCESSOR_METHODS

- (void)setDialNumber:(int)value;
- (int)dialNumber;

- (void)setName:(NSString *)value;
- (NSString *)name;

- (void)setPrograms:(NSArray *)value;
- (NSArray *)programs;

#endif

@end
```

Channel.m

```objc
// Channel.m
//
// Created on Fri Jun 07 19:12:03 PDT 1996 by NeXT
// EOModeler.app Version

#import "Channel.h"

@implementation Channel

#ifdef ACCESSOR_METHODS
```

```objc
- (void)setDialNumber:(int)value
{
    [self willChange];
    dialNumber = value;

}
- (int)dialNumber { return dialNumber; }

- (void)setName:(NSString *)value
{
    [self willChange];
    [name autorelease];
    name = [value retain];
}

- (NSString *)name { return name; }

- (void)setPrograms:(NSArray *)value
{
    // A TO-MANY relationship.
    [self willChange];
    [programs autorelease];
    programs = [value retain];
}

- (NSArray *)programs { return programs; }

#endif

- (void)dealloc
{
    [name autorelease];
    [programs autorelease];
    [super dealloc];
}

@end
```

Suggested Reading

This list names the books we've found most helpful in learning what we know of object-oriented programming and of software development in general. We highly recommend each of these titles.

Business Engineering with Object Technology
> David Taylor
> John Wiley and Sons, 1995
>
> A good introduction, with concrete examples, to the use of object modeling as the first step in building a suite of business applications.

Debugging the Development Process
> Steve Maguire
> Microsoft Press, 1994
>
> A great, practical discussion of how to build and manage successful development teams. The author focuses more on shrink-wrap application issues, but most of what he says is applicable to any software development team.

Design Patterns
> Erich Gamma, Richard Helm, Ralph Johnson, and John Vlissides
> Addison-Wesley, 1995
>
> If you've ever wished for a catalog of good object designs, this is it. Novices and experts alike will benefit greatly from having this book.

The Mythical Man Month, Anniversary Edition
Frederick P. Brooks, Jr.
Addison-Wesley, 1995

This book belongs on the bookshelf of every software engineer and manager. If you don't have it, put down this book and run, don't walk, to the nearest bookstore, buy it, and read it twice.

The Object Advantage
Ivar Jacobson, Maria Ericsson, and Agneta Jacobson
Addison-Wesley, 1995

A solid book discussing how business process reengineering and object technology fit together. This book makes a forceful case for modeling.

Pitfalls of Object-Oriented Development
Bruce Webster
M & T Books, 1995

A useful sourcebook of snags and problems you might run into and some potential solutions. Although a little rough in places, Webster has spent more time than most managing NextStep and OpenStep developers, and he knows what he's talking about.

There's also another book about OpenStep coming out soon. Although we've only had time to skim through it, we're sure you'll want to take a look:

OpenStep for Enterprises
Nancy Craighill
John Wiley & Sons (forthcoming in 1996)

Index

4GL 163

A

abstraction 15
Access layer 182
accessor method 101, 173
action message 63, 108
adaptor (bridge) 231
adaptor, database 183
adopt a protocol 26
alloc method 29
applet 198
archiving 30, 43
aspect, of association 175
assertion handler 43
association 174
AT&T 153
attribute 171
autorelease method 29
autorelease pool 41

B

bash 90
batch fetching 190
Beck, Wirfs-Brock and 220
binding, static/dynamic 19

blind update 187
Booch, Grady 220, 223
Bourne shell 82
bridge 231
Brooks, Fred 222
business application 126
business component 127
business entity 127
business process 126, 216
business simulation 216
bycopy keyword 147
byref keyword 147

C

C 8, 19, 22, 32, 42, 234, 249
C library functions 28
C++ 9, 13, 15, 234, 250
    compared to Objective-C 31
    integrating with Objective-C 33
    performance 249
cell 65
change management 213
change tracking 190
class 17
    anonymous 26
    root 28

class object 27
class property 171
classification 17
Class-Responsibility-
    Collaborator 220
Coad, Peter 220
collection class 10, 46
color 68
Colors Panel 74
component
    business 127
    WebObjects 199
concurrency 156, 159, 249
    debugging 243
configuration management 213
connection death 148
content view 57, 58
control 64
conversation queuing 145
copy method 29
CORBA 152
    services 154
CRC 220
csh 90
customization point 185, 188, 194, 195
cut and paste 75, 87

D

data link 70
data source 55, 194
data, process, and policy 126
dbx 95
dealloc method 29
debugging 211
DEC 153
delegate 55

application 61
database adaptor 185
Distributed Objects 145
window 57, 61
delete propagation rule 191
development model 215
display 59
display group 174, 177, 194
Display PostScript 6, 7, 76, 85, 87
Distributed Objects 10, 48, 133
    concurrency 159
    debugging 243
    interoperability 154, 160
    load balancing 155
    naming service 154
    performance 157
    reliability 158
    scalability 155
    security 155
    transparency 156
distribution 36, 48, 133
drag and drop 75, 87, 104
Draw 76
drawing 58, 59
dynamic binding 19
dynamic typing 19
dynamism 18
    debugging 238, 242

E

Edit 89
editing context 174, 178, 188, 189
    nested/multiple 192
Encapsulated PostScript 68, 76, 91

encapsulation 16, 231
@end 22
enterprise object, definition 165
enterprise object, generic 170
entity 15, 170, 220
    business 127, 216
    inheritance mapping 184
EOGenericRecord 170
EOModeler 169, 183
EPS 68, 76, 91
error handling 42
event handling 58
event message 62
exception 42

F
fault 168, 188, 190
fetching
    batch 190
    pre- 190
File Merge 82
filtering 193
    in-memory 193
first responder 61
font 8, 66, 75
Font Panel 66, 74
formatter 45, 176
    date 176
    number 176
framework 78
    vs. kit 6

G
gdb 80
global identifier 189
gprof 246

H
Header Viewer 96
Hewlett-Packard 153
horizontal inheritance mapping 184
HTML generation 197
hypertext system 197

I
IBM 153
id 21
IDL 153
image class 68
@implementation 24
in keyword 147
independent conversation queueing 145
Informix 185
inheritance 17
inheritance mapping 184
in-memory filtering 193
in-memory qualifier 193
in-memory sorting 193
in-memory transaction 168, 192
inout keyword 147
instance 17
instance variable 16
@interface 22
interface (Java) 26
Interface Builder 11, 53, 77, 81, 96
Interface Definition Language 153
Interface layer 194
Internet 197
invocation 142
Iona 153

iterative development 211, 215, 222

J
Jacobsen, Ivar 220
Java 9
JavaScript 203

K
key window 61
key-value coding 186
kit vs. framework 6

L
lifetime, object 28
lock 159
locking 171

M
Mach 51, 73, 75, 80, 83, 213, 246
machd 75
Mail 14, 84, 89
main window 61
mapping
    entity inheritance 184
    relational-to-object 167
message 16, 21
    C++ 8
    unrecognized 142
method 16
MIME 84, 89
model 166
    business 216
    development 215
    object 164
    relational 164
    WebObjects 200
model file 169, 183
modeling 15
Model-View-Controller 101, 166, 199

N
NetInfo 14, 83
Netscape Navigator 198
NetWare 83
next responder 61
NeXTmail 14, 84, 89
nib file 103
NIS 14, 83
nmserver 76
nonportable API 232
notification 39
Novell NetWare 83
NSConnection 39, 49, 135, 137, 142, 144
NSObject 28

O
object, definition 16
Object Linking & Embedding 149, 154
Object Management Group 152
object request broker 150
object store 188
    multiple 191
Objective-C 5, 8, 9, 15
    compared with C++ 31
    debugging 238
    integrating with C++ 33
    performance 32, 249
object-oriented programming 15

ODBC 185
OLE 149, 154
OMG 152
one-table inheritance mapping 184
oneway keyword 147
OpenStep specification, definition 3
optimistic update 187
Oracle 185
ORB 76, 150
orbreg tool 150
out keyword 147
outlet 108
owner 55

P

panel 57
pasteboard 69
pbs 76
performance 9, 212, 245
    Distributed Objects 157
    Objective-C 32
perl 204
persistent variable 201
pessimistic update 187
policy 126
polymorphism 18
port 142
    receive/send 140
portability 5, 211, 231
portable API 232
POSIX 5
PostScript 6, 7, 58, 59, 68, 76, 82, 85, 87, 91
Preferences 91
prefetching 190

Preview 76, 91
primary key 168, 171
printing 68
@private 23
procedural programming 15
process 126
    business 216
    development 214
    iterative development 225
    waterfall development 214
profiling 246
Project Builder 76, 77, 92
project management 211, 213
property key 175
property list 44, 47
@protected 23
@protocol 26
protocol 22, 26
    Distributed Objects 143
proxy 137
    local/remote 140
@public 23

Q

qualifier
    in-memory 193

R

rapid prototyping 211, 215
reference counting 29
    debugging 239
relational database 163, 165, 181
relationship 168, 171
    construction 189
release method 29
requests, in Distributed Objects 144

responder chain 54, 60
retain method 29
reusable component 200
root class 28
root connection 138
ruler 64
Rumbaugh, James 220
run loop 39, 40, 41, 139
    Distributed Objects 144

S

sampler 246
sampling 246
script, Web 199
self 25
serialization 43
Services facility 71
session management 198, 201
session variable 201
SGI 153
sh 90
shelltool 90
simulation, business 216
Smalltalk 9, 19, 20, 101
snapshot 187
software development process 214
sorting 193
    in-memory 193
SQL 163, 185
static binding 19
static typing 19
stored procedure 163, 185
STRICT_OPENSTEP 233, 234
strong typing 242
subview 58
super 25

superview 58
Sybase 185

T

target 63
target–action paradigm 55
tcsh 90
Terminal 84, 90
text classes 65
TextEdit 76
this 25
TIFF 76, 91
timeout 149
timers 39
timing 246
transaction 184
    in-memory 192
typing
    static/dynamic 19
    weak 242

U

undo 178, 191
Unicode character encoding 35, 67
Unicode text system 67
uniquing 168, 189
unrecognized messages 242
update strategy 187
use case 217

V

validation 168, 193
value class 10, 44
value conversion 185
vending an object 140
version control 213

vertical inheritance mapping 184
vi 89
view 58
view hierarchy 58
virtual machine 198
VT100 90

W

waterfall model 214
weak typing 242
Web page
　dynamic 197
　static 197
WEBOBJECT HTML tag 199, 201, 202
WebObjects 198
willChange method 165
window 57
window manager 86
Window Server 59, 60, 76
Wirfs-Brock and Beck 220
WorkShop OpenStep 13, 85
Workspace Manager 14, 84, 88
World-Wide Web 197

X

X terminal 8, 87
X Window system 85
xterm 90

Y

Yap 82
Yellow Pages 14, 83

Z

zsh 90